Castleman's Corkscrew

including
The Railways of Bournemouth
& Associated Lines

Volume One: The Nineteenth Century

by
B.L. Jackson

THE OAKWOOD PRESS

British Library Cataloguing in Publication Data
A Record for this book is available from the British Library
ISBN 978 0 85361 666 5

Typeset by Oakwood Graphics.
Repro by PKmediaworks, Cranborne, Dorset.
Printed by Cambrian Printers Ltd, Aberystwyth, an ISO14001 and Green Dragon
Level 5 certified printer on paper sourced from sustainable forests.

Dedication

George Arthur Pryer, June 1944-June 2004

George Pryer was born at Swanage on 23rd June, 1944 within sight and sound of the branch railway. Following a spell living in London the family moved back to Dorset settling in Weymouth where, after completing his education, with his interest in railways, he joined the motive power department at Weymouth shed. However, his interest in signalling saw him shortly transfer to the traffic department, where following relief work and a spell at Dorchester South he gained his first appointment as signalman at Broadclyst in 1964. Following promotional moves to Cullompton, Ascot, Salisbury, and Andover he moved to Millbrook where he was back on the Southampton & Dorchester, a line with which he had a particular interest.

The closure of many signal boxes with the introduction of panel boxes saw him on the relief staff in the Southampton area, then as a guard at both Weymouth and Eastleigh before returning as a signalman at Eastleigh panel. His final promotion came as Signal Manager based at Bournemouth, from where for several periods he was seconded to run the signal training school at Waterloo. Taking early retirement he hoped to devote his time to recording signalling history, sadly within a short time ill health intervened and he passed away on 29th June, 2004.

Outside his railway career he was one of the five founder members of the Signalling Record Society in 1965, an organization today recognized as the experts in signalling history. He produced 21 signal box diagram books covering the Great Western and Southern railways, and was the author of *A Pictorial History of Southern Signalling*. His last book was a pictorial survey of LSWR signal boxes, the first of an intended series covering the Southern Railway. Magazine readers have also benefited from his work with a series of articles firstly in the *Railway Modeller*, and later in *Steam Days*. He had also supplied many diagrams and plans for numerous other railway books.

George had also been the joint author of several railway histories and until his untimely death was to be the joint author of *Castleman's Corkscrew*, which he considered to be his home line, therefore this work is dedicated to George Pryer, railwayman, historian, and friend.

Published by The Oakwood Press (Usk), P.O. Box 13, Usk, Mon., NP15 1YS.
E-mail: sales@oakwoodpress.co.uk
Website: www.oakwoodpress.co.uk

Contents

Front cover: A specially commissioned painting by Mike Jeffries of Beattie 2-4-0 No. 159 *Castleman* standing in the up platform of the original Wareham station.

Title page: The Canute Castle Hotel near the docks in Southampton, illustrated in Measom's Guide to the London & South Western Railway of 1856. It was at this point that King Canute allegedly made his attempt to hold back the sea, which was doomed to failure. However, to the left of this illustration the earliest docks were constructed in the 1840s and assured Southampton's future expansion as both a seaport and as an important railway centre. *Author's Collection*

Rear cover, top: A turn of the century view of Bournemouth Central looking west, viewed from Holdenhurst Road Bridge. *Author's Collection*
Rear cover, bottom: The camera captured this quiet moment at Brockenhurst just after the turn of the century, the Morant Arms dominates the scene with the main road to Lyndhurst going away in the centre. The crossing gates are still hand-operated, not yet controlled from Brockenhurst East signal box behind which stands crossing cottage No. 7 dating from the opening of the line. Today busy traffic heads to and from Lymington and its ferries, and Brockenhurst has established a substantial tourist economy. *Author's Collection*

Acknowledgements

To assemble a work of this nature reference has been made to a great many documents, newspapers and other sources. The surviving documents of the Southampton & Dorchester Company and minute books of the LSWR have been consulted, as have the principal newspapers of the area including *Bournemouth Observer*, *Bournemouth Visitors Directory*, *Christchurch Times*, *Dorset County Chronicle*, *Hampshire Advertiser*, *Hampshire Independent*, *Poole & East Dorset Herald*, *Southern Times*, various transport journals including *The Railway Times* and the *LSWR Gazette*.

The assistance of the following organizations is gratefully acknowledged, Bournemouth Central Library, Bournemouth Railway Club, Dorset County Record Centre, Dorset County Museum. The Lens of Sutton Association, The National Archive at Kew, Poole Museum, Ringwood Library, Southampton City Archive, Southampton Central Library, Signalling Record Society, South Western Circle. Weymouth Central Library, Wimborne Railway Club. Thanks are also due to the late George Pryer for his expert assistance on railway matters and his work on the manuscript at the early stages.

The author wishes to thank all who have so generously offered their knowledge and time with various questions that have arisen, in particular, J. Alsop, Mrs Maureen Attwooll, Miss Wendy Brown, Dr J. Boudreau, C.L. Caddy, R.S. Carpenter, C. Chivers, P. Foster, D.M. Habgood, M. King, B. Moody, N. Pomfrat, L. Popplewell, J. Read, the late R.C. Riley, C. Stone, P. Swift, B. Thirlwall and M. Thresh.

Many of the photographs in this work have been provided by various organizations and individuals and have been duly credited. Others have come from the author's collection, which has been accumulated over a number of years, many with their provenance uncertain, so if I have inadvertently infringed anyone's copyright, please accept my apologies.

I should also like to thank the Oakwood team for their help and assistance, and finally my wife for her encouragement and forbearance whilst this work was being researched and written.

The upper part of Weymouth Esplanade depicted around the time of the railway's arrival in the town. The large building in the centre was the Burdon Hotel, a frequent holiday residence of Sir Daniel Gooch of the GWR. Had the Southampton and Dorchester plan for an independent station been proceeded with, it would have approached from behind St John's Church in the background and terminated immediately behind the Hotel Burden (today the Prince Regent Hotel). *Maureen Attwooll Collection*

Introduction

The original railway from Southampton to Dorchester, Castleman's Corkscrew, was a classic of its age. A 60 mile line through a predominately rural area with little hope of obtaining revenue from industry *en route*. Indeed it was also unusual in that all the original Directors and majority of the shareholders were the gentry, whereas most lines could boast a number of industrialists, who saw their railway as a means of transporting the raw materials and products of industry. Therefore one has to ask the question why build a railway at that time into such countryside? One answer is that Dorchester was not the goal, and with Weymouth considered as an afterthought, the aim must have been the desire to progress further west into Devon and perhaps beyond!

Readers might be surprised that this work covers a subject far greater than the original Castleman's Corkscrew. If the true letter of the title were adhered to it would have been an unusual history to compile. Weymouth the eventual end of the line, and at the time the most important town, was served by the Great Western Railway (GWR), with the London & South Western Railway (LSWR) only having running rights from Dorchester Junction, their own plans for an independent branch to the port having been abandoned, thus by default the eventual terminus of the line was on Great Western territory!

Likewise, Bournemouth, which hardly existed in 1845, would be left out along with the lines that eventually served the County Borough which Bournemouth had become by the turn of the century clearly demonstrating its rapid growth, which changed the entire demographic structure of the surrounding area as the evolution of Bournemouth altered the course of history

Today both ends of the original line are still operational, the centre section, in later years referred to as 'The Old Road', has disappeared from the map, a victim of the Beeching era. Therefore to have written this work without referring in detail to the development of the Bournemouth area would have created a large void in the history of the original line. As all these lines became inextricably linked they have been included to provide a complete history.

Weymouth in itself is a complex story, in the main concerning the GWR, and therefore this work has restricted itself to events that concerned the LSWR and its successors for the completeness of their history, as with the branch lines to Lymington, Swanage and Portland. The same applies to that much celebrated line, the Somerset & Dorset Railway. Although not the direct subject of this work, its affairs from its interception with running powers over the LSWR between Wimborne and Bournemouth West are inextricably linked, as part of the rich tapestry that is woven into the railway history of East Dorset.

The Southampton & Dorchester Railway technically commenced at Southampton Junction resulting in all lines west of Southampton tunnel being part of the story. However, not wishing to overload an already complex narrative, the history of Southampton's Western Docks, except where mentioned in context, has been omitted and the author feels that it rightly belongs to Southampton's maritime history.

Over the years the names of a number of stations have been changed; to avoid confusion in the earlier part of the text the later name has been added in brackets after the name in use at that time. The table overleaf shows the name changes of stations:

Original name	New name	Date re-named
Blechynden	Southampton West	July 1858
	Southampton Central	7th July, 1935
	Southampton	10th July, 1967
Bournemouth East	Bournemouth Central	1st May, 1899
Bournemouth Central	Bournemouth	10th July, 1967
Boscombe	Pokesdown	October 1891
Brokenhurst	Brockenhurst	1849
Bishopstoke	Eastleigh	1852
Christchurch Road	Holmsley	1863
Dorchester	Dorchester South	November 1949
Hinton	Hinton Admiral	1st May, 1888
Hurne	Hurn	1897
Milton	New Milton	May 1897
New Poole Junction	Poole Junction	January 1876
	Poole Junction & Broadstone	July 1883
	Broadstone & New Poole Junction	January 1887
	Broadstone Junction	March 1888
	Broadstone	July 1929
Poole	Hamworthy	2nd December, 1872
Poole Junction	Hamworthy Junction	2nd December, 1872
Southampton	Southampton Docks	July 1858
	Southampton Town & Docks	September 1896
	Southampton Town for Docks	November 1912
	Southampton Terminus	9th July, 1923

The complexity of events in the last 160 years also requires that certain events of a national nature are described to assist the reader through the minefield of political and other circumstances that have affected railways over the years. Unfortunately although rail travel had become available to the masses during the Victorian era, photography was still the luxury of the few and was a complex business thus many of the illustrations in this volume are of a later period. Likewise to avoid duplication of material further details of both the Poole Harbour Tramway and the Hamworthy branch can be obtained in *Rails To Poole Harbour* by Colin Stone, also published by Oakwood Press.

A majority of railway history measurements were quoted in imperial, this has been retained in the historic context, consultation of a conversion table will satisfy those who appreciate metric measurements. Also the recorded miles engines travelled was not an exact science, locomotives were not equipped with mileometers, the records were compiled from various daily duty records which at times for a number of reasons could be inaccurate.

Over the years the value of money has changed out of all recognition making the costing and wages of the past difficult to compare. However, economic historians consider £1 in 1851 would equate to about £61.50 in 2007.

The author does not claim this work to be the Alpha and Omega, unfortunately the lack of some early records, drawings and photographs has denied both the author and reader a fuller picture of the early days.

Brian Jackson
Weymouth
2007

Chapter One

Charles Castleman and his Family

Much has been written concerning the great railway engineers and entrepreneurs of the Victorian age. However, little is known of the careers and private lives of the many less famous men who were instrumental in the construction of Britain's railways.

One such man was Charles Castleman, the driving force behind the company which brought the first railway to West Hampshire and Dorset. This line, due to its circuitous route, is known as 'Castleman's Corkscrew'. Unlike the greats of his time, no biography of Charles Castleman has ever been published, thus a little information about the man and his family is relevant to the history of the railway to Dorchester.

The Castlemans were an influential family from the Dorset village of Chettle. William Castleman (1766-1838) moved to Wimborne and established himself in the legal profession, in which capacity he became Deanery Steward to the Hanham Estate. During 1800 he went into partnership with William Dean and George Adams to form the Christchurch, Wimborne & Ringwood Bank also acting as the new bank's legal advisor.

William Dean was a member of the family that later (as Cooper-Dean) developed much of Bournemouth. Dean died in 1812 and was succeeded at the bank by his son-in-law William Clapcott, but by 1818 the bank was making heavy losses, causing William Castleman to resign and withdraw his capital. Shrewd businessman that he was, Castleman then advanced considerable loans to Clapcott over a number of years to alleviate his difficulties.

Well-established at Wimborne, Castleman commissioned architect Jeffrey Wyatt (later Sir Jeffrey Wyattville) to design Allendale House, which became the family home in the town. As in many other families of the period, the Castleman's suffered a high infant mortality rate and of their 10 children only three sons, Henry, Edward and Charles survived beyond their teenage years.

Henry (1805-1863) entered the legal profession and practised at Christchurch, whilst Edward and Charles were also solicitors, setting up in practice as E. & C. Castleman with offices in Wimborne and Ringwood. Following the forming of the Southampton & Dorchester Railway Company, Edward invested £3,500 in shares but thereafter appears to have had little direct involvement in it, concentrating his career on the administration of country estates and becoming steward to the large Bankes estate. He married Ann Fryer, daughter of a local banker and granddaughter of the infamous Dorset smuggler Isaac Gulliver. They lived at Allendale House until Edward's retirement, moving to Chettle House at Chettle, a property his father had purchased in 1826. Edward died aged 61, in 1861.

This branch of the family's unusual claim to fame came in October 1882 when one of his daughters, Edith Mary Hanham, was cremated at Manston House, Blandford, the first recorded cremation in England in modern times. At that time it was uncertain if cremation was actually legal, the first public crematorium not opening until 1885.

Allendale House, Wimborne, the Castleman's family home. Today, after extensive restoration, it is the headquarters of the East Dorset Heritage Trust.   *Author*

St Ives House, Ringwood, the home of Charles Castleman between 1848 and 1862. Photographed during the 1930s, Castleman rebuilt the original house and towards the end of his stay added the conservatory.   *East Dorset Heritage Trust*

Who resided at Allendale House in later years is unclear, in late 1854 the Revd C. Tockington was in residence although it still appears to have belonged to the Castleman family in 1885, as it was sold in May that year following a dispute between parties named Smith and Collis who were relatives on Edward's side of the family. Between 1905 and the 1930s the building was occupied by Wimborne School for Girls and from 1937 until 1974 it housed the offices of Wimborne Urban District Council, after which an antiques company occupied the ground floor, with a restaurant above. In May 2001 a major refurbishment commenced and today East Dorset Heritage Trust occupies Allendale House, which is used for various purposes including an adult education centre.

Charles Castleman (1807-1876) pursued his profession somewhat differently from his brother, combining legal work with a growing interest in transport systems. Through his involvement in the Turnpike Trusts and the maintenance of roads he had realised the importance of a good transport network. There is little doubt at first he undertook the work of instigating the railway scheme purely in his professional capacity at the behest of William Lambert. However, Castleman soon became the driving force behind the formation of the Southampton & Dorchester Railway Company, investing £5,000 in it and becoming the company's Secretary and solicitor. He was appointed a Director of the London & South Western Railway in 1855, Deputy Chairman in 1859 and Chairman in December 1872, his predecessor, Captain Mangles, having resigned through ill health. Unfortunately, Castleman was also to suffer indifferent health and his chairmanship was short. At the half-yearly General Meeting in February 1875, the Deputy Chairman, R.H. Dutton, expressed great regret at the absence of Mr Castleman through illness and shortly afterwards Castleman resigned to be replaced by Dutton.

It is clear from the earliest days of Charles Castleman's professional life that he was a man of courage, prepared to embark on the Southampton & Dorchester scheme and take on the might of the LSWR, the Great Western Railway, and other authorities to achieve his aims for the Southampton & Dorchester company. As an LSWR Director, his first responsibility was to the railway and its shareholders, but he was a humane man and in 1861 he took much time in planning a new superannuation scheme, introduced in 1864 for the company's officers and clerks.

Castleman's private life was as traumatic as his business life had been successful. Even the privileged classes could not avoid the harshness of living in the Victorian era.

He married firstly Martha Jane Henning, at St Mary's Church, Weymouth on 30th April, 1832. She was the only child of John and Diana Henning. The Hennings could trace their roots back to Tudor times and were well established with property throughout the county including Weymouth and Melcombe Regis. An earlier John Henning had built Poxwell Manor and was linked through marriage to the Trenchards, another established Dorset family. Henry Henning had been one of Weymouth's two MPs between 1679 and 1694, whilst Edmund Henning was a banker whose business, the Weymouth & Dorsetshire Bank, failed in the Georgian period.

The only known portrait of Charles Castleman.   *Courtesy Mrs Marie Simcox*

John Henning was the son of Robert Henning of Alton Pancras and around 1800 commenced practice as a solicitor at Weymouth, a town councillor and an Alderman and owned a considerable amount of property in the area. He was the owner of a sulphuretted hydrogen spring discovered at Radipole in 1830, and, following the erection of a pump room, Radipole Spa was in business until the early 1870s when it fell into disuse, the Radipole Steam Laundry later being built on the site!

As a member of the town council Henning was vociferous in the matter of bringing the railways to Weymouth, and with the formation of the Southampton & Dorchester Railway Company took out £1,000 of shares.

In April 1848, Castleman, then described as an 'Attorney of Ringwood', purchased St Ives House, Ringwood. It would appear there were no children from his marriage to Martha and she died of fever, aged 41, at St Ives House on 21st December, 1848. Her body was brought back to Weymouth for burial in the crypt of Holy Trinity Church, where a memorial tablet to her can be found on the east transept wall. In the tradition of many Victorian gentlemen, once a respectable period of mourning had been observed, a second marriage was entered into. On 26th February, 1852 Charles Castleman wed Louisa Elizabeth Hussey at Littleham, Exmouth and from this union a daughter, Emma Jane, was born on 4th October, 1853. The following year fate struck again. Louisa died, aged only 27, from tuberculosis whilst staying at Bonchurch, Isle of Wight. Rather unusually, she too was buried in the crypt of Holy Trinity Church, Weymouth.

Widower Castleman married for a third time on 31st March, 1859 at Ringwood parish church, his bride being Isabel Swinburne. He remained close to the family of his first wife, Martha Henning. Her father, John Henning, died in 1860 and his wife Diana in 1866. Both were buried in a vault in the new Melcombe Regis cemetery, at Weymouth, constructed jointly with Charles Castleman. Castleman was executor of Henning's will in which he left,

> To my excellent son-in-law Charles Castleman of St Ives, near Ringwood, Hants, Esquire, one hundred pounds sterling as a small token of my regards. To my dear little godchild Emma Jane Castleman daughter of the said Charles Castleman, one hundred pounds sterling with my affectionate love.

Following bequests to business partners and friends the bulk of his estate, which included a number of properties in Weymouth, was left to his widow. Upon her death it was to pass to Charles Castleman, a demonstration of the depth of affection which remained between the two families.

In 1862 Charles Castleman moved from St Ives House to Glasshayes, Lyndhurst. He was a Justice of the Peace and a Commissioner of the Deer Enclosures Act for the New Forest, and gave evidence before a Royal Commission in May 1868. His status in Hampshire society can be judged by an arrangement he came to with the local council. Castleman considered that a lane known as Love Lane, which ran alongside his residence, Glasshayes (today the Lyndhurst Park Hotel), impinged upon his privacy. The council agreed to close the lane and Castleman provided a clock (value £300) for the tower of the new parish church!

The Lyndhurst Park Hotel, Lyndhurst, formerly the Grand Hotel. Although now much rebuilt, it was originally 'Glasshays', the residence of Charles Castleman from 1862 until his move to Richmond. *Author's Collection*

The south side of the Lyndhurst Park Hotel, photographed during 2007. *Author*

On 3rd April, 1872 his daughter Emma married Algernon Hay Lushington, also of Lyndhurst, who was described as an Attorney and Solicitor. He was the eldest son of Frederick Actell Lushington and Lady Margaret Julia Hay Lushington, daughter of the 17th Earl of Erroll and from a wealthy Scottish land owning family. The Lushingtons' ancestry can be traced back to the 16th century in Kent and the family's baronetcy to 1791.

By the time he became Chairman of the LSWR, Charles Castleman had moved to the Crows Nest, Queens Road, Richmond, Surrey. Following his resignation from the post he purchased a freehold property, The Grove, Bishopstoke (now known as Eastleigh), but was not to enjoy the pleasures of a well-earned retirement for long, dying of kidney failure on 17th July, 1876.

Castleman was buried in the vault at Weymouth on 20th July, 1876. His Will specifically stated, 'I desire that my funeral may be as plain and economical as my executors can reasonably make it' and it must have been a very private affair, for despite his position in society and the conveyance of his body to Weymouth by train, no mention of his funeral appeared in the local press.

Castleman's Will had been drawn up by Weymouth solicitor George Andrews, former partner of, and successor to, John Henning. It consisted of 25 hand-written pages, plus a two page codicil and gave explicit instructions as to the disposal of his estate. Castleman's estimated wealth was stated to be £18,000, and by today's standards he was a millionaire.

His third wife, Isabel, was bequeathed an annuity of £100 to be divided into quarterly payments. She survived him by four years, dying at Winchester in August 1880, aged 53. After various bequests to friends and household staff, the bulk of the estate was left to his daughter Emma, the will incorporating clauses to protect her, her husband and any children of the marriage.

Charles Castleman did not live to see his first grandchild, Muriel, born to Emma six months later on 19th January, 1877. By 1879 Emma and her family had moved to Sandown, Isle of Wight where on 15th September she gave birth to her second child, Herbert Castleman Lushington. Unfortunately Emma suffered from epileptic convulsions following her confinement and she died aged 26 on 4th October, 1879 and was buried at Sandown.

Her husband Algernon Hay Lushington, remarried on 6th January, 1881. His second wife was Effie Lillian Newall, second daughter of Captain W.E. Newall of the 92nd Gordon Highlanders, and she gave birth to a son Montague Hay Lushington on 24th November, 1881.

The Lushingtons were living in 1881 at Audley House, Culver Road, Sandown and that year's census described Algernon as a 'gentleman income derived from dividends'. The family moved later to Lansdowne, Queens Road, Shanklin. Algernon Hay Lushington died, aged 83, on 13th September 1930. In February 1943 his widow Effie and her spinster stepdaughter Muriel moved into a suite of two bedrooms and a lounge/dining room at the Palmerston Hotel, Shanklin. Effie died on 26th July, 1946, aged 85. Muriel lived to 90 years of age, dying on 7th February, 1969.

Emma's son Herbert Castleman Lushington had a long and distinguished life, serving in the Army in both World Wars. His first son, Henry Edmund Lushington was born in October 1910, but what might be described as the curse of the Castlemans visited Herbert in 1927 when his wife died.

Ten years later Herbert found himself in line to inherit the Lushington baronetcy. His father's cousin, the 5th baronet Sir Arthur Patrick Lushington, died in 1927 having failed to produce a male heir. Next in line would have been Herbert's father, Algernon Hay Lushington, but he had died in 1930, so the title passed to his son, Herbert, by his first wife Emma.

When Herbert, now Sir Herbert Castleman Lushington 6th baronet, died in October 1968, the title passed to his son, who became Sir Henry Edmund Castleman Lushington, 7th baronet. Following his death in 1988 the title passed to his son Sir John Richard Castleman Lushington, 8th baronet, the present holder of the title and the great-great-grandson of Charles Castleman.

During the 1880s there were references at several Weymouth Council meetings to the Castleman Estate, and as late as the 1960s the Lushington family still owned property at Lodmoor Hill, Weymouth, an inheritance from the marriage in 1832 of Charles Castleman and Martha Henning.

Today, walkers and cyclists can explore the countryside along sections of the closed railway line between Ringwood and Poole, which forms the 'Castleman Trail'. At West Moors, where the station once stood, is a sheltered housing complex named 'Castleman Court'. In Ringwood the direct successors of E. & C. Castleman, solicitors, still practice in Market Square, the road built over the site of the old station is named Castleman Way. However, to the railway historian, the name 'Castleman's Corkscrew' will always remain synonymous with the original railway to Dorchester.

Charles Castleman's grave together with that of the parents of his first wife in Melcombe Regis Cemetery, Weymouth. Buried amongst the good and great of the town, the obelisk to the right marks the resting place of Joseph Drew, proprietor of the *Southern Times* and director of Messrs Cosens & Company who brought paddle steamers to the resort.

Author

Chapter Two

A Railway for Dorset

To appreciate fully the impact railways had on the community one firstly has to consider the years prior to their introduction. Travelling any distance involved a journey by horse or horse-drawn vehicle over inferior roads. Prior to 1600 a journey from London to Dorchester on horseback could take three days, whilst by 1658 the London-Dorchester coach took 2½ days. However, by 1769 with improvements to the roads the journey time had been reduced to a day and a half, by 1796 this had been further reduced to 25 hours. Until 1800 Weymouth passengers had to transfer to another coach upon arrival at Dorchester, by 1810 London to Weymouth could be achieved in 18 hours; although there had been a considerable improvement in timings the journey was still a trial of endurance.

The opening of the railway between London and Southampton in 1840 enabled a passenger to leave Dorchester by coach at 5 am and arrive at Southampton in time to board the 1 pm train reaching London at 5 pm; this reduced the journey time to 12 hours. Following the opening of the Southampton & Dorchester Railway in 1847 the entire journey was undertaken by rail in 5½ hours, demonstrating the great advantages of rail travel.

In the decade following the opening of the Liverpool & Manchester Railway in 1830, men of business and industry became fully aware of the benefits offered by rail transport and schemes for new lines proliferated. By the end of 1844, 2,235 miles of railway were in operation in the British Isles with an additional 855 miles authorized, and a further 2,816 miles having been proposed. Some were excellent, some mediocre, but there were also some wildly speculative ideas that had no chance of commercial success. Indeed, it was said at the time that - except for a few established companies - the only money being made out of railways was lining the pockets of solicitors and land agents, which was largely true. The average price of railway shares peaked in 1845 and remained high the following year. Collapse followed in 1847, and many small investors lost their life savings in ill-conceived railway ventures, as it seemed that every town and village in the Country sought a connection with the system, and the era was dubbed the 'Railway Mania'.

Dorset was a very sparsely populated county with a population of little over 65,000 in the mid-1830s, although the seaports of Poole and Weymouth had an attraction to a few interested parties. As early as 1825/26 there was an attempt by Somerset colliery owners to replace the ailing Dorset & Somerset Canal and construct the Radstock, Shaftesbury & Poole Railway to form communication with the English Channel, with a route planned via Frome, Warminster, Shaftesbury, Blandford and Dorchester; as with many other early grand plans little progress was made. The same applied to a proposal in the *Dorset County Chronicle and Somersetshire Gazette* during April 1833 for a railway between Weymouth and Dorchester, the tunnelling through Ridgeway Hill being considered a minor importance. A more plausible scheme was the Bath &

Weymouth Great Western Union Railway of 1836, routed via Bathampton, Freshford, Frome, Witham, Wincanton, Cerne Abbas, and Dorchester, with a number of branches that connected with the Somerset coalfield and the quarries on the Isle of Portland. The mention of Purbeck paving stones and other minerals and commodities in the Prospectus adds conjecture as to what the ambitions of the project were. Unfortunately, as only half the share list had been subscribed the Bill was rejected by Parliament in May 1837.

A further look at Dorset in the early 1840s still does not make it appear a likely candidate for prospective railway schemes. There was a conspicuous lack of heavy industry, no coal mines, a thinly spread population, and - over much of east Dorset and west Hampshire - a poor soil that placed agriculture at a disadvantage. Much of the land between the River Test at Totton and the River Avon at Christchurch was in fact occupied by the New Forest, a vast, lonely admixture of heath land and deciduous woods that William the Conqueror had set aside as hunting country. Though long since freed from the harsh laws of a Royal Forest, much of it remained Crown property under the aegis of the Commissioners of Woods & Forests and development was tightly controlled.

There were a few towns: Lymington, Ringwood, Wimborne, Christchurch, Poole, Wareham, Dorchester and Weymouth, but they were small and well spaced out - and a glance at the map shows the impractibility of attempting to connect them all up with one line of railway. At the time Bournemouth did not even exist, so it is not surprising that the promoters of the Southampton & Dorchester Railway thought it more advantageous to skirt around the northern edge of the Forest to serve Ringwood and Wimborne, rather than face the difficulties of building a coastal line via Christchurch and Poole where the potential route was obstructed by the waters of Poole Harbour.

Despite its status as county town of Dorset, Dorchester was a very small place and unlikely to repay the cost of building a line some 60 miles long in order to reach it, so one gets the immediate impression that something else was afoot - as indeed it was!

The Southampton & Dorchester Railway was unusual in the fact that in its early days it was completely controlled by country gentlemen, without the industrialists and other interested parties that were involved in a majority of schemes. Apart from Southampton, a seaport that was rapidly developing, the line passed through a predominately rural landscape and apart from the small port of Poole only served market towns to terminate at Dorchester. Weymouth was only added as an afterthought which strengthens the theory that a westward extension to Exeter was the main aim of several of the principal investors. Both promoter Charles Castleman and the company's Engineer, Moorsom, were on record as being in favour of such a policy, and there were other factors that raise the possibility of the extension of the line being conceived from the beginning.

Three of the original Directors of the company were distant cousins, De Mauley, Brockner and Lambert. William Charles Lambert (1797-1877) resided at Winterbourne Steepleton, a small village west of Dorchester, which in 1841 was inhabited by 191 people (in the Prospectus Lambert is stated as residing at Wimborne!). Lambert was a very influential person, a barrister at law at the

Inner Temple, a man of influence, wealth and business interests in the West Country, he had reasons for procuring a line to the West, in particular one that passed his house! Although in his professional position he had to be circumspect how he was seen to act in the matter, there is little doubt he assisted his cousins in the raising of the capital, and his legal knowledge was of great assistance when applying for the Acts of Parliament. Fellow members of the legal profession, his personal friend Edward Castleman and his brother Charles were employed to promote the scheme. Charles Castleman was to become the mastermind behind the scheme and was without a doubt influenced by Lambert, soon became deeply involved, perhaps more than he had originally intended, to the extent that his name became synonymous with the railway.

The early date of the Southampton & Dorchester Railway can also be explained by the politics of the day and the frustrated desires of the two major companies of the area: the London & South Western Railway, which had begun life as the London & Southampton Railway, changed its name in June 1839 to appease Portsmouth, and completed its line throughout from the Nine Elms station in London to a terminus in Southampton, near the docks, on 11th May, 1840. The other was an alliance of broad gauge companies led by - and later amalgamated with - the Great Western Railway which, having reached Bristol from Paddington in June 1841, contrived to gain access to the far west over the Bristol & Exeter and South Devon railways (Exeter was reached in 1844).

The LSWR harboured two long-term ambitions above all else: to reach Bristol (which it never did) and to extend westwards to Exeter and Plymouth. For its part the GWR longed to gain footholds in Southampton and Portsmouth. The former was partially realised later in the century but the latter always eluded them - but these ambitions do go some way towards explaining why the canny GWR Board willingly embraced a company rejoicing in the title of the 'Wilts & Somerset Railway' which planned to construct not just a broad gauge line from a point near Corsham (later known as Thingley Junction) to Salisbury but also branch from Westbury to Frome. The latter was intended as a launch into the then-developing Somerset coalfield, but much of the country through which it passed was thinly-populated and distinctly rural - hardly the sort of territory to return a large operating profit - so the GWR's attraction must have been that Salisbury offered possibilities for an extension to Southampton!

Soon after the publication of the Wilts & Somerset's scheme not only did another broad gauge company, the Bristol and Exeter Railway (B&E), make an attempt on Dorset with a line from Durston (near Taunton) to Weymouth via Yeovil, but the Wilts & Somerset enlarged upon its original plan to the extent that the Westbury-Salisbury section was relegated to branch line status with the 'main' line now seen as running from Thingley Junction to Weymouth by way of Frome, Castle Cary, Yeovil and Dorchester. To avoid Parliamentary conflict, the B&E was soon persuaded to terminate its line from Durston at Yeovil. Weymouth was of course a seaport that would have generated traffic in its own right and it had been made a fashionable watering place by George III so some long-distance passenger business could doubtless be anticipated. But again such a scheme involved miles of railway through undeveloped countryside devoid of industry, so the continued support of the GWR can be explained only by the fact that the revised plan furnished them with two chances of reaching Southampton; the short one via Salisbury or the long one via Dorchester and the coast. It was, however, an enthusiasm not shared by investors in general, for the Wilts, Somerset & Weymouth Railway (as the company had now become) always experienced the greatest difficulty in attracting capital, and this was to cause many delays in construction.

Naturally the LSWR grew nervous over the possibility of broad gauge incursion and doubtless longed to give the GWR some worries in return by projecting a line towards Exeter, thus generating exactly the right climate that could be exploited by a clever man. That 'clever man' was Charles Castleman, a Wimborne solicitor.

The Castlemans were part of the local Establishment. William was a solicitor, attorney, and notary of Wimborne, and two of his three sons - Edward and Charles - followed him into the legal profession, setting up a satellite office at Ringwood and becoming clerks to the Wimborne and Puddletown Turnpike. Charles was visionary enough to realise that the future lay with iron roads rather than the turnpike variety and soon drew up a set of proposals for a railway from Southampton to Dorchester, which he placed before the LSWR Board on 2nd February, 1844. Clearly he sensed what was happening behind

Dorchester is a town whose origins date back over four-thousand years, the Romans established the town proper which through the years developed into a market town serving a large rural area becoming the county town of Dorset at which the Southampton & Dorchester Railway arrived in 1847. An illustration from the early 1850s depicts Cornhill, at the top of South Street, showing the Antelope Hotel a long established coaching inn.   *Author's Collection*

A well-known local landmark stood at the entrance to Dorchester station. Officially known as crossing cottage No. 43 it is only conjecture that this would have ever become a proper crossing cottage, assuming any projected extension had taken that route.

South Western Circle, Eyers Collection

the scenes, for he was at pains to explore with them the prospect of extension west of Dorchester and/or Salisbury.

The talk must have been encouraging, for Castleman convened public meetings at Poole and Weymouth to canvass support - although the latter seems rather a tactless choice in view of the fact that the port would not be catered for! These were soon to be followed by a further meeting in Dorchester, by which time enough enthusiasm had been shown for the project to progress. Much of Castleman's support emanated from the 'landed' class, keen to enhance the value of their property; farmers were also quick to see the advantage of a reliable transport facility that would make their produce more competitive.

The meeting held at Weymouth on 6th May, 1844 quickly showed that although Castleman's scheme was of great interest, several of those present had others in view. The meeting was ostensibly called 'For the purpose of taking into consideration the contemplated railway from Southampton to Dorchester and means of giving effect to so desirable a scheme'.

The Mayor Sir Edward Johnson stated,

> There could hardly be a doubt that if a line was brought to Dorchester either by the South Western Company as now proposed, or by the Great Western Company, the terminus would not remain in that town, therefore he would advise them to use every exertion to get Weymouth at once adopted as the terminus, because the expense of the Bill would be the same if Weymouth was left out.

Concern was expressed that if Weymouth failed to become the terminus of the line, the Packet Service between the town and the Channel Islands could well move to Southampton, quoting the recent move of certain shipping services from Falmouth to the rail-connected Hampshire port. It was stated that, 'A railroad direct from Weymouth to London should be of the greatest advantage, but if they could not have this, they must join any branch as best they could'.

TO THE NOBILITY, GENTRY, AND OTHER PROPRIETORS AND INHABITANTS OF THE NEIGHBOURHOOD OF DORCHESTER AND WEYMOUTH.

MY LORDS AND GENTLEMEN,

It having been reported to us that CAPTAIN MACDONALD and MR. TOWNSEND have called Meetings in your Towns for the purpose of inducing you to express a feeling in favor of a Line of Railway from Dorchester towards Stalbridge, to communicate with the projected extension of the South-Western from Salisbury Westward towards Taunton, and that at the Meeting at Weymouth Mr. Townsend stated that this Line was in opposition to the Projected Railway from Southampton to Dorchester, and further that the South-Western Company would give their opposition to the latter Line, we take the liberty of addressing you on the subject.

In the first place, we believe Mr. Townsend to have been misled as to the views of the South-Western Company, as we have what we deem the best grounds for saying, that no opposition is contemplated by them to the Line from Southampton to Dorchester.

Secondly---As Captain Moorsom is proceeding most rapidly with his Survey of the Coast Line, we earnestly entreat of you to withhold any expression of your opinions until after the intended Meeting at Dorchester, on the 19th of July next, when his Report will be laid before you.

And lastly, we would respectfully submit for your consideration, whether far greater advantage would not be derived to your Neighbourhoods by the making of the Projected Line from Weymouth to Bath, than by the proposed Branch from Dorchester to Stalbridge, and that more especially if taken in conjunction with our Projected Line from Southampton to Dorchester.

We have the honor to be,
MY LORDS AND GENTLEMEN,
Your very faithful & most obedient Servants,
EDWARD & CHARLES CASTLEMAN.

Ringwood, 14th June, 1844.

WOODFORD, PRINTER, BOOKBINDER AND STATIONER, RINGWOOD.

A notice published by Edward & Charles Castleman in June 1844 explaining various aspects of the proposed railways in the Dorchester area.

The Revd Urquhart, assistant Curate of St Mary's Church, Weymouth spoke with much enthusiasm of the advantages of railway communication, and continued by stating that 'it was of the greatest importance to lose no time in bringing the line on to Weymouth which he though would be best effected by joining the Great Western Company. This he knew from a letter he had received from this powerful Company desirous of adopting a line to Weymouth'.

Following the introduction of this second scheme into the meeting, there was much delusory discussion between those assembled. Weymouth solicitor and town councillor, Mr John Henning (Castleman's father-in-law) told the meeting if the Reverend gentleman had attended to a letter from Messrs Castleman or had waited until the second resolution had been round, he would have refrained from introducing the question of another line. It was intended that the line should come on to Weymouth and whether the line came from Southampton to Dorchester or Bath to Dorchester the terminal could not stop there, the line must come on to Weymouth. Mr Henning then made the point, had the Great Western ever made any public offer to Weymouth? It was true that a private communication appears to have been made to an individual, or individuals, but this meeting could not take any notice of that, much less to proceed to act on it.

Following further discussion that the main point of the meeting was to support the Southampton & Dorchester scheme, it was decided that representation should be made at the Southampton meeting, which was to be held in three days. However, by the termination of the meeting it was clear that other schemes could be in the offing!

A very well attended public meeting was held in Southampton Town Hall on 9th May, 1844, at which Castleman said he now wanted to test the soundness of the scheme by appointing a committee to examine every aspect in detail before taking positive steps in the formation of a company. The proposed route was also discussed; it emerged that the intended junction with the London-Southampton line would be at Northam. From here the line would run along the shore of the Test estuary to Redbridge where the river would be crossed on a viaduct, thence through the very heart of the New Forest to Wimborne before reaching Dorchester by way of Bere Regis and Puddletown - a distance of 52 miles.

A provisional Committee was formed without delay - and included a few notables such as Lord Malmesbury (who owned large estates south of Ringwood), Lord de Mauley of Canford near Wimborne, and Colonel Henderson, the Mayor of Southampton. Also included were representatives from the towns en route and, to ensure the continued interest of the LSWR, the Chairman of that company, William Chaplin.

On 30th May the committee appointed an Engineer, William Scarth Moorsom, to make a survey of the line and submit detailed costings as quickly as possible. Moorsom had been an assistant to Robert Stephenson during construction of the London & Birmingham Railway and Engineer in Charge of the Birmingham & Gloucester Railway, so he certainly did not lack experience. His report was presented to the committee at the Crown Inn, Wimborne, on 18th July, 1844 - and it recommended a number of changes to the original plan.

The wording of the report by today's standards could well be described as verbose. However, it does clearly illustrate the thoughts and circumstances of the time, and is therefore recorded as written in 1844.

With reference to your instructions conveyed under date of 4th June [I] have examined the country generally between Southampton, Dorchester, and Weymouth and I now reply first, specifically to the points named, and secondly, shall give my general recommendation upon the line of Railway to be adopted.

All the lines laid down upon your map possess the advantageous feature of connecting, in a very direct manner, the proposed termini; but they do not appear to have been drawn with much regard to the expense of construction, nor to that facility of communication between the different intermediate towns and villages which I consider essential in a railway such as this now under consideration. The principal objections in regard to the former points are - that these lines run over considerable elevations, which would require expensive cuttings, or even tunneling, to reduce them to their proper railway planes; and with regard to the latter point, the only intermediate towns closely approached by any of them are Redbridge, Lyndhurst, and Wimborne, while the no less important places of Lymington, Ringwood, Poole, and Wareham, were left at more or less inconvenient distances. I have therefore considered - secondly, the lines by which all, or nearly all, the intermediate towns may be most conveniently served with due regard to the ornamental and other properties which might be injured by an injudicious position of the line; and after thus weighing the whole of the interest, and conferring as fully as time admitted with the proprietors and other parties interested, Save to recommend that the line should pass from Southampton, by way of Redbridge, within a mile on the south of Lyndhurst, by Brockenhurst and Ormansby Ford, to the south of Burley Beacon, by Crow to Ringwood, thence in a nearly direct course north that of Lions Hill to Wimborne, thence across near to Hamworthy Church and Poole, by Oakley and the Delph, thence by Rockley Point to Wareham, and onward by the vale of the Frome and Winfrith valley to Dorchester, terminating at the first bridge there.

The line onwards to Weymouth will be of a totally different character, for as I have understood that a direct connection with Dorchester would be material in the view of the inhabitants, both with reference to the existing traffic, and for facility of further connections onwards, it appears that a line directly over the hills, making the distance eight miles, and laid out for atmospheric traction, would be preferable to the alternative of tortuous deviations or expensive tunneling, which must be resorted to if a comparatively direct line were attempted for locomotive traction. Hence I should recommend that from Dorchester to Weymouth, the line be carried almost direct by Bincombe, and the terminus made at the Royal Terrace, a position which gives perfect facility for good connection with the principal part of the harbour.

At Southampton it would appear that at least two modes of entrance may be recommended. The most simple would be, to take generally the line of the abandoned canal, swerving a little where the exact line would interfere with ornamental property, and thus passing by a short tunnel, (one of small dimensions being already constructed), to join the South Western Railway at the bridge of the Fareham Road. Another entrance extremely advantageous for the town, as well as for a railway terminus, may be found by taking generally the line of the Western shore, and ending at the north end of the pier, from whence a tram line laid along the quays would give every necessary facility for uniting with the South Western Company's station, and provided that the various local authorities will cooperate with the provisional committee in procuring an easy right of access in the latter direction, I should recommend it in preference to the former; but without such assistance it may probably be found comparatively difficult and expensive, and therefore in such case the former should be preferred.

Wareham a small town dating back to pre-Roman times showing St Mary's Church Wareham, alongside the River Frome which once served the town from the sea. The arrival of the railway in 1847 was to provide the town with a new prosperity.

Author's Collection

The line which I recommend would thus pass within 4 miles of Lymington, 6 miles from Christchurch, and about the same from Bournemouth, while the stations at Ringwood, Wimborne, Poole, Wareham, and Dorchester, will be either in or near the entrance of those towns. The total distance exclusive of the Weymouth portion will be upwards of 59 miles. Thirdly with reference to communicating lines (by which I presume your instructions means branches). It does not appear to me necessary at present to lay down any branch from the line above recommended, for the facilities of access will by the main line be great without any branch, but it may probably hereafter be desirable to connect with Lymington by an easy branch about three miles long, and with Christchurch a similar connection may readily be formed should the traffic require it. With Blandford nothing is easier than to connect it if necessary.

Fourthly I have examined the country with a view to a junction with Salisbury rather than with Southampton. No difficulty would exist merely with reference to the country itself, but it might be difficult to avoid objectionable interference with the family seats of Lord Normanton and others of the nobility and gentry, while at the same time the public would be worse served than by the way of Southampton. The distance from Christchurch would be increased, Lymington, Beaulieu, and Redbridge would be excluded, and the populous neighbourhood of Lyndhurst otherwise so well accommodated would loose the advantage now contemplated. In addition to this the distance not only to Southampton but to the Metropolis, which is one of the main objects of this railway, would be increased, and the town of Southampton would lose a most advantageous connection, whilst Salisbury itself would not be proportionally benefited, inasmuch as the junction with Bishopstoke and Salisbury branch would be 3 miles distant from that city. In the event of any unforeseen difficulties occurring at Southampton, and if the owners of property should be desirous that a line of railway should be carried along the vale of the Avon, an easy line might be made in this direction.

Fifthly - may I state that the levels of this line are extremely favorable, the greater portion will be practically level, and the maximum inclination will not exceed one in 200, except for a short distance between Poole and Wimborne, where it may be desirable to increase the inclination to one in 100, so as to approach those towns more nearly and at less expense than could be otherwise done; and as a pilot engine would in all probability be stationed thereabouts necessarily from other considerations, this inclination would cause no difficulty in the practical working of the line. Your railway should unquestionably be a single track, provided with proper passing places, as is done on the Peterborough and other lines. The surface of the country between Southampton and Dorchester is remarkably favorable for a line of this character, and there is no one work upon the whole line, worth speaking of as presenting any feature other than is ordinary. The material is excellent, being with hardly any exception sand and gravel.

I have already observed that between Dorchester and Weymouth a totally different character of country is found, and this will be met by means of the atmospheric planes, which will involve works of only ordinary magnitude, and by which the traffic will be arranged with particular economy.

The expense of the line between Southampton and Dorchester will be about £450,000, and I feel confident, provided the original plans are adhered to, that I can procure tenders from responsible contractors, who will compete for executing the line at an amount so much within this as to leave you reasonable evidence that the total need not be exceeded.

The portion between Dorchester and Weymouth will probably require the addition sum of £104,000 including engines and necessary apparatus.

Sixthly - With regard to the traffic, persons have been stationed on the roads, and the whole of the information collected has been submitted to Mr Pare, whose report will be laid before you, and I am quite sure from the experience of 13 years on various railways, and now knowing this country, that the calculations which Mr Castleman made will be found to be under rather than over stated.

Seventhly - The opinions here given are based upon your desire, that the railway should be laid out with the utmost economy with good workmanship.

Eighthly - I have assumed for my calculations, that you adopt the ordinary construction. If by the time you come to execute the works there should be found no necessity for connecting with the iron railways now laid down, you may use wooden rails with considerable economy; and indeed if you were to adopt the latter construction, it would not prevent the ready transference of your traffic at the terminus. Arrangements of this nature must, however, depend upon the existing company with whose line you intend to connect.

Although not specifically alluded to in your instructions, I have pleasure in stating that the line has been laid so as not to interfere prejudicially with any ornamental residence in the country that I am aware of. Certainly there is no case of reasonable objection that has yet reached my notice - and it is impossible to avoid the conclusion that this line bringing every part of this coast in direct communication with the metropolis, passing through the heart of our great timber preserves, and from thence leading directly to our great Naval Arsenal, must be viewed as not only affording local convenience, but also as ensuring great national advantages.

It would then appear that every facility exists for making a substantial, and at the same time a cheap railway from the traffic of which a fair profit may be expected, but it should be remembered that to do this with due advantage to all parties is necessary that the influence of these counties should be combined in the undertaking, a fair proportionate interest locally taken up, is the best, and indeed the only assurance you can give to capitalists that you have a proper confidence in your own measure. By adopting this course you will be able to take upon yourselves the local management, which is extremely important for your own interest, whereas a contrary course would put in jeopardy the local accommodation, and may place the management in the hands of parties interested less for the undertaking than for other connections.

Moorsom's report was followed by a short report by Mr William Pare concerning the estimated traffic the line could generate:

I have at your request made an estimate of the probable traffic, and the revenue to be derived there from, which would pass along the proposed line of railway between Southampton and Dorchester, by way of Brockenhurst, Burley, Ringwood, Wimborne, Poole and Wareham, and I herewith hand you the result.

Taking such proposition only of the present traffic, along the route of the proposed railway, as experience fully warrants me in doing, and assuming, as is usual in these cases, that the number will be doubled in consequence of the facilities afforded by the railway, and which is the lowest ratio of increase on existing railways, I arrive at the gross annual revenue from this department of £37,659.

The revenue to be derived from the carriage of general merchandise, coal, timber, and agricultural produce I estimate at £9,000 of which £7,000 is derivable from produce now carried by land.

The income from the conveyance of cattle, gentlemen's carriages and horses, mails and small parcels, is calculated at £2,100. The total gross revenue as above stated will be £48,752 per annum, which after deducting 40 per cent for working expenses will leave a net income of £29,252 available for a dividend.

I have further at your request, made an estimate of the additional revenue, which would probably arise from an extension of the line from Dorchester to Weymouth, which may be fairly taken upon the same principle at £10,500.

In conclusion, I have to observe, that in framing the above estimate, I have carefully excluded all traffic respecting which doubts may be reasonably entertained, and from information already in my possession, I have no hesitation in saying that more extended enquiries and observations will not only fully confirm the present estimate, but will justify its increase.

Armed with these facts and figures the meeting voted to accept the Engineer's report.

Perhaps not surprisingly, the people of Weymouth were less than pleased with the scheme, being fearful that a railway terminating eight miles away on the opposite side of a high range of hills would render the port uncompetitive in the face of better-equipped Southampton. Moorsom had been at pains to address their concerns, but pointed out that as the intervening hills reached a height of some 400 feet they represented a considerable obstacle to railway building. However, he considered that - for £104,000 - a line to be worked on the 'atmospheric' system, which allowed much steeper gradients than conventional motive power could deal with, might furnish the answer. It was a bold statement, bearing in mind that the 'Atmospheric' system was something of an untried novelty at the time. Later practical experience, notably in South Devon, proved it to be disastrous: it was one of Brunel's few, yet very conspicuous, failures!

Fanciful as the idea of an Atmospheric line might have been it was enough to calm the agitated Weymouth faction and, at a public meeting in Dorchester the following day (19th July), Moorsom's proposals were approved. As another sop to Weymouth the name of the company was changed (rather subtly) to the Southampton and Dorsetshire Railway (a title used for a short period).

The Revd Urquhart speaking at the meeting, not mentioning his previous interest in the plans of the Great Western company, suggested a line approaching Weymouth from the east. He wished to ask Captain Moorsom if, in his survey, he had directed his attention to Warmwell Cross and Weymouth, because he believed there could be a good line that way. The Reverend gentleman said he thought that town and port entitled to more consideration than it had received. He enlarged upon the importance of Weymouth as in population and traffic and begged to suggest that the title should be altered so that the line might be called the 'Southampton, Dorchester and Weymouth Railroad'. As to leaving the line to Weymouth to the possibility of the atmospheric principle, he thought from the doubtful reports of this new principle, it was a contingency upon which the inhabitants of Weymouth ought not to rest, for if they did they might not ever have a line at all by atmospheric traction.

Captain Moorson said that he had already stated that he had surveyed the whole area of country within the range of the line. His attention had been directed to that part alluded to by Mr Urquhart and he was decidedly of opinion that it would be injurious to divert the line in any such direction. As to the little village of Warmwell, it was out of the question to look to such places particularly being of great consequence in such an undertaking, and he would at once say, considering the position of Dorchester as the county town, the traffic and other circumstances, it would be more advantageous to those who had property in the neighbourhood of Weymouth, to have the present line than to divert it in the direction pointed out by Mr Urquhart, or in any other direction suggested. With respect to the atmospheric principle he did not think it so uncertain as the Reverend gentleman did, but he was not now called on to discuss that point.

The fact that the proposed line from Southampton was to end at Dorchester gave little comfort to the inhabitants of Weymouth, who had formed a Railway Committee to forward their interests. The situation changed following a meeting in the town on 30th October, 1844 attended by representatives of the prospective Wilts, Somerset & Weymouth Railway, with the meeting being addressed by none other than Mr Brunel.

There was much lively debate and the spectacle of some leading towns-people attempting to wear two hats at once and change horse in mid-race. Despite the meeting also being addressed by Charles Castleman strongly putting the case for the Southampton & Dorchester scheme, there was much support for the GWR-backed line, resulting in the following resolution:

> That the prospectus of the proposed Wilts, Somerset and Weymouth Rail Road having been explained it be resolved that his line merits the support of the inhabitants of Weymouth, who hereby pledge themselves to give it their most strenuous aid, and they will request the County Members and also the Members for Weymouth to support a Bill for this line in the House of Commons. And that the interests of this port and harbour as well as that of the neighbouring ports and the County of Dorset generally will be most effectively promoted by giving our undivided support to the Wilts, Somerset and Weymouth Railway in conjunction with the Southampton and Dorsetshire Railway.

The commitment of the Wilts, Somerset & Weymouth company was further advanced when the *Dorset County Chronicle* for 14th November, 1844 announced that the company was accepting subscriptions for shares. Indeed there must have been strained family loyalties at Weymouth, as Messrs Henning and Andrews were appointed the local solicitors for the company. However, if the inhabitants thought they had secured a swift place on the railway map, they were in for a long frustrating ride.

Chapter Three

The Politics of the Railway Age

It was not only the inhabitants of Weymouth who were eager to join whichever faction would guarantee them the best chances of obtaining a railway for, during the past year, Castleman had also played a game of brinkmanship.

By this time the country was well and truly in the grip of the Railway Mania and Castleman doubtless felt assured that he could play off the existing major companies against one another to receive the best possible terms. After all, his line could either be seen as a westward drive for the LSWR or as a possible means of approach (albeit a little indirect) to Southampton for the broad gauge faction - but his machinations were somewhat negated when the Government, anxious to save valuable Parliamentary time, appointed a committee known as the 'Five Kings' to examine all railway Bills and weed out the obvious non-starters! The committee consisted of Lord Dalhousie (Chairman), Samuel Lang, G.R. Porter, Captain Coddington, and Captain O'Brien, and over the next few years, they were to exercise great influence over the emerging pattern of railways in Britain.

The race to the West was on and Castleman obviously thought that he had matters well in hand - but the Five Kings thought otherwise. Perhaps it should be explained that competition between the two major companies (the GWR and LSWR) was the more intense because of the difference in gauges. A break of gauge was inconvenient for passengers, forcing upon them a change of trains, but for goods traffic it was an absolute disaster! Everything had to be unloaded from the wagons of one gauge and reloaded in those of the other, this double handling not only causing severe congestion and delay but also more instances of breakage and petty pilfering.

There was also the cost of construction, a tunnel on the broad gauge had to be made six feet wider than that of the standard gauge. Added to this there was the cost of land, it was estimated that the broad gauge required an extra three quarters of an acre per mile. However, in 1846 Parliament ruled that with the exception of the Great Western all railways would adopt the standard gauge of 4 feet 8½ inches for future construction. In 1869 the first of Brunel's 1,456 miles of broad gauge was converted, a process that was to come to a costly conclusion 23 years later, whilst today scholars and historians still continue to argue its advantages and disadvantages.

Small wonder that ports like Southampton and major manufacturing towns championed any scheme that promised to circumvent this nuisance, so although Exeter was already joined to Bristol and London that city was keen to encourage the standard gauge. Furthermore, the LSWR had by now obtained an Act for a branch from Bishopstoke (later known as Eastleigh) to Salisbury which, although at first glance likely to have little impact on the Southampton & Dorchester, did in fact have considerable bearing upon its future. Construction of this line was delayed by bad weather and it was 27th January,

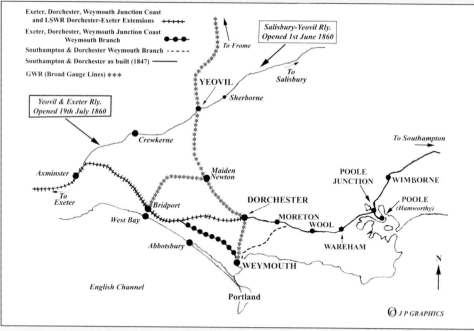

The Southampton & Dorchester Railway and its projected branches and other lines including the GWR broad gauge in the Dorset, Somerset and Devon area.

The existing railways and others under construction in 1848. Note the territory west of Dorchester open for development. The heavy black lines show the broad gauge GWR and constituent companies including the Wilts, Somerset & Weymouth Company.

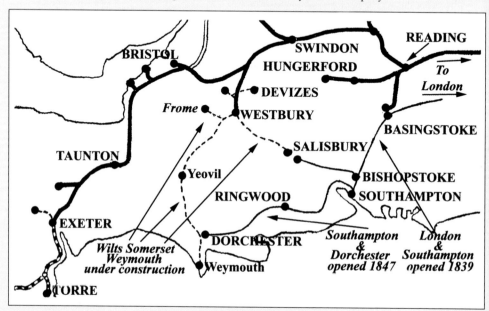

1847 before the first goods train rumbled into Salisbury, but thereafter it was that city and not Dorchester that was seen as the ideal launch point for a westward thrust. Although the LSWR did retain some interest in Castleman's line, they saw it now in more local terms and as a means of keeping the GWR out of the area.

It would seem that Castleman had been advised of this at the meeting of February 1844 but had chosen to ignore it. Almost certainly the acceptance of a seat on the Southampton & Dorchester Board by Chaplin was to allow him to keep an eye on things, but when the LSWR Chairman found that his name was being used as evidence of his company's support for a coastal route to Exeter he was furious and issued a statement that this was not the case. Incidentally, the LSWR now had ambitions reaching well beyond Exeter, Falmouth being mentioned as a possible goal!

In an effort to secure the position of his railway, Castleman then made the mistake of attempting to dictate the policy of the major company by refusing to enter into further negotiations unless the LSWR undertook to promote no lines west of Yeovil. This was rather like the tail trying to wag the dog and Chaplin's Board were in no mood to comply. There thus began a period of considerable friction between the two companies, in the course of which Castleman decided to explore his alternative option - the GWR! Accordingly he wrote to that company's Chairman, Charles Russell, on 30th July:

> It will no doubt be known to you that some gentlemen in the South-West part of the County of Hants and the Southern part of the County of Dorset have caused a survey to be made for a line of railway from Southampton to Dorchester, and it is of course palpable to everyone that should this line ever be made it must ultimately be continued to Exeter. We shall of course in the first instance be anxious to connect ourselves with one of the existing Companies and the South Western is undoubtedly the one to which, from its position, we might be expected to offer a lease of the line in the first instance. An act, however, of undoubted duplicity on their part makes me fearful to trust them, as they have a scheme of their own for supplying the County of Dorset by means of a line from Salisbury, passing through the upper part of the County with a branch from Salisbury to Dorchester and Weymouth.
>
> I now come to the reasons for your Company agreeing to treat with us for a lease of the line, even in the present early stage of our proceedings.
>
> First then, I would submit to you that it is impossible for you to prevent one line [being constructed]. A line parallel with the Great Western, between it and the coast, would clearly do you less injury than a more central one.
>
> Secondly, with the projected lines emanating from the Great Western and going North and South, particularly those from Taunton to Bridport, Bath to Weymouth, and Corsham to Salisbury, the whole of the central part of the country might be considered as supplied, whilst the base line along the coast would act as a feeder to the cross lines and would be sufficient ground for an opposition on the part of Great Western to the more central route proposed by the South Western, and as it is known that the Government are most anxious for the continuation of a coast line, their support might be depended upon for furthering our project.
>
> Thirdly, if I am right in assuming that you would be unable to prevent the formation of one line parallel to the Great Western, then I presume that it would be better for you to have control over that line and be receivers of a part of the profits, which would otherwise be wholly taken away from you. I am of course ready to adopt the wide gauge

and extend the line from Dorchester to Exeter. My proposal would be that, after satisfying you as to our plans, estimates, and traffic, if we can show a return of not less than 6% upon the contemplated outlay, you should agree to take a lease of the line at an amount sufficient to pay the shareholders 3% and divide the net profits with them afterwards. It is of course clear that the sooner such a step as this, if decided on at all, is adopted, the better will be the means in our power of frustrating the South Western Company's object.

Castleman's true objective was now clear: he would build a cheap line in what he saw as a strategic position and then pit the two major companies against each other in order to obtain the most favourable terms - whilst at the same time enhancing the value of property in the area of his home town by placing it securely upon the trunk line to the West!

Paddington initially showed considerable interest in this suggestion and at a Board meeting on 3rd October it was voted that a draft agreement for a lease be prepared. Of course, this document stipulated that the Southampton & Dorchester would be broad gauge and that a junction with the Wilts, Somerset & Weymouth line would be made at Dorchester.

News of these negotiations caused panic in the LSWR Boardroom, for not only was their monopoly of Southampton now seriously threatened but an occupation of that area by the GWR would affect their expansionist dreams into Devon and Cornwall! It was therefore decided to counter with a plan of their own under the title of the Salisbury & Dorsetshire Railway, which envisaged a line from Salisbury to Weymouth by way of Fordingbridge, Wimborne and Dorchester. Although much of this route was later destined to be occupied by railways in a piecemeal fashion, at the time it drew the hostility of several landowners because it destroyed good agricultural land in the Avon Valley; whereas the proposed route of the Southampton & Dorchester crossed mostly infertile heath and was therefore largely unopposed.

At a Board meeting on 2nd August, 1844 the LSWR considered an alternative line from Salisbury to Taunton via Shaftesbury, Sherborne and Yeovil, with a branch from the latter to Weymouth, any decision about extensions further West being left for another occasion.

However, it is indeed an ill wind that blows nobody any good, so whilst the LSWR were obviously disenchanted with Castleman's behaviour the people of Weymouth were delighted by it! The Borough had come out strongly in favour of the Wilts, Somerset & Weymouth line as it was felt that GWR involvement in the Southampton & Dorchester would ensure the future prosperity of the port, the LSWR being too wrapped up in Southampton to encourage shipping traffic at Weymouth. Doubtless the idea of the 'Atmospheric' line and associated change of trains at Dorchester also contributed to their lack of support for the LSWR. At a public meeting in the town on 30th October Castleman was warmly applauded when he said that the proposed Salisbury & Dorsetshire line was nothing more than a nuisance that the promoters had no intention of building, its sole purpose being to frustrate the GWR!

There can be no doubt that at this stage Castleman held all the trump cards: he enjoyed the unqualified support of the communities along his line, the tacit approval of Parliament who wanted to see a coastal railway as an aid to defence, and he was even being cheered on by the business interests of Southampton. The latter were anxious to break the LSWR monopoly and obtain a route for traffic consigned to broad gauge stations that did away with transhipment. Naturally Castleman did everything in his power to foster these sentiments, dismissing the difficulties likely to arise from a break of gauge at Southampton as 'a mere bugbear'.

The Southampton & Dorchester Railway Prospectus named Lord de Mauley as Chairman with John Mills of Bisterne Park, Ringwood, as his deputy. Castleman himself was the 'Secretary and Solicitor' - duties he encompassed in the legal practice he shared with his brother Edward, although the latter does not seem to have taken much interest in railway matters. Other local Directors were the Hon. Colonel George Dawson Damer MP of Came House near Dorchester, Colonel Mansell of Smedmore House, John Morant of Brockenhurst House, Edward Greathed of Uddens Park near Wimborne, Captain Joseph Garland of Wimborne, Richard Brouncker of Boveridge House, R.H. Swaffield of Weymouth, E.A. Wood of Osmington, John Cree of Owermoigne, William Lambert of Wimborne, William Fryer of South Lytchett House, William Voss of Puncknowle, between Dorchester and Bridport (probably attracted to the scheme by the promise of an extension to Exeter), and Francis Bryant of Parkstone near Poole.

The shares were set at £50 apiece, with a deposit of £2 10s. on each, carrying a dividend of 3 per cent guaranteed by the GWR - and it was reported that 3,500 had already been applied for. Some adjustments were made to the original Southampton & Dorchester plans, and both these and the plans for the Salisbury-Weymouth line were now ready for presentation to Parliament. The route of the former no longer turned sharply south into the town of Poole but served that ancient seaport by a branch from a point north of Turlin Moor to a terminus on the quay wall on the south side of the harbour - a spot subsequently known as Hamworthy Quay. At Southampton two alternatives were suggested: one route running along the Western Shore to near the Royal Pier, whence a tramway would connect the Southampton & Dorchester line to the LSWR terminus, the alternative was via a tunnel under part of the town to join the LSWR at Northam.

Southampton Council supported the route on an embankment along the waterfront to a station near Royal Pier. To this end Castleman pledged to the Council that the Southampton & Dorchester company would use every endeavour to construct the line to the pier and onward along the shore to the LSWR terminus. Early in 1845 a letter from the company to the Town Clerk stated:

The Company will run their line of railway from the Bath House at Millbrook to Mr. Gabletts premises at West Quay at an average distance of seventy feet from high water mark to form an esplanade twenty feet wide outside the railway with crossings over the railway at such points as may be agreed on and to make the land within the line solid to the level of the esplanade. The land within the line to be the property of the town. The Company to maintain the sea beach and the esplanade. The Company to form such sewer springs underneath the railway as the town may require. The esplanade to terminate at Mr. Gabletts premises and the railway to be continued thence to the pier gates on embankment and viaduct without an esplanade.

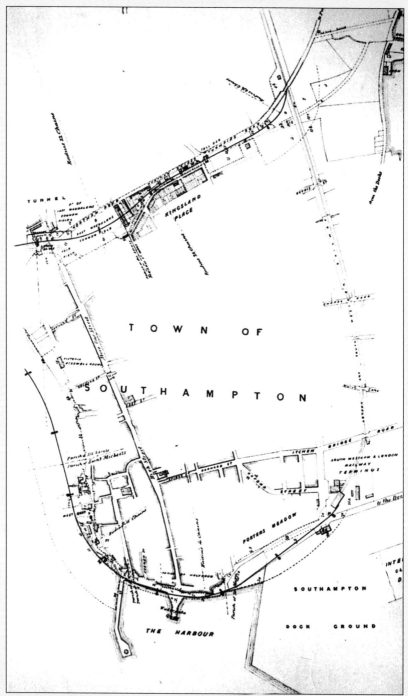

Plan showing the two proposed alternative routes into Southampton, the lower around the Western Shore to the Terminus Station and the upper through the tunnel under Marlands.

Courtesy Dorset History Centre

However, the Pier and Harbour Commissioners were totally opposed to the use of steam locomotives on the section of the line that would have been constructed from Royal Pier along land adjacent to the Town Quay, both of which came under their jurisdiction, a matter that was resolved at a Commissioners meeting on 3rd May, 1845.

The Commissioners had effectively killed the route via the waterfront, so that when the Bill came before Parliament it was dropped in favour of a tunnel under the town, and to enable this option to be exercised at minimum cost, Moorsom envisaged making use of the derelict canal tunnel for this purpose.

Returning to the general politics of the railway, just as Castleman must have thought that everything was going his way, the 'Five Kings' made their pronouncement in a report dated 31st December, 1844: the Bristol & Exeter branch from Durston to Yeovil should be constructed, as should the Wilts, Somerset & Weymouth and the Southampton & Dorchester, but the Salisbury & Dorsetshire and Salisbury & Yeovil should be discontinued. The 'Kings' initial report made no reference to the gauge question and Castleman must have been delighted at the success of his scheme over those of the mighty LSWR, but his elation was short-lived. A follow-up report from the 'Kings' stated that the GWR should transfer their interest in the Southampton & Dorchester to the LSWR - which in turn meant that the gauge would automatically be 'narrow' (the term then often used for the standard gauge). This left Castleman with the somewhat tricky business of changing horses in mid-stream and re-establishing

Dating from the early 1850s this illustration of Southampton shows 'God's House' looking towards Town Quay. Had early plans proceeded the Southampton & Dorchester Railway would have used this section of the highway to lay their line from the Terminus Station towards Millbrook. *Author's Collection*

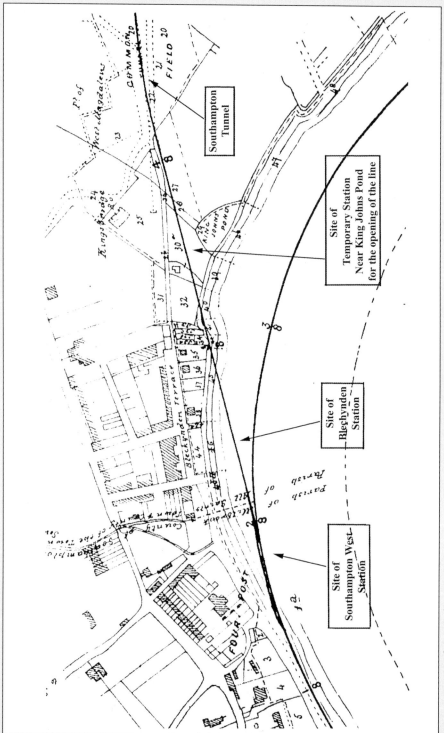

Deposited plans showing the proposed alternative routes to the west of Southampton, the line across the plan going through Southampton tunnel, the line curving towards the right bottom corner proceeding to Southampton Docks (Terminus) via the Western Shore. The later positions of the various stations have been superimposed over the original drawing.

Courtesy Dorset History Centre

a working relationship with a company he had recently done so much to undermine. But solicitors are ever resourceful in such matters - and at least he had the consolation that the LSWR projects west of Salisbury had been vetoed, thus improving his bargaining position and allowing his dream of extending the line from Dorchester to Exeter to remain alive.

He was in fact eased out of this difficult situation by Lord Dalhousie who wrote to the three interested parties on 16th January, 1845 with the helpful suggestion that they should sign a tripartite agreement which allowed both the GWR and LSWR to support the Southampton & Dorchester and the Wilts, Somerset & Weymouth Bills then before Parliament and subsequently keep each other fully advised about any westward extensions. For the GWR this meant anything west of Hungerford and for the LSWR anything west of Salisbury. Furthermore, the Southampton & Dorchester would undertake not to promote any line beyond Dorchester without the full compliance of both the major companies.

This suggestion was accepted, and once the agreement was signed Castleman set about the preparation of documents leasing his railway to the LSWR. The larger company was to pay the Southampton & Dorchester an annual rent of £20,000 plus 50 per cent of the net profits, this arrangement being endorsed by the GWR on condition that local traffic between Dorchester & Weymouth was worked solely for the benefit of that company.

Several points came up for debate when the Bill was presented to Parliament in April 1845, the most contentious being the route of the line through the New Forest. Feelings ran as high about this as they would today at a motorway enquiry! The MP for South Hampshire, Henry Compton, was also a Verderer and was vehemently opposed to any railway whatsoever crossing the Forest, but the Member for Lymington, Mr Mackinnon, took a more enlightened stance by arguing that the Forest was public land under the management of the Crown and should therefore be subservient to the Public good. In his opinion, if Parliament had the power to order a man's private land to be cut through in the common interest, publicly-owned land should be treated in the same way. When George Banks, a Dorset member who had actively supported the Salisbury & Dorsetshire line, gave rather grudging evidence in favour of the line it became clear that Compton stood alone, withdrawing his objection after Lord Palmerston had said a few words in support of the scheme. The Bill received its second reading on 21st April.

During the Committee stage Moorsom was questioned closely about his apparently very low estimate for the cost of construction, but he continued in his assertion that the line would cost no more than £8,000 per mile: £2,500 for a single line of rails and £5,500 for land, earthworks, and general materials. When asked whether he thought the line would be profitable he replied that he had enough faith in it to be a substantial shareholder! A vast amount of Committee time was occupied by discussions on the line of route at Southampton, there being the two alternatives already mentioned. The 'shore line' envisaged a station near the Royal Pier with a tramway linking the Southampton & Dorchester line with the LSWR to facilitate the exchange of traffic - though it has to be said that this did not furnish a through line suitable for use by passenger trains. Although this route promised less disturbance to the town of Southampton the junction arrangements were a major weakness, the fate of this route being virtually sealed by the Pier & Harbour Commissioners and the Town Council who refused to vote any money towards it even though it would have reclaimed for development a large area of mudflats.

The inland ('tunnel') route with its junction north of the LSWR terminus came in for criticism by Mr Deacon, the Town Clerk, on the grounds that it would cross the Lammas Lands - an area recently earmarked by the Council as a public park which would be totally ruined by the deep cuttings necessary to convey the railway. In response the railway offered to lengthen the tunnel from the original 160 yards to 528 yards, but as it still severed a portion of the Lammas Lands the offer was rejected. As a result of this dispute the Bill did not specify the length of the tunnel, an omission that was to cause more arguments later. However, the council did succeed in inserting a clause into the Bill requiring a station to be erected at the western end of the tunnel ('Blechynden') in lieu of the one that would have been provided at Royal Pier had the shore route been adopted, but failed in their attempt to make it a compulsory stop!

Three sections of the Act clearly set out the requirements at Blechynden:

33. It be enacted that the Company shall before the opening of the railway for public use, make at such points on or near the shore of Southampton Water and near the eastern end of Blechynden Terrace, aforesaid, as shall be agreed on between the Company and the said Mayor, Aldermen and Burgesses and afterwards maintain, a station with all such houses, warehouses, offices, yards, apparatus and other works and conveniences as the Engineer of the said Company shall consider to be requisite for the proper accommodation of the public and that adequate provision shall be made by the stoppage of a sufficient number of trains for the purpose of taking up and setting down passengers and goods at the said station.

34. Construct and maintain for two years a public walk on the southern or south-western side of such part of the railway as shall be made on the shore and mudlands of Southampton Water.

39. The Company shall construct and maintain a good carriage road or causeway in continuation of the street call Blechynden Street in the town and County of Southampton up to and across the line of the railway.
   The Company to construct and maintain a good and convenient public landing place and steps and mooring posts etc.

Although it would seem that these discussions ironed out most of the problems facing the railway, several other schemes were promoted during 1845, at the height of the Railway Mania, that could have had a profound influence on the Southampton & Dorchester - but they had little chance of success. The LSWR consulting engineer, Joseph Locke, suggested a 'Exeter, Yeovil, and Dorchester Railway' which had as its main route a line from Basingstoke to Exeter via Andover and Yeovil, Dorchester being reached by a branch from Crewkerne to Bridport, whence the already authorized Bridport branch of the Wilts, Somerset & Weymouth Railway would take it to its destination by the provision of mixed gauge track. Moorsom countered with an extension of his line from Dorchester to Exeter via Bridport under the grandiloquent title of the Exeter, Dorchester & Weymouth Junction Coast Railway which also included a southerly branch line through Portesham and Abbotsbury that terminated at Weymouth, to be followed almost immediately by the publication of a Prospectus for a South Western & South Devon Coast Junction Railway along similar lines. Furthermore, the Southampton & Dorchester visualised an easterly route into Weymouth from Moreton instead of sharing the metals of the Wilts, Somerset & Weymouth from Dorchester, this scheme including a tramway to the harbour.

At this stage it also seemed likely that Poole would become the terminus of a line from the North. There were plans for a Manchester & Poole Railway which would have left the proposed Manchester & Southampton at Ludgershall, and Locke surveyed a similar route that would have used a section of the Southampton & Dorchester line to reach Poole. He also surveyed a Salisbury, Wimborne & Poole Railway that would have joined the Southampton and Dorchester at West Moors.

Poole was further favoured by the wide-ranging Bristol, Poole Harbour & Lymington Junction Railway for which a Prospectus appeared showing a line from Bristol via Pensford, Clutton, Timsbury, Shepton Mallet, Wells, Bruton, Castle Cary, Wincanton and Blandford, with a spur at Bruton connecting with the Wilts, Somerset & Weymouth, thence to Poole. From here the line to Lymington ran directly along the coast through the area later to be occupied by Bournemouth and the ancient town of Christchurch.

Between 1845 and 1847 no less than 25 schemes appeared featuring Southampton, such was the optimism over the town's future as a port, but most were ill-conceived and some competed directly with each other and were bought off by stronger rivals. Many approached the port from the north and east and so do not concern us here, but an important exception was the Manchester & Southampton Railway which - despite having a title designed to make one think of railway-building in the grand manner - made use of existing lines between Manchester and Cheltenham. The 'new build' was a line from Cheltenham to Redbridge (where it would have joined the Southampton & Dorchester) by way of Cirencester, Swindon, Marlborough, Andover & Romsey - a route later completed by other railways - with a branch to Salisbury, Ringwood, and Poole. The LSWR responded with a short line from Redbridge to link up with its Salisbury line at Romsey, but both were rejected by Parliament.

In the wake of this defeat the LSWR tried to save the day by offering to take over the Manchester & Southampton between Andover and Redbridge, making use of running powers over the Southampton & Dorchester from the latter to the junction at Northam. But even with this reasonable offer and the enthusiastic support of both Southampton and the industrialists of Manchester the scheme died. It would have been a superior version of what later emerged as the Midland & South Western Junction Railway - and perhaps it was ahead of its time!

Meanwhile, back on the Southampton & Dorchester proper, there remained some unfinished negotiations. The exact route through the New Forest was subject to the outcome of talks with the Commissioners of the Royal Woods & Forests, details having been omitted from the Bill to prevent delay, but Queen

Victoria had given her personal consent to the use of Crown land in Hampshire and that belonging to the Duchy of Cornwall in Dorset. In this rather incomplete state the Bill received the Royal Assent on 21st July, 1845 - and that afternoon Castleman drove into Ringwood to a tumultuous welcome, his carriage being met and escorted into town by the local band. An archway of roses spelling out 'Castleman forever' spanned the door of the Red Lion Inn and later that same evening a dinner in his honour was given at the Crown Inn.

The Act authorized a capital of £500,000 divided into £50 shares, calls being limited to £10 per share at intervals of not less than three months. There were also powers to raise another £166,000 in mortgages and bonds as soon as half the authorized share capital had been subscribed.

Amongst the many clauses and provisions within the Act, the question of the gauge was not well defined: 'The railway shall be formed of such gauge as according to such mode of construction as will admit of the same being worked continuously with the London South Western Railway'. Likewise when referring to the Wilts, Somerset & Weymouth Railway the exact gauge was not stated!

Set out in legal terms were the agreements that,

> ... should the Wilts, Somerset, and Weymouth Railway construct their line, they are required to construct upon equitable terms and conditions such works or accommodations at the junction between their railway and the Southampton & Dorchester Railway as may be necessary and expedient for facilitating an interchange of traffic as may be agreed upon between the Companies, in the event of disagreement between them, as may be determined by the Board of Trade.

A further clause covered the provision of additional rails where necessary for the convenient interchange of traffic. There was also a requirement for the Wilts, Somerset & Weymouth company on their railway between Dorchester and Weymouth to lay down rails to accommodate the engines and carriages of the Southampton & Dorchester Railway. Likewise the latter had to lay a third rail to accommodate the engines and carriages of the Wilts, Somerset & Weymouth Railway for a distance not exceeding eight miles to the east of Dorchester Junction.

The Directors must have been well satisfied with their financial progress, £380,000 being already paid up when the Act was obtained, but in fact little of this came from local investors. John Mills of Bisterne Park (Ringwood) was by far the largest local shareholder with a stake of £25,000, Castleman and Lord de Mauley both holding a comparatively paltry £5,000 apiece, but others connected with the line were not afraid to put their money into it. Chaplin (the LSWR Chairman) invested no less than £65,000! Samuel Morton Peto, whose company - Messrs Grissell and Peto - had been awarded the construction contract, not only agreed to take shares to the value of £25,000 as part payment of the quoted price of £420,000 but also advanced £800 from his private coffers to facilitate the immediate start of work. Indeed, it was this type of financial involvement that was to see the downfall of this entrepreneur in later years. Samuel Morton Peto (1809-1889) had with Grissell constructed a number of railway works including the Eastern Counties Railway, and public works including Nelson's Column

The seal of the Southampton & Dorchester Railway Company, incorporating the arms of Southampton, Dorchester and Poole.

and the rebuilding of the Houses of Parliament. In 1846 Peto rearranged his affairs, the partnership with Grissell being dissolved on 2nd March allowing Grissell to specialise in building work and Peto to concentrate on railway construction.

The first general meeting of the shareholders took place at the Crown Inn, Ringwood on 20th August, 1845, with John Mills as Chairman. The first business was to appoint Captain F.A. Griffiths as Secretary to the company at an annual salary of £525 and Messrs John Randall and William Royal were elected as company auditors. The Directors were empowered to receive calls in anticipation, in order to facilitate the progress of the work up to £60,000.

The Directors felt it their duty briefly to advert to the transfer of the lease of the line from the Great Western to the London & South Western Railway Company. This transfer was made at the instance of the Board of Trade and as, in addition to an increased rent of one half per cent on the capital, the independence of the company was ensured, and the amount required for the works guaranteed, the provisional Committee had no hesitation in making such transfer. The guarantee of the South Western company was for £20,000 a year, being equal to four per cent upon the estimated capital of the company. The amount subscribed to the undertaking by them was £325,000, in respect of which they were to have the power of nomination of four Directors, the other shareholders appointing eight Directors out of the twelve.

The Directors had much pleasure in stating that the terms of the lease to the South Western company (with the exception of two or three parts of minor importance) had been agreed upon, and that the whole of the capital was subscribed.

The Chairman submitted for consideration the proposition for laying down a double line of rails instead of a single line. Castleman favoured this course of action stating that the additional cost would only be £80,000 compared with £200,000 if doubling was carried out later. However, the South Western company had a £320,000 share in the local concern and would only agree to the doubling of the four mile section between Southampton and Redbridge including Southampton tunnel; all bridges over the line were to be constructed to accommodate double track as were three viaducts including the one at Wimborne over the River Stour.

Unfortunately, by the end of the year the triple agreement was already dead in the water! The London & South Western was already considering schemes to proceed west of Salisbury towards Yeovil and Exeter, there was also the possibility of that company becoming involved in a scheme for a line from Salisbury to join the Southampton & Dorchester near West Moors (an earlier version of the later Salisbury & Dorset line). There were also the machinations of the Great Western, which had also breached the previous agreement, to consider.

These events had resulted in a number of vitreous letters between De Mauley, Chairman of the Southampton & Dorchester, and Chaplin, Chairman of the London & South Western, a number of which were published in the press.

On 4th December the Secretary of the Southampton & Dorchester Company wrote to the London & South Western Chairman stating:

> The Board has under its consideration today the correspondence between the Great Western and South Western Companies and the official advertisements of the South Western Board, expressive of their intention to support certain lines westward of Salisbury, which appear to be almost identical with schemes rejected last year by the Board of Trade, upon the ground that 'of the two great schemes then before them, only one could be supported from the resources of the district', and in which decision the South Western Company acquiesced, such an acquiescence being a part of the consideration upon which this Company consented to the transfer of the lease of their line from the Great Western to the South Western Company
>
> I am directed to inform you that this Board views with the greatest alarm the proposed junction of the South Western Company with schemes competing with this line, and which, if carried, must have the effect of seriously injuring the shareholders of the Southampton and Dorchester Company. And I am desired to request the favour of your informing me whether the South Western Directors are prepared to make any communication to this Board upon the unexpected changes which they have thus brought about without any intimation to the Directors of this line, and to urge your early reply to this letter to enable the Board to determine on their future proceedings.

In reply the Chaplin the South Western Chairman, justifying their position stated,

> It is, indeed a subject of regret to our Company that its conduct in this transaction has nor received that sanction from the Board of Trade which we feel convinced would have been given to it had the Board of Trade thought fit to interfere; but we feel satisfied that, when the proper period shall arrive, we shall be able to establish, in the clearest manner, the integrity and consistency of the principles upon which we have acted; and we trust that in the meantime we shall not be prejudiced in the minds of disinterested parties, by the circulation of statements which we have already pledged ourselves to refute.
>
> In making these remarks, however, it is far from the intention of the Directors of this Company to imply that the course into which the change of circumstances had led them with reference to the promotion of the Salisbury and Yeovil line, exonerated them from giving to the claims of your Company every such equitable consideration as the relations of our respective Companies entitle you to expect.

It is evident to us that your shareholders will obtain a degree of protection against the effects of the new line to Yeovil if constructed under the influence of the South Western Company which they could not look for had it been promoted by an independent company, or one whose interests are less nearly allied with your own than those of the South Western.

A further letter from the Southampton & Dorchester Board to Chaplin on 18th December opened up the matter of the previous triple agreement and the Board of Trade's opinion at the time:

In your letter to Mr Castleman on the 29th July, 1844, in the whole process of investigation before the Board of Trade, and in all the subsequent conferences, it was admitted by you that two lines to the west, through the South Western railway district, could not co-exist; that the traffic would not justify the construction of both; and consequently that the one or the other would be rendered incapable of maintaining itself to be worked efficiently. This was very distinctly stated in two paragraphs of the Board of Trade report, by which your Company agreed to be bound, and which I here quote in corroboration; 'It soon become evident to us, from the statements of the parties and from the estimates of traffic, that one of the two great schemes above described, only one could be supported by the resources of the district. The coast line and other lines of the Great Western scheme, could only hope to exist by combining with the local traffic such portions of traffic towards the metropolis as would be diverted from them by the construction of a more direct central line; and on the other hand, the central line, passing through a district comparatively destitute of local traffic, could only be supported by drawing into it the whole traffic toward London'.

We beg to remind you, that so entirely have the promoters of this scheme been impressed, from the earliest period of their proceedings, with the correctness of the views thus taken by the Board of Trade and yourself, that when a lease of this line was transferred to your Company on the 17th September, 1844, one stipulation was that you should desist from prosecuting any extension of your line west of Salisbury, and upon your declining to come under this condition, the treaty was broken off.

However, despite all the correspondence the London & South Western company was not to be impressed by the protests of the Southampton & Dorchester Board. It held a substantial financial interest in the latter company which was to increase, and it was the beginning of the end of Castleman's aspirations of a direct railway to the West!

The two proposed routes for the Southampton & Dorchester Railway, the upper one being selected. Had the lower line been constructed it would have preceded the Bournemouth direct line by over 40 years and the development of Bournemouth might well have happened in a shorter time. There would also have been the problems of crossing Poole Harbour to form a junction at Hamworthy. Like a majority of proposed lines one can only speculate as to their eventual success.

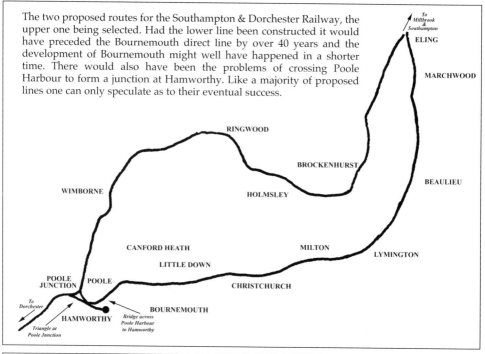

The completed Southampton & Dorchester Railway through the New Forest crosses the top of the map with the two diversions proposed by Thomas Page in 1845 below, the broken line being the coastal route to Poole.

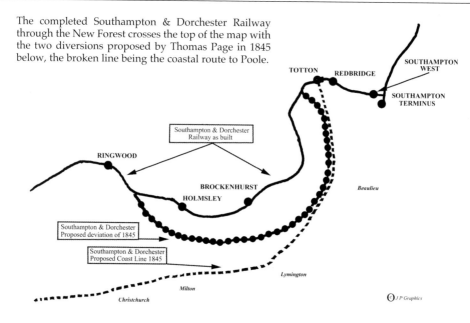

Chapter Four

Construction Commences

Peto (the contractor) took the far-sighted step of shipping some materials into Hamworthy whilst the Act was progressing through Parliament with the intention of building the Poole (Hamworthy) branch first and then working out in each direction along the main line as land and resources became available.

During a meeting on 2nd August the solicitor reported that he had directed the resident Engineer to furnish a plan of the tram road to Eling Wharf, which the Directors sanctioned and ordered, and the solicitor to endeavour to obtain the necessary consents with Sir John Barker Mill. At a further meeting held on 20th of the month a petition from the inhabitants of Eling was read requesting the erection of a station at Eling instead of Redbridge. In reply the Directors stated they could not entertain the subject until they had some more definite knowledge of the intentions of other companies proposing to bring railways in that direction!

At the first company meeting on 20th August it was announced that a considerable portion of the land had been purchased, and that work on three or four parts of the line were in progress, with arrangements for the purchase of further land being negotiated. By the end of August more than a mile of embankment had been raised across Hamworthy Common, but work further inland was deliberately delayed until after the gathering of the harvest to avoid excessive compensation payments. By September work had commenced between Redbridge and Southampton, work was also being undertaken at Moreton where on 8th December William Coles a horse driver was killed when run over by a train of wagons,

By the end of February 1846 the Engineer reported that he was satisfied with progress, 12½ miles of track had been laid, and that 606,706 cubic yards of earthworks had been excavated. It also transpired, during February, that Mr Locke, the Engineer of the LSWR, made a demand that turntables larger than those provided for in the specification approved by him be considered by the Southampton & Dorchester Board, a matter to which they had no objection provided the lessees pay the interest on the additional outlay.

However, by that time cracks were appearing in the unity between the Southampton & Dorchester company and the London & South Western. These were brought to a head at the half-yearly meeting of the Southampton & Dorchester company held at Southampton on 28th February, 1846 where a number of grievances were brought to the fore. Firstly, there were the difficulties concerning the route of the line through the New Forest, a matter that had yet to be resolved with the appointment of Brunel to arbitrate in the matter. Although few doubted Brunel's unimpeachable eminence as an engineer, they feared his connections with the Great Western could prejudice both the Southampton & Dorchester and the LSWR companies.

This matter, the previously mentioned collapse of the triple agreement and other disagreements caused Chaplin, the LSWR Chairman, to state, 'if they were rival companies, they could not have acted in a greater spirit of opposition'. Insisting that the Board required 'new life to be infused into it, he therefore proposed four new Directors all with LSWR connections, Sir John Guest, Captain Breton, Colonel Henderson and Mr Maddison to replace local Southampton & Dorchester Directors, Bond, Bryant, Garland and Jones. The existing four London & South Western nominees, Boothby, Smith, Uzielli and Chaplin remained. Following the voting which the LSWR nominees won by the number of shares held by the London & South Western company, there only remained four local Directors, De Mauley, Mills, Brouncker and Lambert, giving the LSWR eight of the 12 elected Directors!

Castleman objected to this move and had earlier instituted a Chancery Court case in the name of Edward Greathed, a former Director, to prevent the LSWR from obtaining additional shares in the Southampton & Dorchester company. The hearing was begun on Friday 27th February before the Vice Chancellor of England. The object of the plaintiff, who himself held 10 shares, was to prevent the LSWR from voting in respect of 2,500 shares in the Southampton & Dorchester Railway which the LSWR Directors had purchased in addition to the 6,600 which they held under the agreement. On the Saturday the Vice Chancellor decided in favour of the LSWR, the result of the case being transmitted from London to the half-yearly meeting by electric telegraph.

This action had called Castleman's loyalties into question, he insisting that he acted for Greathed in a private capacity. However, Chaplin remarked that, 'the Company's solicitor could act for the Company on some occasions and against it on others'! There is little doubt that this situation forced the LSWR into obtaining a greater control of the local company although they already held three-fifths of the shares; however, a number of further shares had become available and were acquired by them.

Mr Castleman proceeded to refer to the purchase of shares by the LSWR made under his advice. He stated that:

> Mr Edward Mills who held 1,300 shares in trust for the contractors, requested him to find a purchaser for them, and accordingly he mentioned the circumstances to the South Western solicitor, and the shares were bought. He had no instructions in this matter from the Board, and so friendly were the two Companies at the time, that he verily believed, if the South Western Directors had told him they wished to purchase shares, he would have done all he could to procure them.
>
> Afterwards, however, came out the correspondence with the Great Western Board, and supplying as that correspondence did, clear proof of a breach of faith towards the Southampton and Dorchester company on the part of the South Western, could it be wondered at that a want of harmony should arise - could it be wondered at that there should be an absence of free and full communication? Was it not natural that they should suspect those who had committed one breach of faith as likely to commit others.
>
> [Mr Castleman continued, and] disclaimed all personal reference to the South Western Directors, the plans had been refused by him under the authority of the Directors, because the Directors of the South Western had refused to put the branch line on the same footing as the original line. With respect to the Chancery suit, it was instituted by Captain Greathed; and he was not aware that professional etiquette should have prevented him from acting for that gentleman, more especially as he himself had a strong opinion that the independence of the line ought to be preserved, and that the

votes from these shares would destroy it. He begged to add that if the amendment was carried, it would be utterly impossible for him to act with the new Board, and therefore he must tender his resignation. He did not mean however to do this vexatiously. He would assist whatever gentleman be appointed; but he could not consent to be the instrument of carrying out views so totally opposed to his own.

Following much discussion over Castleman's announcement, the Southampton & Dorchester Railway Chairman begged to express the entire satisfaction of his colleagues and himself with the conduct of Mr Castleman throughout. His services had been most valuable not only as the first promoter of the company, but also in arranging with so much talent and so much zeal the various matters affecting the undertaking. He was convinced that but for Mr Castleman's assistance the company would never have reached its present position, and he only hoped that they would find a successor equally able and energetic.

However, there appears to have been a change of heart by all parties, as the *Railway Record* for 28th March reported that,

> ... an amicable understanding has been come to between the old and new members of the Southampton Board, and that Mr Castleman has at their unanimous request resumed the office as solicitor to the company, and that he shall not be called upon to do anything which is in his opinion contrary to the original agreement between the two companies.

In April 1846 it was reported that the line was progressing well in the direction of Wareham - despite some difficulties in obtaining solid foundations at Rockley, where the route crossed an inlet of Poole Harbour and some pile driving was necessary - but to the east of Poole Junction (Hamworthy Junction) little had been done. Later that month the *Poole Herald* commented that the work was at a standstill due to bad weather, adding that the townsfolk of Wimborne were still awaiting a firm decision on the site of their station. The Southampton & Dorchester company had wanted to build it on the Canford bank of the River Stour, close to De Mauley's estate at the spot later occupied by the Somerset & Dorset engine shed, but the LSWR favoured a position on the other side of the river closer to the town centre.

Calls were made on shares as construction proceeded. Following a meeting at the LSWR offices, Nine Elms, on 30th April, 1846, a notice appeared in the press for a call of £5 per share, payable before 30th May. At this point the personal intervention of the contractor, Peto, again arises. For reasons unknown Peto in May 1846 purchased a small five-acre estate to the east of Dorchester, known as Syward Lodge. The north edge of the land was required for the line of the railway, whether the landowner was difficult about selling a small portion of his land to the railway or the company lacked finance to make the purchase is unknown. However, following the opening of the line Peto sold the strip occupied by the railway and Syward crossing gate lodge to the LSWR for £100 in January 1848, the remainder of the estate being sold for £73,456 17s. 9d. Whether Peto acquired the estate as a financial investment or because of difficulties between the former owner and the Southampton & Dorchester company, there is little doubt the deal was to Peto's advantage.

Syward Crossing east of Dorchester, built to a higher standard than many crossing cottages on the line, no doubt to appease the owners of the nearby estate.
South Western Circle, Eyers Collection

Once the weather improved work was prosecuted with vigour - although again most of the activity was concentrated at the western end of the line. The cuttings taking the line through Fordington Fields and into Dorchester were in hand by July and materials for the construction of Dorchester station and the associated railway cottages had been delivered to the site, whilst the bridge carrying the Wareham road over the line at the eastern end of the town was also being erected

By August Moorsom had informed both the Southampton & Dorchester and the London & South Western companies that the section between Dorchester and Ringwood would be ready for opening in the November. The LSWR replied that it was not prepared to carry out a partial opening of the line (*see below*).

Despite the optimism over the western section there were difficulties to overcome with the section through the New Forest between Ashurst and Brockenhurst. Moorsom's line would have been constructed to the north of the line that was eventually constructed, passing nearer to Lyndhurst with a proposed station at Pondhead. However, the Commissioners of the Royal Woods & Forests were fearful of the fire hazard to the timber plantations which at that time supplied vast amounts of timber to the Royal Navy; they also wished to protect animals, in particular the Royal deer which all roamed on unenclosed land. The Commissioners therefore preferred a route which skirted around the edge of the Forest, and engaged an experienced civil engineer, Thomas Page, to survey alternative routes for the railway.

On 31st March, 1845 Page submitted his report to the Commissioners outlining two routes (see page 42), the first would have completely changed the character of the Southampton & Dorchester Railway. Leaving the proposed route at Eling (Totton) it would have proceeded towards the coast passing to the north-west of Beaulieu then across Beaulieu Heath, then curving west to the north side of Lymington, before proceeding westwards through New Milton, passing just north of Christchurch before crossing Littledown and the south side of Canford Heath before running alongside the Wimborne Road into Poole where it would have crossed the harbour to join the proposed line at Hamworthy. To enable trains to proceed towards Dorchester a westward facing curve would have been constructed at Hamworthy Junction.

This choice would have removed two market towns, Ringwood and Wimborne from the route, although an equal amount of traffic would have been derived from both Lymington and Christchurch. Bournemouth, at that time a mere hamlet, would have had no impact on the route of the line, for nobody could have foreseen the rapid development that was to later change the area. The Southampton & Dorchester company would also have had to purchase extra land, added to which there would have been the expense and delay in obtaining an additional Act of Parliament.

The second choice of route would have turned west on Beaulieu Heath, passed Boldre and then turned northwards to join the proposed line near Kingston Common, east of Ringwood.

Moorsom rejected both of Page's lines, resulting in Brunel being employed for a fee of £210 to arbitrate on the matter. Brunel suggested a route from Ashurst, which ran between the proposed route and Page's route and rejoining the proposed route at Latchmere Pond (later Lymington Junction). There would have been several steep gradients particularly south of Brockenhurst, and the route crossed two tracts of land outside the ownership of the Crown.

Firstly there was the Bishop of Winchester's purlieu, north of Beaulieu, but the Bishop agreed for the railway to cross his land subject to £50 compensation. The other landowner was John Morant of Brockenhurst Park, a shareholder in the Southampton & Dorchester company and previously a member of the provisional committee. He had accepted the original proposed line, which would have passed close to the front of his residence, however, he objected to the revised route although it was further from his property, refusing permission for Page's surveyors to enter his land, in a move that could be construed as having been backed by the company. Eventually a compromise route was agreed and in July 1846 an agreement was signed between the Commissioners and the Southampton & Dorchester company who paid £12,000 for the land they required.

The conclusion of these arrangements came just in time for Peto, for further delay could well have forced him to disband his workforce, and with navvies in short supply owing to the amount of work available, difficult to replace. To encourage Peto to complete the work by the 1st May the company offered him a bonus of £5,000. The winter of 1846-1847 was noted for severe frosts and heavy rains which in turn held up work. In the New Forest the nature of the soil proved difficult, in a single week a total of 13 horses became stuck in the mud and had to be destroyed, 11 of them in the section between Brockenhurst and Ossemley Ford (Holmsley).

It would appear that the shareholders of the Southampton & Dorchester had lost interest in the affairs of their company or were satisfied with the progress made for insufficient members attended the third half-yearly meeting of the company at Southampton in August 1846 to allow it to proceed under the rules of its constitution. The Directors' report being forwarded to the shareholders, it stated that the line in the New Forest had been adjusted to the satisfaction of the Commissioners of Woods & Forests, and would entail expenses in excess of the original estimates and cause a delay of some months in the opening of the railway. The financial sheet showed receipts to the amount of £160,035 1s. 9d. and expenditure to the amount of £156,719 2s. 6d. The Engineer stated that from the western boundary of the New Forest to Dorchester might be opened in two months, and the whole would be opened by the following May. He spoke highly of the works and the conduct of the labourers employed on them. He also stated that some branches were in contemplation with a view to feeding the traffic of the trunk line.

It was clear that the local company had lost control of its line, the minutes of the LSWR Board for August 1846 stating, 'that the secretary of the Southampton and Dorchester Railway be informed that this company are not prepared to carry out partial opening from Dorchester to Ringwood as proposed by Captain Moorsom'. The LSWR solicitor Mr Bircham was also requested to give his attention to the subject of bylaws to be adopted for the Southampton and Dorchester line.

On 5th September, 1846 the Chairman of the LSWR intimated that the Southampton & Dorchester Board had, subject to the approval of the LSWR Board, ordered the construction of branches from Wimborne to Blandford, Brockenhurst to Lymington and Moreton to Weymouth, and that the Secretary inform the Southampton & Dorchester Board that they approve the steps they have taken. However, at the same meeting the Secretary was ordered to intimate to the Southampton & Dorchester Board that the LSWR did not consider it expedient to lay down a second line of rails at present. At a meeting a week later Mr Locke, the LSWR Engineer, advised the Board of dispensing with the Moreton-Weymouth branch!

Although the line passed through easy country and lacked any spectacular engineering features, there were no safety rules in those days and several navvies were killed or injured. In May 1846 a labourer was seriously injured at Dorchester when he fell from a plank, and on the morning of Monday 2nd June a workman by the name of Bundy was killed at Ringwood. Bundy had loaded some sleepers onto a wagon and, as he bent forward to set the vehicle in motion with a push, struck his head on a protruding sleeper. Falling across the rail, he was run over by the wagon. A young boy named John White fractured his right arm whilst working on the line between Wareham station and Worgret on Monday 15th June, and the following day another young man was fatally injured when knocked down by a horse working on the tip site. Both his legs were broken and he died after a few hours. There was yet another fatal accident at Worgret on Tuesday 27th October, when a navvy was crushed between a moving wagon and the side of the cutting. Then 17-year-old George Cherret was killed when he fell on the tip at Canford: in all seven men lost their lives - two of them in Southampton tunnel - and at least 10 were seriously injured during the construction of the line. The life was hard and the hours long, but at least Peto paid wages regularly in coin of the realm

The average weekly wage was 15s., but £1 could be earned in Southampton tunnel! It seems little enough today, but it was very good at a time when a farm worker took home around 9s. for a week's labour. A Dorset newspaper at the time commented on how it was causing unrest amongst the farm labourers, some of whom left the land for increased wages.

Amongst the contractors of the period Peto was one of the better organized, on the Southampton & Dorchester line he employed an agent, Beatty, who had to deal with sub-contractors. A practising Methodist, Peto was opposed to the 'Truck System' used by many contractors to pay their men, and gave evidence before a Government Committee on the matter. Peto also cared for the education, health and spiritual needs of his men and created a loyal workforce, resulting in the work on the Southampton & Dorchester line not being marred by outbreaks of drunkenness, violence and other social problems that beset so many other lines.

Whilst most places along the line were enthusiastic about their new railway, the townsfolk of Poole lost a great deal of interest in the project once it emerged that they were going to be by-passed by the main line and served by an inconvenient station at the end of a branch. It was not that the proposed terminus was particularly remote from the commercial centre of Poole - indeed, on a map it appeared to be almost central - but that it was sited on the opposite side of the harbour and could only be reached by a lifting toll bridge which in practice showed a disconcerting tendency to be open for passing ships at the wrong times, causing many intending travellers to miss their trains! This, plus the nuisance value of changing trains at Poole Junction (Hamworthy Junction), led the town to think that it deserved better. Their disenchantment spawned a number of rival schemes, the most notable being a Bristol & Poole Harbour Railway Company. On 5th November the *Poole Herald* announced the provisional registration of this company and wished to inform the public that a Prospectus would shortly appear for the undertaking under the direction of 'an influential committee of management', several letters appearing in the local press at the time in support of the scheme.

Poole Town Council soon came out in favour of this project. At a meeting held on 9th December, 1846 the proposed railway from Bristol to Poole was discussed and a resolution carried to the effect that such a communication would confer most important advantages upon the Borough and be of immense public utility, since it would be a means of connecting the Bristol and English Channels and thereby avoiding the tedious and frequently dangerous navigation around Land's End. It was, according to the report, 'in contemplation to convene a public meeting of the inhabitants on this important measure'. It was claimed at the time that 'the whole of the plans and books of reference of the Bristol and Poole Harbour Railway' had been deposited.

It would appear that in the opinion of the LSWR there were construction problems with the Southampton & Dorchester line. In December 1846 a letter to the London & South Western Board from their Committee of Ways and Works recommended that a communication be made to the Southampton & Dorchester Board as to the state of the works on the line, the cuttings of which were reported to be in a backward state, and the ballast in many cases bad in quality and deficient in quantity. And they further recommended that the site reported by the deputation as best suited for the coke ovens at Poole be adopted and authority given to purchase the land near the entrance of the harbour.

Later in the month the LSWR Board received a letter from the Secretary of the Southampton & Dorchester company accompanying a report on the state of the works on the line and applying for payment of a promised temporary loan of £25,000, which was granted and a cheque issued.

Equally frustrating to the proprietors and contractors alike were the problems of Southampton tunnel. Moorsom had been persuaded to extend the tunnel in order to protect the Lammas Lands, but in order to obtain a straight bore he would have to realign the railway beyond the authorized limits of deviation to take it across part of East Magdalen Field - part of the area earmarked for development as a public park but not then in the possession of the Corporation. However, the Town Clerk offered to approach the current owners to obtain their permission for the line to pass beneath the land, but soon became involved in a dispute over ownership of part of the site.

Castleman was infuriated by the delay and threatened to revert to the original plans (which featured a shorter tunnel), whereupon the Town Council had to remind him of his pledge before the House of Commons Committee. Thereafter the Corporation had sufficient doubts about the company's scruples to appoint a committee in November 1845 to watch over their interests and to 'take such steps as they may deem necessary to compel the performance of the undertaking and, if necessary, to apply to Parliament for that purpose'. The Southampton & Dorchester company came in for some strong criticism at a public meeting held on the 7th of that month, one speaker referring to them as 'a band of thieves, who are trying to get possession of the land they need without paying for it'.

It was voted to make an appeal to the Court of Chancery, but in December Moorsom rendered this unnecessary by suggesting that the company should buy the land and resell it to the Corporation as soon as the tunnel was completed. This was accepted on condition that the sum involved did not exceed £4,000.

The tunnel was not a long one by railway standards, but it was destined to give the contractors and the railway endless worry and expense right up to the present day. Only a short section under Thorner's almshouses was driven in the conventional way, the remainder being built by the 'cut and cover' method in which the soil was backfilled after completion of the brick arch. Cornish miners played a large part in the driving of the ordinary tunnel section so inexperience was not a problem, but a combination of unstable soils and the close proximity of the derelict canal tunnel - which actually crossed the railway tunnel at a very oblique angle just one foot below it - certainly was! Heavy rain in 1846 caused a build-up of water in the derelict canal tunnel, saturating the surrounding sands and gravels - a situation aggravated when the sewers of Portland Place overflowed and ran into the workings. In January 1847 a subsidence above the tunnel caused the movement of the almshouses, resulting in both their demolition and that of Aslett's Carriage Bazaar nearby.

Further financial transactions took place when on 1st January, 1847 the Southampton & Dorchester Secretary sent a letter to the LSWR Board intimating that a large number of additional shares had been allocated to the London & South Western as its share of the new capital and requested acceptance and payment of a deposit of 10 per cent within two weeks. Needless to say, with the chance to obtain more control of the local line the shares were accepted and the deposit paid!

Peto looking forward to the line's completion had written to the LSWR Board early in January 1847, proposing to maintain the permanent way and works on the line for three years from the date of its opening for the sum of £185 per mile per annum, an offer declined by the Board.

It was reported that the construction of the line had quickly exhausted all the local stocks of bricks and supplies from further afield were expensive and difficult to obtain owing to other railway and building works taking place. This resulted in the Southampton & Dorchester Board authorizing Peto to construct wooden bridges on the line in order to effect its opening in May. However, they stipulated that in the event of it being determined that Peto was by the terms of his contract required to construct brick bridges, the expenses of later alterations would have to be defrayed by the contractor.

At the beginning of March work had stopped on Wimborne viaduct awaiting a decision by the LSWR Board. The Southampton & Dorchester company stated that a saving of £490 would be effected by constructing the viaduct for double track as compared with the expense of making the alterations at a later date, a request the LSWR agreed to. In the same month the Southampton & Dorchester requested that in order for the company to provide for the payment of the forthcoming contractor's certificate, a deposit of £1 per share on the 8,516 additional shares accepted by the LSWR company the previous month be paid, such were the financial circumstances of the local company.

On 3rd December, 1846 a notice in the *Poole Herald* issued by the Southampton & Dorchester Railway announced an extraordinary general meeting of the company, to be held at the Nine Elms terminus of the LSWR on Thursday 10th December at 4 pm. This was for the purpose of taking into consideration resolutions submitted and sanctioning application to Parliament in the next session for powers to deviate railways in the New Forest, together with the making of branches from near Moreton to Weymouth, Wimborne to Blandford, and to Lymington and Eling Wharf. The same matter was discussed at the half-yearly general meeting on 11th February, 1847, in more defined terms:

A Bill for making a branch railway from the Southampton and Dorchester Railway at Moreton to Weymouth, and for other purposes, with power to transfer same to the London & South Western Railway Company, capital £193,000.

A Bill for making a branch railway from the Southampton and Dorchester Railway to Blandford and for other purposes, with powers to transfer the same to the London & South Western Railway Company, capital £150,000.

A Bill for making an alteration in the line of the Southampton and Dorchester Railway, and certain branches there-from to Lymington and Eling, and for other purposes, capital £60,000, and for the amalgamation of the Southampton and Dorchester Railway Company with the London & South Western Railway Company, and enlargement of powers of such Companies.

A Surveyor's Court was held at Matchams Hotel on 10th February, 1847 to enquire into the New Forest deviations and the proposed Lymington and Eling branches. The question of the site for the proposed Brockenhurst station arose during March, the company having planned to construct a station at Latchmere (later the site of Lymington Junction). However, Mr Stewart the MP for Lymington had forcibly represented the desire of his constituents to have the station in Brockenhurst village, although Moorsom, the company Engineer considered Latchmere the preferable site. The Board with the sanction of the Commissioners of Woods agreed to the village location.

At the time work on the line was not progressing very well as Southampton tunnel was causing problems. Two of Thorner's Almshouses at the southern end - though underpinned with massive timbers - had settled considerably, showing the treacherous nature of the soil underneath. A shaft had been sunk to the rear of these properties and another large one made at the entrance to Northam Road. After expending several thousand pounds in excess of his original undertaking, the sub-contractor engaged on this section of the works felt obliged to give up!

By early March works had been completed in the Wareham area and during the first week of April it was reported that a large number of workmen were engaged in the completion of the station buildings at Dorchester in readiness for the opening of the line. However, there was scant progress with the promised Blechynden station at the west end of Southampton tunnel, which seemed to have been quietly forgotten. In August 1846 Castleman admitted, 'that the Company had no wish to construct a station near Blechynden Terrace but there appeared to be no alternative except by the common wish of the people of Southampton'.

At that time the proposed Manchester & Southampton Railway was before Parliament and there were suggestions that a decision be deferred with the possibility that only one station need be constructed for the use of both companies!

During early 1847 with the opening of the line imminent there was a flurry of activity to construct a station; there were problems with the site which was marshland and partly tidal. On 13th March, 1847 Moorsom had written to the Town Clerk of Southampton stating:

> I am under the belief that I shall have to occupy permanently that portion of King John Pond which has already been marked out for the station and perhaps rather more; as the time is now very short for getting up the buildings and I have been increasingly delayed by different obstacles being put in the way by other parties - will you oblige me by procuring for me immediate entry (under the assurance of course that I then keep permanent possession).

It would appear that either the Council were tardy in their reply or Moorsom was impatient to proceed as on the 19th in a letter to Southampton Council, Moorsom stated:

> I wrote several days ago to your clerk requesting a copy of the minutes - but I have substantially agreed with you that the station is to be partly in King John Pond I intend to carry that agreement out by building the house. This I won't do till you have complied with your part of the agreement by putting me in possession of the land.
>
> I therefore have ask you to put me in possession under such form of assurance as will suffice for immediate entry to build and secure my building from seizure as being on your land after it is up, and I offered to have the valuation made at once. Is this not quite plain?

It appears that access was granted to the site without the correct authority resulting in construction being halted whilst the legal process was proceeded with, the contractor having acted prematurely in entering the ground and commenced the erection of the station having done so with the consent of the person who rented the feed of the land. An injunction was obtained as no agreement had been reached by the parties on both sides, as to the compensation to be paid to Mrs Pilgrim (the tenant) for her interest.

The *Hampshire Advertiser* for 24th April, 1847 reported that solicitors for the Southampton & Dorchester Railway had made an application to Southampton Borough Magistrates under section 85 of the Land Clauses Consolidation Act to be enabled to go upon land occupied by Mrs Maria Pilgrim as tenant by lease of the Corporation:

> The land in question adjoining King Johns Pond at the commencement of the approach to the railway tunnel and on which the railway company has commenced erecting a station covenanted for by the Town Clerk when the Bill was in committee and from which a road is proposed to be made along the shore to Manchester Street leading up to Windsor Terrace, Portland Place etc. so as to secure an entrance into the town for those passengers who may not choose to be carried through the tunnel and all the way down to the Marsh Terminus.

The Corporation now, with the opening of the line imminent, fearing that the Blechynden station (required under section 33 of the Southampton & Dorchester Railway Act) would not be provided, initiated proceedings to prevent the opening of the line until it was constructed. The Council minutes recorded that on 29th May two Directors of the Southampton & Dorchester company had waited upon the Mayor stating,

> ... it was the intention of the Company to stop a certain number of trains daily at Blechynden Terrace and that instructions had been given to construct a temporary station for the accommodation of the public until the proceedings in Chancery with reference to the site for the permanent station at Blechynden Terrace were brought to a close.
>
> With the view of amicably settling the present law proceedings that the site for the station should be altered and that the same should be at the dwelling house in the field belonging to Major Fotheringham adjoining the railway and near Blechynden Terrace. The Company to contribute £300 for roads to the site now proposed by him for the station upon condition that the Company has such part of King John Pond conveyed to them as they may require for their use at the station.

The resulting temporary station was erected at King Johns Pond and premises in Blechynden Terrace known as Ivy House were leased from a Mr Purkis for use as offices, although there was still disagreement concerning the various approach roads.

However, other works along the line were almost complete, and on Saturday 1st May Peto travelled on a locomotive from Lyndhurst station - which he left at 11.30 am - to arrive at Dorchester at 2.45 pm after calling at several stations *en route*. The return trip commenced at 4.15 pm. Peto was reported as having used six engines during the construction of this line, the one run on this first trial trip being named *Samuel Morton Peto*. The same engine was used on Tuesday 4th May when a special train left Lyndhurst at 8 am conveying a party of engineers and officers of the company, including Moorsom himself. This time all stations were inspected, the train not arriving in Dorchester until just before 1 pm. Some of this extended journey time was caused by obstructions on the line, as nobody had apparently been notified that the special was running and sections of the line were strewn with debris and wagons that had to be removed before the train could continue! Following arrival at Dorchester, the party adjourned to the King's Arms Hotel, there to enjoy a 'superior luncheon, accompanied by champagne and other wines in profusion', the success of the Southampton & Dorchester being drunk with great enthusiasm. At 2.30 pm the party left Dorchester on their return journey, this time travelling down the Poole (Hamworthy) branch.

Meanwhile affairs at the Southampton end were not proceeding well, a spectacular collapse taking place on 2nd May, 1847 when 10 yards of the tunnel under London Road caved in, taking two bystanders down into the workings. Fortunately neither suffered any injuries and, as in a Laurel & Hardy film, they were able to walk out of the eastern entrance, apparently none the worse for their experience!

Repairs to the tunnel resulted in the Board of Trade inspection of the completed line being postponed, this eventually being undertaken by Captain Coddington, on Thursday 20th and Friday 21st May, 1847. Of the tunnel the Captain stated that it was 'a very well executed work, the joinings [sic] of several lengths being perfect. It shows no appearance whatever of failure and weakness'.

The *Western Flying Post* reporting on the inspection stated:

At twelve o'clock the *Reindeer* engine with a first and second class carriage, horse box and luggage trucks &c, left the Blechynden Terrace station and proceeded through the Southampton Tunnel, which has caused so much trouble to the contractors but is now satisfactorily completed, to the terminus of the South Western Railway, whence after a short delay it started en route for business. The examination of the line was throughout minute, more particularly that of Southampton Tunnel in which considerable time was spent. Every bridge under and over the line was also carefully inspected.

Progress was slow, Wimborne not being reached until 5 pm when it was decided to take hotel accommodation for the night. The following morning the train departed from Wimborne at 9 o'clock and upon arrival at Poole Junction (Hamworthy Junction) the Poole branch was inspected. A rather unfortunate

'REP' unit No. 3014 emerges from the east end of Southampton tunnel with a Bournemouth-Waterloo semi-fast service. It was at this end of the tunnel on 2nd May, 1847 where 10 yards of the tunnel under London Road caved in.

Peter (Hussey) Smith, Bournemouth Railway Club

accident took place upon the train's return to Hamworthy when a pointsman relinquished his grip of a lever prematurely and sent the front and rear sections of the train in different directions and derailing the first and second carriages. Clearly 'Spring' points were involved here! Fortunately there were no injuries and within a quarter of an hour the derailed vehicles were back on the rails; ample evidence of the light construction of contemporary rolling stock. The train then continued towards Dorchester, where a crowd greeted its arrival at noon.

Following luncheon the train again departed at 1.45 pm and returned to Southampton in about three hours, stopping at most stations and changing engines at Poole Junction (Hamworthy Junction). It was reported that 'the second mile from Dorchester was traversed in 68 seconds' - a rate of travel that must have seemed truly amazing to most of those on board!

Thus the first railway to penetrate Dorset passed its official inspection. The report is extremely concise, and bears no comparison with the mountain of paper that would be generated in later years by lesser events, and for that reason alone it is worth quoting in its entirety.

29 Great George Street,   *22nd May 1847*
Sir,
I have to report for the information of the Commissioners of Railways that I inspected on the 20th and 21st inst., the line of the Southampton and Dorchester Railway preparatory to its being opened for public traffic. The notices given by the Company bear date the 30th March and the [???] Respectively.

I was accompanied during the inspection by Captain Moorsom, the Engineer in chief and his assistants, Mr. Campbell, Secretary to the London & South Western Railway, Mr. Albinus Martin, their Engineer, Mr. Peto who has executed the whole of the works and by several other gentlemen - and I received from them whatever information I required. The length of the main line is 60½ miles and the Poole Branch about 1¾.

Curves: The course of the line is very serpentine, the curves amounting to rather more than half the total length, and the straight portions being separated into 48 distinct places. The curves are however in general moderate, and in all instances wherein they differ from the Parliamentary Plan, have been improved. The following are all the curves, which have a radius less than half a mile:

The junction curve at Southampton, which will be particularly referred to;

Three curves of 20 chains radius, all in the town of Southampton and within a quarter mile of the junction, where speed must be moderate under any circumstances;

One of thirty chains radius close to Redbridge Station;

One curve of 35 and two of 30 chains radius, on each side of Wimborne Stn;

One of 30 chains radius at Poole Junction, and but three others of 30 chains, on any part of the line remote from a Station;

The junction curve of the Poole Branch is 15 chains radius and one other is 30 chains.

Gradients are favourable. There is no great extent of level; the line is broken into a vast number of undulating planes, or flat inclinations and for short lengths, not steeper than 1 in 200 with the following exceptions:

4 Planes, aggregate length 6 miles 13 chains, are at inclinations between 1 in 175 and 1 in 185.

4 Planes, aggregate length 3 miles 63 chains at 1 in 150;

2 Planes, aggregate length 1 mile 27 chains at 1 in 130 and 1 in 113;

and 3 Planes, aggregate length 3 miles 32 chains at 1 in 100, the longest of the latter being 1 mile 20 chains.

On the Poole Branch is one inclination ¾ mile at 1 in 100.

Cuttings and Embankments are of moderate extent, and in total amount to very far below an Average. Captain Moorsom gave me the total amount at One Million and three quarters cubic yards, which spread over a distance of 62 miles gives only 28,226 cube yards per mile. The soil is favorable, consisting of a mixture of marl and clay overlaying fine white sand in the eastern half of the line, and gravel over the western half, terminating in chalk. None of the cuttings are of formidable dimensions; the heaviest are in the New Forest, and were attended with some difficulty while cutting through the clay and marl from the quantity of water they contained, but as soon as the substratum of sand was reached it acted as a natural drain and in a few weeks they became quite dry. The slopes were in nearly every case trimmed off and showed no tendency to slip. They have been provided with slopes of 1½ to 1 and the embankments 2 to 1.

There was but one cutting incomplete at Sett Thorns in the New Forest. It is almost wholly through fine white sand. Enough has been removed for the completion of the permanent way, and though the sides have not been removed to the intended slopes, I do not apprehend any danger. The sand appears of the same description as that found in Kent and examples exist near Greenwich, Woolwich and along the Thames of its standing almost vertical for years, at considerable height. It will be all removed in the course of about a fortnight.

On the Poole Branch is a cutting 41 feet deep through sand, which is quite dry, trimmed off and sown.

Bridges over the Railway: Owing to scarcity of other material, timber has been extensively used. Stone is scarcely to be procured and it was stated that all the bricks in the County around had been used up. The span is generally 28 feet, and there are 5 bridges of 26 feet span and 4 of only 23 feet. These latter, though not exactly dangerous, are in my opinion injudiciously narrow, being even of less width than tunnels are ordinarily made where the enormous expense attendant upon their construction induces the smallest convenient opening.

There are but 7 bridges over the line constructed initially of masonry. They are built with arches of brickwork, when on the square set in lias mortar and when on the skew set in cement. The abutments and wing walls are either brickwork or coursed rubble Purbeck stone. Their foundations are either gravel or coarse road sand; they are substantial and well proportioned and executed structures.

There are 15 other bridges over the line. They have brick piers and abutments, and a superstructure either of iron flat girders each in a single casting (proved to 25 tons) or else a flat timber Truss with several principals and cast iron and Tie Rods and Rings with cast iron shoes. The latter are principally for occupation and other roads of light traffic.

Bridges under the line: There are but 3 bridges under the line composed of masonry, equally executed as those over it, and 8 composed either partly of masonry with iron girders for superstructure or else entirely of timber being supported on piles driven to refusal, with longitudinal timbers to carry the rails. When the bearing has been under 15 feet a single 13 inch baulk has been used, between that and 20 feet a split back with wrought iron tension rods between the parts, and for 25 feet bearing, 2 whole timbers one above the other, strutted in addition from the supports. The whole of these bridges were very firm and steady in passing over.

Viaducts: There are 11 timber viaducts, some of considerable length, with bays or openings varying from 5 in number to 45. They are of 3 classes, having openings of 11 feet, 18 feet and 25 feet. 3 of them only have been made for a double line of rails. The supports of all have been treated alike, consisting of whole piles driven till they would go no further - when the height has been made under 20 feet, 2 piles sloping towards each other with a batten of about 3 inches to 1 foot have been connected at their heads by a cross sill, forming a Trestle which carries the longitudinal timbers - when the height has been 20 feet and upwards, these piles have been stiffened by diagonal braces, and when the height exceeds thirty feet, a construction in all respects similar to that upon the Bricklayers Arms branch of the London & Brighton Railway has been adopted. Then as to bearing distance, the 11 feet openings have a longitudinal whole timber for each rail. The 18 feet openings have two timbers one above the other, and the 25 feet openings have 2 whole timbers with struts extending from a waling piece bolted to the piles diagonally upwards meeting underneath the centre of each opening. These viaducts are all of excellent materials and workmanship, and are strongly bolted together and strapped at every point of meeting.

In addition to these Viaducts there are a great number of small timber constructions of similar character only a few feet in height, where the railway crosses low ground. They are instead of culverts and to allow the free passage of water in the event of floods.

The whole of this construction and works of art, upon the line, reflect much credit upon the Contractor and his assistants as regards their execution.

Level Crossings: These are very numerous. All the public and turnpike roads have proper gates, so constructed as to enclose either the road or the railway, and have lodges for the accommodation of the Gate Keeper.

Tunnels: There is one tunnel in the town of Southampton: its length is 528 yards. It does not appear that any other cause than avoiding residential damage produced this tunnel. The amount of earth over the top of it does not exceed 18 feet. With the exception of a very short length under the Alms houses, it was all constructed as an open cutting, the tunnel formed like ordinary bridge buildings, and the earth replaced over the top of it, in doing which too soon the last constructed length of 10 yards which had only been finished 4 days and there, as I am informed being very wet, fell in. That portion has been reconstructed using cement for the arch, and this work created some apprehension in Southampton as regards the tunnel generally. I examined it carefully, and consider it a very well executed work; the joinings of the several lengths were perfect. The [???] was quite regular, the arch dry and it showed no appearance whatever of failures or weakness, indeed from its construction as an open work, none of the difficulties of tunneling had to be encountered.

Permanent Way: Is single throughout with the exception of the first 3 miles from Southampton to Redbridge, and a short piece of from 20 to 100 yards at the intermediate Stations. The gauge is 4 feet 8½ and the middle interval when double is 6 feet. The rails, chairs and sleepers are the same as the South Western Railway: depth of ballast 22 inches, formation level 28 feet (double) 14 feet (single) in cutting and 30 and 15 feet on embankments.

The Company have sufficient land to make the line double when required. The bridges {over} are also intended to accommodate a double line as well as the Wimborne Viaduct.

Turntables and Switches: There are turntables at the Termini capable of turning an engine when uncoupled from its tender, and turntables at most of the intermediate stations, which will turn carriages or trucks, but not an engine, There is no turntable at the extremity of the Poole branch capable of turning an engine, on that short distance therefore, it must travel tender foremost in one direction.

The Switches are of Fox's patent with balance weights. The line being single, all the points will face the traffic either in one direction or the other.

Fencing: Generally post and rail set upon a low earthen bank, but in the New Forest the Commissioners of Woods and Forests have ordered a fence consisting of posts 8 feet apart and seven galvanized steel wires stretched between them. I am informed that some delay has arisen in obtaining the decision of the Commissioners as to what kind of fence should be set up, and that the decision has been so recently obtained that time has not enabled the Company to complete it. It was in an advanced state of progress when I made the inspection, and a large force was employed upon it, but still some parts of the line were unenclosed. The part of the Forest through which the line passes may be looked upon as uninhabited, and I do not think the absence of the fencing involves risk to the public using the line, and need not interfere with the opening unless the Commissioners of Woods & Forests object on the score of the animals.

Stations: There are 13 intermediate stations as follows:

Name	Distance from Southampton
Blechynden	¾ of a mile
Redbridge	3¾ of a mile
'Ashhurst' (A)	7 miles
Beaulieu Road	10 miles
Brockenhurst	14¼ miles
Ossemsley (B)	19½ miles
Ringwood	23¼ miles
Leonards Bridge	29¾ miles
Wimborne	34½ miles
Hamworthy & Poole Junction (C)	40½ miles
Wareham	45 miles
Wool	50¼ miles
Moreton	55 miles
Dorchester Terminus	60½ miles
Terminus of Poole Branch	1¾ from Junction

(A) later 'Lyndhurst Road', (B) later 'Christchurch Road', (C) later 'Hamworthy Junction'.

At all the stations the permanent buildings containing booking offices and waiting rooms were erected and covered in. Most of them were completed and all sufficiently advanced to afford shelter and accommodation to the public. The passenger platforms were all made.

Signals: At all the stations the lamp signals for night use were up and those for the day were either up or on the ground in readiness. The line being single, these signals are but of secondary importance. The necessity of a previous arrangement of waiting places for all trains, and the impossibility of deviating from the arrangement when made, render a single line independent of fixed signals.

The curves and gradients have all been constructed within the limits of deviation permitted by Parliament, and as I have already stated, where altered have been improved.

The junction curve at Southampton is the smallest radius I have met with upon the main line of any railway that I have inspected, being only 5 chains.

A strong wooden guardrail plated with iron has been added on the inside of the curve. In passing the engine round it, the straining and grinding were very apparent and without the guardrail I do not think it could be safely traversed. It offers an example to be avoided, but it is marked upon the Parliamentary Plan and of course I could not object to it. However Mr. Martin the Engineer of the South Western informs me that, on the line passing into their hands, (which it does when certified by the Commissioners), this curve will be done away with and one of 9 chains leading to a different point of their line constructed in lieu of it.

On referring to the Southampton & Dorchester Railway Act, 8 & 9 Vic. C, 98, I observe that power is vested in the Railway Department to require a double line of rails to be laid down on the whole or any part of the railway if the traffic thereon shall in their opinion render such double line of rails necessary. I feel convinced that the convenience of the traffic will induce the Company to double the central portion of the line: say from Ringwood to Wimborne or to Poole long before its necessity demands it. This railway is (I believe) the longest, which has ever been constructed in England with a single line. The Newcastle & Carlisle Railway was 60 miles and the Northampton & Peterborough 43 miles - in both cases the Companies doubled portions of the line almost immediately after the opening and eventually doubled the whole of them.

The Brighton Company is also doubling its lines between Portsmouth and Hastings as fast as it can.

The circumstance that any irregularity which occurs upon a single line not only deranges that train but affects the whole of the subsequent trains on that day, renders the working of so great a length as matter of much difficulty, which is aggravated if the traffic is to be worked in unison with other railways, as in this case.

The efficiency of this (a coast line) in a military point of view, is crippled by the impossibility of sending special or extra trains over it without much time and previous arrangement.

The works on the line are well executed, the permanent way completely laid, well ballasted and consolidated, and I am not aware of any thing affecting the public safety which should prevent its being opened for public traffic.

The line will be worked with the Stock of the South Western Company, whose property it becomes on opening. I annex a numerical list of the Staff to be employed at the Stations.

I. Coddington, Cap. R.E.
Inspector of Railways

The line having successfully passed the Board of Trade inspection everybody was confident that it would be open for traffic without delay. Timetables were

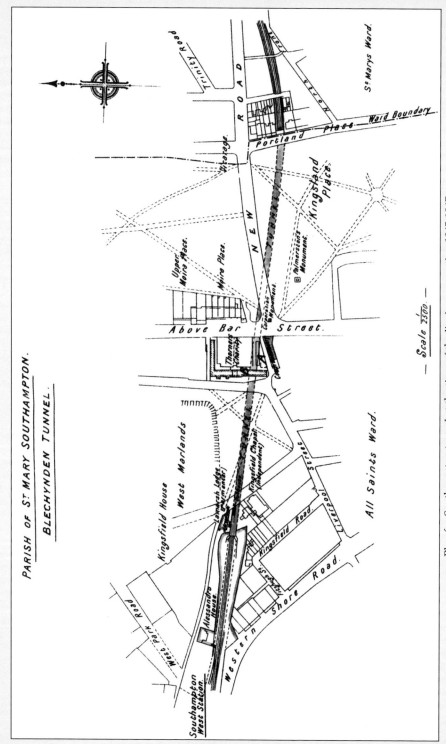

Plan for Southampton tunnel at the time of the line's construction 1845-1847.

displayed and other preparations put in hand for opening the line on Tuesday 1st June, but on the preceding Sunday the tunnel at Southampton again caused concern by showing signs of movement. The following day a bulge in the brickwork revealed that a 60 ft section of the wall on one side of the tunnel had started to sink. A further inspection by Coddington, accompanied by both Moorson the Engineer and Peto the contractor, revealed the cause of the problem as being the abandoned canal tunnel.

In his subsequent report Captain Coddington stated:

> About fifty or sixty years ago a tunnel was constructed for canal purposes, which proved a failure and was abandoned, I enquired what precautions had been taken at the crossing and was informed that the old tunnel had been completely taken out, and that in addition a length of twenty feet of the old tunnel on either side of the new one had been built up solid with rubble masonry.
>
> It appears that Mr Peto, for the accommodation of those parties whose property lies above the line of the old tunnel, agreed to strengthen it by building a certain number of cross walls at short intervals. The mode adopted in doing it was to drive a small gallery laterally from the site of the new tunnel to reach the old one at a point some distance beyond the twenty feet which had been solidly built up. Through this gallery the materials were introduced and three, four, or more cross walls about ten feet apart were built within it.
>
> The old tunnel having been on a level and open at its extremities, whatever percolation of water entered it, either from the sides or above, flowed out at both ends. The crossing of the new tunnel in no way affected this drainage, but by the filling up solid of a portion of it, leaving a hollow interval, the accumulation of water in seeking an egress has entered into, saturated and sodden the clay upon which the new tunnel stands, and it is now incapable of supporting its weight.

As early as December 1846 one of Southampton Corporation's surveyors, Mr McAdam, had expressed doubts about the stability of the tunnel and the town's Improvement Commissioners had refused to reopen London Road, which had been temporarily diverted to avoid the workings after cracks and depressions started to appear. Following the serious collapse of 30th May the Commissioners asked for a copy of Coddington's original report on the tunnel, but the Board of Trade supplied only extracts. They were not satisfied with this and sent McAdam to make an inspection on their behalf. He visited the workings on 24th June and reported that the spaces between the cross walls in the old canal tunnel had been filled with brickbats, but the volume of water still running down the north side suggested that 'the cause of the mischief' had not been removed. The situation came in for a good deal of discussion at subsequent meetings, but the Improvement Commissioners eventually let the matter drop.

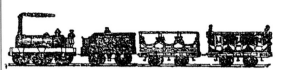

LONDON AND SOUTH WESTERN RAILWAY.

ON and after MONDAY, JUNE 7th, 1847, the TRAINS are intended to RUN as follows:—

DOWN.

Class.	From Nine Elms at	From Southampton at	Arriving at Dorchester.
1st and 2nd......		7 45 a.m.	10 50 a.m.
1st, 2nd, and 3rd..	7 30 a.m. }	12 35 p.m.	3 40 p.m.
1st and 2nd	9 0 a.m. }		
1st and 2nd	11 0 a.m. }	2 50 p.m.	4 45 p.m.
1st & 2nd (Express)	12 30 p.m. }		
1st and 2nd	3 0 p.m.	*6 30 p.m.	9 40 p.m.
1st and 2nd, (Mail)	8 50 p.m.	12 30 p.m.	3 30 a.m.

UP.

Class.	From Dorchester at	From Southampton at	Arriving at Nine Elms.
*1st, 2nd, and 3rd	7 15 a.m.	11 0 a.m.	1 50 p.m.
1st, 2nd, and 3rd..	11 10 a.m.	{ 3 0 p.m.	5 50 p.m.
		{ 4 0 p.m.	8 0 p.m.
1st and 2nd	3 40 p.m.	7 0 p.m.	10 35 p.m.
1st and 2nd, (Mail)	10 5 p.m.	1 15 a.m.	4 25 a.m.

* This is 3rd Class between DORCHESTER and SOUTHAMPTON only.

On SUNDAYS, commencing JUNE 6th, 1847.

DOWN.

Class.	From Nine Elms.	From Southampton.	Arriving at Dorchester.
1st and 2nd		7 45 a.m.	10 50 a.m.
1st, 2nd, and 3rd }	7 30 a.m.	1 35 p.m.	4 40 p.m.
1st and 2nd . .. }			
1st, 2nd, and 3rd..	10 0 a.m.	6 30 p.m.	9 40 p.m.
1st and 2nd, (Mail)	8 50 p.m.	12 30 a.m.	3 30 a.m.

UP.

Class.	From Dorchester.	From Southampton.	Arriving at Nine Elms.
1st, 2nd, and 3rd..	7 15 a.m.		
1st, 2nd, and 3rd..	12 10 p.m.	4 0 p.m.	8 0 p.m.
1st and 2nd	6 0 p.m.		
1st and 2nd, (Mail)	10 5 p.m.	1 15 p.m.	4 25 a.m.

By order,
P. LAURENTZ CAMPBELL,
Secretary.
308]

Timetable published in the *Dorset County Chronicle* for 7th June, 1847 following the opening of the Southampton & Dorchester Railway.

Chapter Five

Open for Traffic and Amalgamation

The situation created by the collapse of Southampton tunnel threatened to cause the cancellation of the opening of the line planned for Tuesday 1st June, 1847. The stations were ready and all the staff had been appointed to take up their duties for the advertised opening, but it was abundantly clear that it would be impossible to work trains through the tunnel. It was therefore decided to commence operations with a skeleton service between Dorchester and the station in Blechynden Terrace (on the Redbridge side of Southampton tunnel) only, passengers and their luggage being transferred across Southampton to and from the LSWR's station by road. The locomotives and rolling stock had not been delivered onto the line, so they had to be drawn through the streets of the town by teams of horses between the LSWR's terminus and the Blechynden Terrace station. Enough equipment was delivered in this manner to allow two trains to run from Southampton and one from Dorchester on the opening day, but they were not patronised to the anticipated extent as news of the tunnel problems had leaked out and caused many to think that the opening would be postponed.

On the following day (Wednesday), two trains made the journey in each direction, the first leaving Dorchester at 11.30 am and returning from Southampton at 3.30 pm, and the up Mail train, which left Dorchester at 10.05 pm and returned from Southampton at 30 minutes past midnight. The company hoped to increase the service as soon as more stock and motive power could be transported onto the line. Trade quickly picked up, the *Hampshire Advertiser* for 12th June reporting in what without a doubt was an overstated report:

> Southampton and Dorchester Railway Station. The stopping of the trains at Blechynden Terrace has made the neighbourhood as lively and full of business as it was dull before - omnibus and railways are rattling to and fro all day.

Although the dinner arranged at Ringwood to celebrate the opening was cancelled in view of the situation, the townspeople were determined not to lose their holiday and the shops closed at 1 pm to allow everyone to join in the festivities. A celebratory dinner was eventually held at the Crown Hotel on Tuesday 8th June, 70 guests sitting down to an excellent meal accompanied by all the toasts and speeches customary at such functions.

Celebrations there might have been to mark the opening of the line, but below the surface there was unfinished business. It would appear that the station house at Wimborne was either not ready or unsuitable for occupation. At a Traffic, Locomotive, and Coaching Committee meeting on 2nd July, 1847 the question of the station agent Mr Hilditch renting a house was raised, the same gentleman also enquiring about a settlement for the crops in the garden of his previous house at Esher! It was agreed that Hilditch be allowed 10s. a week for his rent and Mr Martin was to report fully as to what was necessary at the several stations on the Dorchester line to make the station homes habitable.

An illustration of Wimborne station at the time of the opening of the line in June 1847 viewed from the south bank of the River Stour. The perspective of several buildings are imprecise and the details of the viaduct are open to question. However, it conveys the atmosphere of the time when railways were a new arrival on the landscape.   *Author's Collection*

An illustration of Dorchester station at the time of its opening in 1847 viewed from Maumbury Rings. Although the perspective is slightly imprecise, the main station building stands in the centre, the covered arrival platform to the left with the engine shed to the extreme right. In the background is St George's church, Fordington.   *Author's Collection*

Parliamentary matters were also outstanding, the Act retrospectively authorizing deviations within the New Forest being passed on Friday 2nd July. Although these deviations had been legally authorized, there remained doubt as to the substituting of bridges for level crossings at several locations. The deposited plans showing underbridges at Hayes Lane, and Holme and an overbridge at Moreton, whereas at Wool alterations to the route of the road would have reduced two crossings to one, and the crossing at Dorchester (No. 42) near Culliford bridge was not mentioned in the plans!

Meanwhile, despite the somewhat sparse service the operation of the line had not been entirely without incident. During the evening of Tuesday 8th June two crossing gates at an unspecified location were 'dashed through by an engine'. The crossing keeper, being new to his duties, had gone to his club and left the gates closed! It almost certainly was not the kind of 'club' to which gentlemen resorted, so one wonders about his likely whereabouts; the identity of the crossing might furnish a clue. The following evening three cows were killed on the line because of unfinished fencing, then - in the early hours of Friday 11th - the 'Down Mail' was derailed at Ringwood by a pointsman who pulled a lever in error and sent the train into a siding. This incident not only made the Mail very late arriving at Dorchester but also delayed the first up train of the day, booked to leave Dorchester at 7.15 am, for almost two hours!

Work on repairing the tunnel was put in hand without delay and a test train passed through on 29th July. Through services were commenced after the passage of the mail train on 6th August, and an announcement appeared in the *Poole and Dorset Herald* to the effect that the tunnel had been opened. Trains for Dorchester now left the LSWR's Southampton station at 7.45 am, 12.35, 3.50, 6.50 pm, plus a mail train at 12.30 am. Completion of the repairs also allowed the running of a through goods train for the first time. Until this became possible there had been very little income from freight traffic, as the need to transport everything across Southampton in road carts had been a great hindrance to efficient working, but thereafter traffic of all types quickly increased. Indeed, the number of passengers conveyed over the next couple of months even exceeded expectations, the Poole (Hamworthy) branch in particular proving so popular that there were reports of passengers riding in open goods wagons for want of proper accommodation!

Popular as the line was with the majority of people, the running of Sunday trains brought an outcry from the Sabbatarians who sent several letters to the Board expressing concern that not only the public but also the company's servants would be lured away from religious observance. The arrival of the railway quickly brought about the demise of the stagecoach, a scene soon repeated across the country as the railways changed transport habits. Locally the *Poole Herald* noting the passing of such services as 'The Forester' (Southampton-Bridport), 'The Emerald' (Southampton-Weymouth), and 'The Avon' (Southampton-Poole), but on the other hand a few new services were introduced. For example, 'The Avon' now plied between Christchurch and Salisbury, calling at Christchurch Road station (Holmsley), and 'The Emerald' between Weymouth and Yeovil via Dorchester and Sherborne. The railway also brought about the introduction of the 'Station Bus' - usually running between

One of the excellent illustrations by Philip Brannon depicting the railway and esplanade between Millbrook and Southampton the telegraph alongside the line and the entrance to Southampton tunnel are clearly depicted capturing the atmosphere at the time of the line's opening.   *Southampton Record Office*

Looking north from the footbridge at Southampton Junction, directly ahead is the original main line of the London & Southampton Railway running from St Denys to Southampton Terminus (behind the photographer). Curving sharply left is the connection to the Southampton & Dorchester, when originally constructed its five chains radius was remarked upon by the Board of Trade Inspector. The 1858 Northam curve runs across the back left and centre of the photograph; Northam station is centre right.   *B. Moody*

Blechynden (Southampton West) looking westward viewed from the top of Southampton tunnel. This early illustration shows the limited siding facilities in the foreground. Beyond the station the level crossing and the water coming up to the formation of the railway towards Millbrook can be seen.   *B. Moody Collection*

Wagons stand in the small goods yard at the original Southampton West station (Blechynden). The water area behind the wall was later reclaimed for the construction of the Corporation power station.   *South Western Circle, Hutson Collection*

A pre-World War I view of Lyndhurst Road looking towards Southampton, clearly showing additions to the original structure, firstly the canopy attached to the station building, then the additional structure to its right and the covered footbridge which was of timber construction.

G.A. Pryer Collection

Holmsley station looking towards Ringwood. Named Christchurch Road until 1863, it lost its importance with the opening of the Christchurch branch and the Bournemouth Direct line. Apart from a flurry of activity in two World Wars it remained a quiet wayside station until its closure in 1964.   *Author's Collection*

Ringwood station looking east around 1900, in the foreground is the second-hand footbridge obtained from Woking. The covered Christchurch branch bay is to the right.
Author's Collection

Ringwood station looking towards Wimborne, to the left is the covered bay of the former Christchurch branch. Behind the up platform canopy are the two water tanks that supplied the needs of both the station and visiting engines.
Author's Collection

The exterior of Wimborne station photographed in later years, the various extensions to the main building can clearly be seen. Already the signs of neglect are starting to show as the station's importance in the community fades away.   *G.A. Pryer Collection*

Lytchett Crossing, Upton, looking west, photographed around the turn of the century with the ground frame hut to the left and crossing keeper's cottage to the right. In later years this quiet scene on the main A35 road between Bere Regis and Poole was noted for its congestion. Upton Cross was situated on the brow of the hill in the background.   *Author's Collection*

the better-class hotels and the station. At Poole such a service operated between the London Tavern and the terminus at Hamworthy, whilst at Dorchester both the King's Arms and Antelope hotels ran station buses. Dorchester, the terminus of the line also took on a new role as a railhead for coaches meeting trains for Weymouth, Bridport, Lyme Regis, and Yeovil, all towns still awaiting the arrival of the railway.

When first opened the line was not equipped with the electric telegraph, the working of trains over the single line with passing loops at stations being simply controlled by the timetable. The dangers of this system were demonstrated by a series of events near Wareham on the night of 20th September, 1847. The last down train of the day had become derailed on pointwork at Wool station at 9.09 pm; the engine and tender together with two first class carriages and a wagon stayed on the rails, the next two coaches and the guard's van leaving the track. A messenger was sent on horseback to Wareham to inform the station master of the situation, it was at this point that the first error occurred. The station master being under the impression that the up mail train had become derailed, instructed that the contractor's 'muck' engine, which was at Wareham, be prepared for the purpose of bringing on the train. Shortly after 10.30 pm steam had been raised and *Peto* started out towards Wool. In the meantime the carriages at Wool had been placed back on the rails and departed for Dorchester at 10.20 pm, where, upon its arrival, the up mail train started out for Southampton. Without the electric telegraph nobody could tell anybody else what they were doing, the result being that in the deep curved cutting at Worgret *Peto*, travelling tender first, was confronted by the up mail. Both drivers saw each other when the engines were about 100 yards apart but, despite them both shutting off steam, a violent collision occurred. The tender of the muck engine was crushed and forced under the mail engine the driver of which had jumped clear, his fireman being thrown off the engine was buried in coke and struck by a jack that fell off the engine. The fireman of the muck engine suffered severe bruising and had the toes of one foot crushed, the three passengers and the guard on the train were unhurt.

When news of the collision reached Wareham the station master sent a messenger to Poole Junction (Hamworthy Junction) for the engine and carriages that were kept there. The messenger arrived at 1.30 am and within an hour and a quarter the engine had raised steam and proceed down the branch to Poole (Hamworthy) to collect the carriages and take them to Wareham. By 3.45 am the passengers and contents of the mail train had been transferred and the relief train started out for Southampton, arriving at 6.20 am. The down mail had been waiting at Redbridge for the arrival of the up train not knowing of the drama further down the line. They eventually proceeded to Wareham where they waited for the line to be cleared, arriving at Dorchester four hours late. At the time of the accident the poles for the electric telegraph had only been erected as far as Ringwood, but the criticism following the accident caused the work on installing the equipment to be completed to Dorchester by the end of the year.

Four days after the collision at Worgret, the dangers to persons involved in shunting operations was demonstrated at Wareham when Robert Brown, who was employed as a gate keeper, was crushed to death between buffers whilst

The original Hamworthy Junction station in 1887 looking east, to the right the down side waiting shelter is just visible along with the water tank. Part of the original station building was incorporated into the rebuilding for the opening of the Holes Bay curve in 1893. Standing in the up platform with a goods train is well tank No. 185 in her rebuilt form of 1885. Built in 1863, she was withdrawn from service in June 1895.   *Author's Collection*

The original Hamworthy station, later Hamworthy Goods. In this view the canopy remains on the down platform and the shelter can just be seen on the up side platform, with the signal box just visible at the end of the down platform.

OLD STATION AT HAMWORTHY.

assisting in coupling a van to the down mail at 3.30 a.m. The following month there was an incident when a passenger train ran into a wagon standing on the track unloading poles for the electric telegraph. Nobody was injured but Wareham magistrates fined the foreman of the gang 10s. for his carelessness.

One of the first attempts to construct a branch to Swanage was considered shortly after the opening of the Southampton & Dorchester Railway. Wareham solicitor Thomas Phippard proposed the construction of a line from Wareham to develop Swanage as a holiday resort and also carry stone and china clay from the quarries and pits. He also suggested the idea of a steamship service between Swanage and Cherbourg. Moorsom surveyed the route and estimated the cost of construction as £85,000; although plans were deposited in October 1847 the scheme was not proceeded with.

As the Southampton & Dorchester Railway had been worked and managed from its opening day by the LSWR, which also held a majority of the shares, it is not surprising that the line quickly lost its few vestiges of independence.The matter had been discussed for a considerable time; Bircham the LSWR solicitor had written to the Board in June 1847 suggesting the payment of £1,352 to scriptholders of Southampton & Dorchester new shares to enable the Secretary of that company to call in those shares. At a LSWR Board meeting on 15th July, 1847 the following proposition was submitted to the Southampton and Dorchester Board:

> That the South Western Company will give for each £50 original share paid up in the Southampton and Dorchester Railway a £50 share in the South Western Railway to be considered fully paid up and to be entitled to the same privileges as the £50 shares of that Company formed out of the tenths in 1846 it being understood that such of the sellers as may hold scrip for new shares shall bring them in and cancel them on being repaid the amount of the deposits thereon with interest at 4 per cent.
>
> The shares thus offered to be given bear 4 per cent per annum interest from the 1st July 1847 to the 31st December 1848 and from that time will enjoy precisely the same privileges as the old South Western shares.
>
> The consequences of thus purchasing the shares in the Southampton and Dorchester line will be to cast on the South Western Company all the liabilities of the Southampton and Dorchester Company.
>
> This offer stands until the first day of September 1847 and is made on the condition of its being accepted by all or at least by 9850 of the present shares and 3850 of the new script or shares including those of the South Western Company on or before that day.

The first moves to finalise the matter followed a LSWR Board meeting on 29th October, 1847 when the officers of the Southampton & Dorchester Railway were instructed to hand over all deeds and documents.

At the half-yearly meeting of the Southampton & Dorchester company held on 24th February, 1848 it was stated:

> The Directors feel assured that the shareholders will admit that success has hitherto attended the Southampton and Dorchester line; and the invariable unanimity of the conjoint Board may be accepted as a guarantee that the line could not be placed in better hands than those of the London South Western Company. For some time past the shareholders have been fully prepared for the amalgamation of the two Companies; The London South Western Company having, moreover (with the exception of very few

shares), become the virtual and almost entire owners of the line, the Directors have little to add on this subject. A Bill for the amalgamation of the Southampton and Dorchester Railway Company and the London South Western Railway Company, is now before Parliament, and the shareholders will be requested to give their final assent thereto at the special meeting on the 14th of next month.

On the 9th March the Southampton & Dorchester Secretary informed the LSWR Board that he was concluding a treaty for the purchase of the remaining shares of the company.

Having proceeded through Parliament, the Bill for the amalgamation of the Southampton & Dorchester Railway into the London & South Western Railway received the Royal Assent on 22nd July, 1848. The final meeting of the local company took place on Wednesday 11th October when the undertaking was conveyed to the LSWR, Sir John Mills being appointed to a specially created seat on the LSWR Board. Thus ended the short history of a local company, which had lasted a mere three years and three months. However, it had constructed 62¼ miles of railway into west Hampshire and south Dorset that formed the backbone of all future developments.

At this point it is convenient to add a footnote concerning the many railway schemes that were at that time either just simply suggested or proceeded with, some of which either duplicated existing routes or failed to reach their estimated traffic potential. During the late 1830s the Duke of Wellington expressed concern as to the incoherent way in which railways were developing suggesting state ownership, but in the free enterprise culture of those times Government intervention was not considered necessary. That, however, was not the end of the matter: in 1844 Gladstone, then the President of the Board of Trade, attempted to bring order to the industry fearful that the railways would create monopolies. He brought a Bill before Parliament with strict controls including purchase by the state of strategic lines. In the event a diluted Bill gave the Government powers to acquire lines built post-1844 if they made excess profits, the Bill also providing for troops and police to be conveyed at times of unrest. The powers to purchase were abandoned following recommendations by the Royal Commission in 1867.

Although during the second half of the 19th century an enormous amount of Parliamentary time was taken up discussing various Railway Bills, the Government's main concern became the improvement of working and safety through regulations implemented by the Board of Trade. Hence, from the earliest days the chance was lost to have given the entire country a first class internal transport system and avoid the unnecessary duplication of lines that only served the considered needs of the individual companies.

Whilst the LSWR Board had been busy removing the last vestiges of the local company to obtain full control of the new line, other events of an important and historic nature had been taking place. As Poole (Hamworthy) was situated immediately alongside a harbour, it was not long before there was talk of shipping services to the Continent in connection with the trains. Indeed, within a few months of the opening of the line the steamship *Waterwitch* was plying across the channel. However, her stay was short, as the LSWR had already established a service from Southampton and was in no mood to encourage competition. There were also legal difficulties at that time for railway companies seeking to become involved in shipping, as in most cases - including that of the Southampton and Dorchester - their Acts of Parliament did not include powers to operate steamships. A loophole could usually be found by the formation of a separate company, and the fact that the list of Directors and shareholders closely resembled that of the railway with which it connected apparently did not matter! Accordingly a company trading under the name of the South Western Steam Navigation Company was floated in September 1846 to operate all shipping services connected with the LSWR.

On 2nd May, 1848 the paddle steamer *Dispatch*, a vessel with a gross tonnage of 320 tons and an overall length of 166 feet, which had been delivered from the builders, Messrs Ditchburn & Mare, sailed from Poole to the Channel Islands and France on her Maiden voyage. She was, of course, registered as the property of the 'Navigation' company. The *Dispatch* only made two sailings from Poole, being replaced by the *South Western*. The *Poole and Dorsetshire Herald* reported that 'The South Western will sail through the summer to Jersey and on to St Malo', and an advert in the same publication trumpeted:

London to the Channel Islands via Poole in eleven hours. Unrivalled steamships will leave Poole Harbour with goods and passengers for Guernsey and Jersey every Tuesday and Friday morning at Three o'clock which is immediately after the arrival of the London mail train, returning from Jersey every Wednesday and Saturday morning at 8 o'clock

This vessel also sailed from Jersey to Granville on Friday afternoons, returning the following morning at 6 o'clock. The fare between London and either Guernsey or Jersey, first class on the train and main cabin on the boat, was 34s. but the same facilities on the boat could be obtained for 31s. if the rail portion of the journey was second class. Those who did not object to roughing it in a third class carriage and a second class cabin could complete the trip for a mere 20s. 6d. The steamer fare between Poole and the Channel Islands was 21s. in the main cabin or 14s. in the fore cabin, the first leg of the journey to Guernsey taking five hours. The advert concluded 'The South Western trains leave Poole for Dorchester five times daily, from where coaches start for Bridport, Yeovil, Taunton and Exeter'. By this time some of the tradesman of Poole were beginning to feel the benefits of both the railway and the shipping services. George Knight, proprietor of the Antelope Hotel situated next to the offices of the South Western Steam Navigation Company at the bottom of the High Street, was advertising facilities for travellers which included a coach to meet every train from Poole station. His main competitor was William Furmage, agent for the LSWR and proprietor of the London Tavern and Commercial Hotel also in the High Street, who not only offered this service but also declared that he would run a road coach to Poole Junction station to meet the night mail trains.

On 14th August, 1848 the LSWR obtained Parliamentary authority to operate its own shipping services, and this brought to an end the fiction of an independent company for that purpose. The South Western Steam Navigation Company was formally absorbed by the LSWR in February 1849, but even before this the status of Poole as a cross-channel port suffered a blow with the

LONDON TO THE CHANNEL ISLANDS

Via POOLE, in TWELVE HOURS,
WITH A BAG OF LETTERS FROM H. M. POST OFFICE.

Alteration of Time on and after Aug. 1.

THE NEW STEAM **COMPANY'S**

SOUTH-WESTERN NAVIGATION **UNRIVALLED**

STEAM SHIPS,
Will Leave POOLE HARBOUR,
WITH GOODS AND PASSENGERS, FOR

GUERNSEY & JERSEY

Every MONDAY and THURSDAY Nights, at ELEVEN o'Clock,
Immediately after the arrival of the Up Mail Train from Dorchester;
Returning from JERSEY, every WEDNESDAY Afternoon, at Three o'clock,
and SATURDAY Morning, at Eight o'clock.

The Passage to or from POOLE and GUERNSEY will not exceed **FIVE HOURS AND A HALF,**
THEREBY OFFERING TO THE PUBLIC,---
THE MOST RAPID COMMUNICATION BETWEEN THE CHANNEL ISLANDS AND THE METROPOLIS.

FARES to and from LONDON to GUERNSEY and JERSEY, the same as via SOUTHAMPTON, viz:---
**First Class Rail & Main Cabin, 35s. 6d.—Second Class Rail & Main Cabin, 31s. 6d.
Second Class Rail and Second Cabin, 24s. 6d.—Third Class Rail and
second Cabin, 20s. 8d.**
BETWEEN POOLE AND GUERNSEY AND JERSEY,—
**Main Cabin, 21s.— Fore Cabin, 14s.—Carriages, £3.—Horses, £3.—Dogs, 5s.
STEWARD'S FEES.—Main Cabin, 1s.—Fore Cabin, 6d.**
1 Cwt. of Personal Baggage is allowed each Chief Cabin Passenger, all above that weight will be charged 6d. per cubic foot.

PASSENGERS EMBARK AND DISEMBARK AT POOLE FREE OF CHARGE.

Goods by the COMPANY'S VESSELS are carried at very REDUCED RATES.
To Merchants and Shippers this route offers peculiar ADVANTAGES OVER EVERY OTHER PORT.
Merchandize of every description may be Imported or Exported at the low local rate of 3d. per ton only, while the facilities are equal to any Port in the United Kingdom.

THE COMPANY'S VESSELS LEAVE

JERSEY FOR ST. MALO,

*Every TUESDAY Afternoon, returning every WEDNESDAY Morning,
at Ten o'clock. Also, from*

JERSEY TO GRANVILLE,

Every FRIDAY Afternoon, returning every SATURDAY Morning,
ACCORDING TO TIDE.

The SOUTH-WESTERN RAILWAY COMPANY'S TRAINS leave POOLE for DORCHESTER, Five times daily—
from whence Fast Coaches start for Bridport, Yeovil, Taunton, Exeter, &c., &c.

Also, from POOLE first-rate Conveyances for Blandford, Shaftesbury, Bath, Bristol, &c., &c.

*THE NEW SOUTH-WESTERN STEAM NAVIGATION COMPANY will not be responsible for any damage
or loss of Baggage, nor for Delays, Accidents, or Sea Risks of any kind whatsoever.*

New South-Western Steam Navigation Company's Office,   **JOHN BROUGHTON, Agent.**
162, High Street, Poole, July 27th, 1848.

Poster announcing the commencement of the steamer service between Poole and the Channel Islands from 1st August, 1848, unfortunately its operation was short-lived.

withdrawal of the service with the sailing on 30th September, 1848. The *South Western* running aground in Poole Harbour marked the occasion. Her passengers were soon transferred to another vessel, but she remained stuck fast until the next spring tide. On the face of it there was every indication that the LSWR intended to expand the port facilities at Poole, as the Act empowering the company to operate steamships included a section authorizing the purchase of land for additional railway accommodation at Hamworthy and the erection of warehouses, wharves, landing places, approaches, and other works. There were several objectors to the proposals, including the Admiralty who thought that the wharves would impede navigation, several ship owners of the Borough who feared that the railway company would monopolise the port, and Poole Corporation. The latter's objection - at a period when most coastal towns were actively encouraging commercial docks - seems rather odd, but the civic authorities had never been particularly happy with the railway and were by now becoming positively hostile. There was deep resentment of the fact that Poole, by far the most important centre in the area, was served by a dead end branch line, and that the site of the station was so inconvenient. It could only be reached from the town over a private toll bridge, which, as previously mentioned, was often raised immediately prior to the departure of a train, thus causing many intending passengers to miss it! The somewhat spartan facilities offered at Poole Junction (Hamworthy Junction) were another source of complaint. It also seemed probable that the Corporation doubted the sincerity of the LSWR - who were deeply committed to the development of Southampton, and would hardly need two major ports to serve much the same area - and feared that the waterfront would be defaced with half-completed works for many years to come.

The Southampton & Dorchester line had settled down to the uneventful life of a rural railway backwater, a peaceful existence that was not seriously disturbed until the mushroom growth of Bournemouth wreaked havoc on the established traffic patterns of the district some 40 years later. However, its bucolic nature did not deter the Ringwood overseers from rating that portion of the line which passed through their parish at £2,400 - an enormous sum that was reduced to a more realistic £300 10s. following an appeal by the company to the Queen's Bench.

The haste and economy with which the line was constructed had caused trouble almost straight away, the irregularity of the curves causing severe wear to the wheels of the locomotives. Within a year of its opening Peto, was eventually granted a contract to carry out all maintenance for a period of three years, had been instructed to take remedial action.

On 4th August, 1849 a cheap day excursion - the first on the line - was run from Dorchester to Southampton at return fares of 1s. 3d. third class, or 2s. 11d. first class. A large crowd presented themselves at the station despite the early hour, many of them leaving their native Dorset for the first time, and 21 carriages and 41 open trucks had to be marshalled into a mammoth train to accommodate them. In those days the motive power available at Dorchester consisted of two Sharp, Roberts 2-2-2 engines, No. 7 *Venus* and No. 10 *Aurora*, both of which were attached to the excursion. However, it was soon realised that a train of such weight needed further assistance, and No. 50 *Buffalo*, an 0-6-0 goods engine which was waiting to depart with the morning up goods, was duly commandeered. This huge triple-headed train left Dorchester at 5.18 am for what appears to have been an enjoyable if somewhat tiring day for its passengers. On arrival back in the County town at 2.10 am the following day, many of them were found to be soundly asleep in the carriages. Those in the open trucks were allowed to remain undisturbed until dawn. The up goods eventually departed from Dorchester almost 24 hours late!

The fact that Weymouth was the closest port on the English coast to the Channel Islands (Guernsey 70 miles, Jersey 80 miles) and the French port of Cherbourg (62 miles) was always in Weymouth's favour as a channel port, and with the conditions on the spartan vessels of the period the less time spent at sea the better! The first regular service from Weymouth had been commenced in February 1794 operated by Post Office Packets, a service that continued despite many difficulties until May 1845 when it was transferred to Southampton, a port already connected to London by railway.

Having failed at Poole the LSWR decided that a further attempt should by tried from Weymouth to St Malo via Guernsey and Jersey. This commenced on 14th August, 1850 with the paddle steamer *South Western*. However, as the railway terminated at Dorchester and passengers had to continue their journey to Weymouth Quay by horse bus it failed to attract sufficient patronage and was withdrawn in the December, the LSWR concentrating its shipping interests on Southampton.

Although the Southampton & Dorchester Railway was running well, plans for expansion were not progressing. The 1846 scheme for an independent branch to Weymouth had been dropped, and plans for a westward expansion from Dorchester were constantly overshadowed by the prospect of the direct line from Salisbury and Yeovil to Exeter. Thus this state of affairs during the late 1840s and into the mid-1850s, with the only railway in the west of England being the Bristol & Exeter company passing through Taunton *en route* to Exeter, placed Dorchester as a convenient railhead for stagecoach services over a large area, including the seaport and resort of Weymouth, eight miles away. For its railway connection both Weymouth and the LSWR relied on the GWR which was having difficulties constructing the Wilts, Somerset & Weymouth Railway. This situation was not resolved until January 1857, and in the November of the same year a branch from Maiden Newton to Bridport was opened giving that town the rail connection that it demanded.

In the north of the county the LSWR main line between Salisbury, Yeovil and Exeter was completed on 9th July, 1860, finally bringing to an end any hopes Castleman and other interested parties still entertained of gaining trunk line status for the Southampton & Dorchester line.

The delays in construction of the Wilts, Somerset & Weymouth line were unfortunate, whilst the Southampton & Dorchester whose line ran through comparatively easy countryside had constructed its 60 mile railway to Dorchester in two years. The Wilts, Somerset & Weymouth , with the construction of 70 miles of railway excluding the branches to Bathampton, Salisbury and Radstock, faced a far greater challenge. Unable to commence work quickly following the passing of its Act, the company soon found itself victim of the Railway Mania and subsequently had difficulties in raising the required capital. With only part of the northern end of the line completed work was brought to a standstill in June 1849 through lack of funds, the result being uncompleted earthworks throughout the counties of Wiltshire, Somerset and Dorset.

The Great Western Railway as guarantors of the Wilts, Somerset & Weymouth company was forced to take the company over in March 1850. This was followed by legal action in an attempt to have the work restarted and led to the formation of the Frome, Yeovil & Weymouth Railway Company in 1852 to complete the work. However, this was unsuccessful and the GWR, faced with the possibility of the LSWR seeking new powers and reaching Weymouth alone, and obtaining a monopoly of the trade including the Channel Island traffic, was obliged to complete the works at any cost. The GWR Board authorized the completion of the works on 23rd September, 1852, although it was still to be a drawn-out affair.

At Dorchester the work of excavating the cutting between Dorchester Junction and the LSWR station was the responsibility of the GWR as the latter owned that particular section of line, indeed, it owned a considerable amount of surrounding land including the site of the later (1879) down platform of the LSWR station. By October 1853 the cutting and the bridge over it carrying Maunbury Road had been completed, the latter receiving criticism over its construction following the collapse of the nearby bridge over the Wilts, Somerset & Weymouth line that same month.

Already served by one railway, the people of Dorchester were less vociferous than those in Weymouth who held a public meeting in February 1854 when a resolution was passed to urge the GWR to complete its line to Weymouth. Work had recommenced by the April when there were reports of difficulty in obtaining labour locally, and in July the *Southern Times* reported construction of the earthworks was progressing and that materials had been brought to Weymouth by sea. An Act of Parliament allowing an extension of time to complete the works was passed on 31st July, 1854. There was optimism that the works would be quickly completed. Mr Dodson, the contractor for the Weymouth section, and also a member of the town council, stated at a meeting in March 1855, 'That judging by the progress made upon the works to the present time, he believed we should be able to travel by rail from Weymouth to Dorchester and Yeovil before the expiration of the year'.

However, Dodson's optimism was a little over stated; in mid-June it was reported that the operation of laying the permanent way was proceeding slowly owing to a delay in the arrival of materials. Construction of Weymouth station buildings commenced at the end of August, and earlier in the month Dodson had stated that he thought that the narrow gauge portion of the line would be completed by September instead of October.

Although there was considerable progress at the Weymouth end of the line, there was a significant section uncompleted, the northern end having not yet reached Yeovil. The townspeople of Weymouth were annoyed with the tardy progress in construction, and further frustrated by the fact that a mere eight miles away at Dorchester the LSWR line had been open since June 1847.

Taking into account the fact that the section of mixed gauge railway between Dorchester Junction and Weymouth was almost completed, general opinion was that this section should be opened to allow the LSWR access to the town. Two public meetings were held in an attempt to obtain answers from both companies for the delays in completion of the line. However, there was little that could be done, correspondence that had taken place between the council and the companies clearly explained the situation. Communication had been made with the LSWR requesting a representative be present at the first meeting. The following reply was received from Mr Scott the traffic manager: 'Mr Crombie is not at home. I can't leave London tomorrow. The Directors will be glad to give due consideration to the resolutions passed at the Weymouth meeting, when they receive them'.

Col W. Lockyer Freestun, one of the two Members of Parliament for Weymouth, a military man more used to action than words had personally checked the line between Weymouth and Dorchester. He reported that he had checked the tunnel and that the rails were laid throughout and that the eight miles of railway might be opened within 10 days. In the early part of August the Colonel had an interview with Mr Chaplin of the LSWR concerning the expediency of opening the standard gauge rails between Weymouth and Dorchester. He also communicated with the GWR requesting that they complete the narrow gauge works so as to allow the passage of LSWR trains.

Following a considerable amount of correspondence a reply on 6th September from Mr L. Crombie the Secretary of the LSWR stated:

I am directed to inform you that the Board has today had under its consideration the advisability of applying to the Great Western company to complete that portion of the Wilts, Somerset & Weymouth Railway which lies between Dorchester and Weymouth.
I am to state that they feel great difficulty in originating any such negotiation.
They have less reluctance in arriving at this conclusion as you and your constituents can no doubt, by a direct application to the Great Western Company bring about some settlement which will be satisfactory to the interests to the town of Weymouth.

A letter two days later from the Secretary of the GWR was equally as unhelpful:

The Directors have used, and are still using every means to get the works of the line finished to Weymouth, and nothing but uncontrollable difficulties with contractors of the works in the first instance, and with iron-masters etc. who undertook to supply the rails and materials, have hitherto baffled the efforts to complete and open the whole.
The Board persevere in the same course, and will to the utmost extent accelerate the opening. But they do not see any advantage to the Company in retarding one part of the line, in order to complete another part, and especially as they will only thereby debar themselves for a longer period from obtaining the Weymouth traffic over their line.
The great sacrifices made by the Great Western shareholders already in providing the funds for the Weymouth line are such as to entitle them to reap the benefit over their own line rather than to postpone it for the benefit of another Company.

A further letter addressed to the Mayor of Weymouth on 6th October from Spencer Walpole, Chairman of the GWR simply repeated the comments raised previously in stronger terms:

We cannot hesitate to admit the expression adverted to of a very decided opinion sincerely entertained at the time by this Board and their principal engineer, as to the earlier opening of our line to Weymouth than has since proved to be the result. We are most anxious to accelerate the construction of the line, and have never failed to impress upon Mr. Brunel the importance we attach to it. But unforeseen circumstances over which the Directors had no control, have delayed, and must still retard, the final completion of the works, and it is not within our power at present to fix the 'precise' time for opening it.

As to the suggestion of our assisting to open the line from Dorchester to Weymouth for the South Western traffic the Board merely remark that they feel naturally unwilling to take any steps which may postpone even for a day, the opening of the whole line between Frome and Weymouth, and as such might be the case to the detriment of their shareholders if they divert to one portion of the railway, the Directors could not feel justified in acceding to that proposition.

The inhabitants of Weymouth, however, may rest upon our renewed assurance that the Directors will spare no exertions to obtain the requisite quantity of rails for the construction of the entire line, which in fact constitutes the main difficulty in its progress to completion.

Additional correspondence from the LSWR referring to a letter sent accompanying copies of resolutions passed at a meeting held at the Town Hall, Weymouth on 27th October, stated:

…that the South Western company are as anxious as the inhabitants of Weymouth can be that the line from Dorchester to Weymouth shall be opened as speedily as possible. It is a matter, however, that does not rest with them. The South Western Company have no control over the construction of the line which has to be completed by the Great Western Company, with whom they have frequently communicated on the subject.

The tone set by both companies although put in diplomatic terms was clearly 'railway politics'. The GWR were not going to allow the LSWR to steal the edge on them by allowing access over the Dorchester Junction-Weymouth section until they could compete on even terms. Whilst the LSWR, who were by Act of Parliament merely allowed running rights over the completed section of line, had to wait, no doubt they were involved in negations with the GWR over other parts of the system where both companies had a shared interest, and did not wish to create any animosity by pressing for favours at Weymouth!

Thus Weymouth had to wait, a victim of circumstance and the policy and pride of the railway companies. However, work on the construction of Weymouth station was proceeding well, the *Southern Times* on 17th November reporting that some portion of the building was undergoing the process of roofing, and that piles were just being driven for the construction of the goods shed which would extend from the passenger station nearly to the Backwater.

Work was still progressing slowly in Wiltshire and Somerset; the section from Warminster to Salisbury opened on 30th June, 1856 giving a connection with the LSWR, albeit with all the complications of a change of gauge. Work on the 26 miles between Frome and Yeovil were completed later that summer and opened to traffic on 1st September.

Whilst the GWR was completing the Yeovil-Dorchester section of its line, other legal formalities were taking place. At the half-yearly meeting of the LSWR held on 7th August, 1856 it was stated:

(FOR JANUARY.)

UP TRAINS.

DAILY.	1 & 2 Class	1 2 3 Class	1 & 2 Class	1 & 2 Class (G)	1 & 2 Class (N)	1 & 2 Class (G)	2 3 Class	1 & 2 Class (Mail.)
From	A. M.	A. M.	A. M.	A. M.	P. M.	P. M.	P. M.	P. M.
WEYMOUTH ...al	6. 0	8. 0	11.55	2.45	4.15	5.45	0.45	
DORCHESTER ...	6.25	8.25	12.20	1.15	4.40	6.30	10.15	
Moreton	M	8.35	12.35	1.45		6.45	10.25	
Wool	M	8.45	12.47	2. 0	N	7. 0		
Wareham	6.51	8.55	12.59	2.30	5. 7	7.20	10.45	
Poole Junction..	7. 3	9.10	1.13	3. 7	5.19	7.42	10.57	
POOLE ....ar.	7.20	9.20	12.35	3.20	5.30	7.50		
,, ...dp.	6.50	9. 0	12.10	2.55	5.10	7.35		
Wimborne........	7.18	9.20	1.20	3.30	5.34	8.15	11.15	
Ringwood	7.30	9.40	1.48	4. 1	5.54	8.45	11.35	
Christchurch	7.51	10. 5	2. 1	4.26	6. 7	9.11		
Brockenhurst ...	8. 0	10.16	2.12	4.46	6.16	9.31	12. 0	
Beaulieu Road		10.30		5. 8		9.45		
Lyndhurst Road..	R	10.37		5.21		10. 0		
Redbridge	8.30	10.40	2.34	5.40	6.44	10.18	12.23	
Blechynden		10.55		6. 7		10.30		
SOUTHAMPTON ar	8.40	11. 5	2.50	6.20	7. 0	10.40	12.40	
,, dp	8.50	12.30	3. 0		7.10		1.30	
WATERLOO	11. 5	5. 0	5.55	9.20	9.55	10.20	4.30	

SUNDAYS.

	1 2 3 Class.	1 and 2 Class.	1 & 2 Class Mail.
WEYMOUTH	6. 0	1.20	...
DORCHESTER	6.25	1.45	10.15
SOUTHAMPTON	9.30	6. 0	1.30
WATERLOO	1.35	9. 0	4.30

G. These are Goods trains from Dorchester to Southampton, to which Passenger Carriages are attached.

N. This train will stop at Wool on Saturdays only.

R. This train will stop at Lyndhurst Road on Tuesdays and Saturdays by signal.

M. This train will stop at Moreton and also at Wool on Mondays, by signal.

DOWN TRAINS.

DAILY.	1 & 2 Class A	1 2 3 Class	1 & 2 Class	1 & 2 Exp. Class	1 & 2 Exp. G	1 Class Exp.	1 & 2 Class	1 & 2 Class Mail.
From	A. M.	A. M.	A. M.	A. M.	A. M.	P. M.	P. M.	P. M.
WATERLOO	...	6. 0	9.40	10.15	11. 0	3. 0	5. 0	8.30
SOUTHM..ar.		10.10	1.10	1.10	1.20	5.20	7.35	11.30
,, dp.	8.30	10.30	1.30			5.40	7.45	12. 6
Blechynden ...	9.10	10.36						...
Redbridge ...	6.50	10.46	1.42			5.52	7.57	12.20
Lyndhurst...	7. 8	10.56	1.52			6. 0	8. 5	...
Beaulieu Rd.	7.25	11. 5						...
Brockenhurst	7.50	11.17	2.12			6.17	8.20	12.48
Christch.	8.28	11.29	2.22			6.29	8.32	...
Ringwood...	8.50	11.44	2.34			6.41	8.45	1.19
Wimborne...	9.20	12. 7	2.53			7. 0	9. 3	1.45
Poole Junct.	9.52	12.23	3. 7			7.13	9.17	2. 5
POOLE .. ar.	10. 0	12.35	3.20			7.27	9.30	...
,, ..dp.	9.40	12.10	2.55			7. 7	9. 5	...
Wareham ..	10.28	12.35	3.21			7.26	9.28	2.19
Wool........	10.48	12.47				L		...
Moreton ...	11.18	1. 0					9.53	...
DORCHESTER	11.40	1.20	4. 0			8. 5	10.10	3. 0
WEYMOUTH	12. 0	1.40	4.20			8.25	10.30	...

SUNDAYS.

	1 2 3 Class.	1 and 2 Class.	1 & 2 Class Mail.
WATERLOO..............	9.15	10.15	8.30
SOUTHAMPTON	1.45	1.45	12.6
DORCHESTER	4.40	4.40	3. 0
WEYMOUTH.............	5. 0	5. 0	...

A. Goods Train from Southampton to Dorchester, to which Passenger Carriages are attached.

G. This train conveys First Class Passengers only, with the exception of servants in actual attendance upon their employers.

L. This train will stop at Wool by signal only.

Timetable published in the *Southern Times* on 24th January, 1857 showing the full LSWR service through to Weymouth following the opening of the line to Weymouth four days earlier.

The Company in pursuant to the provisions of the Act as to the mixed gauge, have also laid down an additional single rail for a distance of eight miles from Dorchester towards Wareham, to accommodate the broad gauge traffic.

How this little exercise in quid pro quo was to benefit the GWR it is difficult to see as the mixed gauge line ended east of Moreton on open heath land, a section of line that history does not record a broad gauge train ever traversing, and was removed by 1863 when that section of line was doubled. However, at a cost to the LSWR of £16,309 honour and the spirit of the Act had been carried out to the letter!

During October it was reported that the final link in the Wilts, Somerset & Weymouth was complete as the rails had reached Dorchester, and the finishing touches were being applied to Weymouth station.

On Monday 22nd December a broad gauge locomotive arrived at Weymouth having travelled from Yeovil over the completed railway. During the first week of January 1857 several GWR locomotives passed over the line, which was inspected by Col Yolland of the Board of Trade on 15th January. It was recorded that an experimental trial was run over the line between Dorchester and Weymouth on Monday 19th January by the LSWR.

On the following day Tuesday 20th January, 1857 the completed railway opened. On a cold wet morning the first train departed at 6.15 am with the second departure hauled by *Otho* at 8.30 am, the first LSWR departure taking place at 11.55 am. Thus the railway to Weymouth had opened, after many struggles both political and financial, 11 years after the original Act of Parliament had been passed.

The opening of the Wilts, Somerset & Weymouth line gave both Dorchester and Weymouth two direct routes to London, the GWR via Swindon to Paddington 168½ miles and the LSWR via Ringwood to Waterloo 147¼ miles.

Services on the LSWR were speeded up with timing alterations to several trains. The *Southern Times* for 10th January reporting in its Dorchester column:

...the train which formerly left Dorchester at 11.45 am and arrived at Waterloo at 5.55 pm by the recent arrangements leaves Dorchester at 12.20 pm arriving at the Waterloo station at the same time as under the old arrangements (5.55 pm) by which a saving of 35 minutes is effected - consideration to the commercial portion of the community. Many other important improvements have also been effected.

With the extension of the line the previous seven up trains now commenced from Weymouth, although of the six down trains only five were extended to Weymouth, the 8.30 pm mail train from Waterloo terminating at Dorchester at 3 am, a pattern that was to continue for the next 113 years.

Finally the LSWR had obtained access to Weymouth although it was only through running rights over the line of their rivals, the GWR. However, goods traffic had to wait a few more weeks as the goods facilities at both the Great Western station at Dorchester and Weymouth station did not open until Monday 2nd March, with Weymouth then enjoying the full facilities offered by both companies.

Had not common sense prevailed the connection at Dorchester Junction might not have been brought into use. The single line spur between Dorchester Junction

A general view of Weymouth station around the time of its opening in January 1857, although the track in the foreground leading to the goods shed does not appear to be laid to completed standard. Standing outside the station's overall roof is an LSWR 2-4-0 believed to be 'Hercules' class No. 40 *Windsor*.   *Author's Collection*

Looking around the curve from Dorchester South to Dorchester Junction; a BR Standard 4-6-0 heads off the Western Region line across the junction towards Weymouth in March 1967, the GWR Dorchester Junction signal box is seen on the right. Had a scheme of 1895 been adopted the land ahead of the engine would have been the site for a joint LSWR/GWR station.

C.L. Caddy

and the LSWR terminus was partly situated in a cutting on a severe curve; in those days of elementary signalling its operation was fraught with difficulty and caused concern to the Board of Trade, so much so that it almost stopped the opening of the connection. At Dorchester Junction where the double junction curved away it was controlled by a points man, after a short distance where the line became single a second points man was employed. The 20 chain single line section then continued around the curve to join the single line of the London & South Western as it approached the Dorchester terminus

On his inspection of the Wilts, Somerset & Weymouth line in January, Col Yolland had expressed dissatisfaction with the arrangements, stating:

...that some arrangement should be made with the South Western Railway Company, by which the proper dispatch of trains between Dorchester Junction and Dorchester South Western station should be regulated over the portion of single line intervening between these points until a satisfactory arrangement of this nature is made, I am of the opinion that the portion of single line between Dorchester Junction and Dorchester South Western station cannot by reason of the incompleteness of the works be opened for traffic without danger to the public using the same.

It was not until the 19th January that agreement was reached that a travelling porter should ride on all engines passing over the junction until some other arrangements could be made. Indeed, this arrangement was to continue for a considerable time, a letter from the Board of Trade to the LSWR in October 1859 stating: 'The use of a porter for pilot duty at Dorchester Junction was to continue for the time being'.

The new arrangements also created operational difficulties for the LSWR at Dorchester where complicated shunting moves were required for all up and down Weymouth trains; indeed, the operation of the extension to Weymouth was not without difficulties.

The mixed gauge track between the two towns allowed the standard gauge stock to travel using the near side rail with the off side set of wheels running on the third rail placed between the broad gauge running rails, this arrangement allowing stock to stand correctly alongside platforms. There was, however, complicated pointwork at crossovers between up and down lines to ensure that the standard gauge stock crossed to the near side rail.

Matters were further complicated at Weymouth there being broad gauge lines, mixed gauge lines and standard gauge lines. To begin with all points were operated by hand levers without any form of interlocking, in addition staff had to ensure stock from either gauge did not come into contact with each other as the buffering and couplings were spaced at different distances.

However, there would also appear to have been a delay in the construction of the LSWR engine shed at Weymouth. At the half-yearly meeting of the company held in February 1858, the construction of a new engine shed at Weymouth was listed in the works department account for the past half-year.

A general arrangement drawing of Dorchester for the period between 1868 and 1878 showing the unusual terminal arrangements and the single line to Dorchester Junction, also the engine shed in its original two-road form.

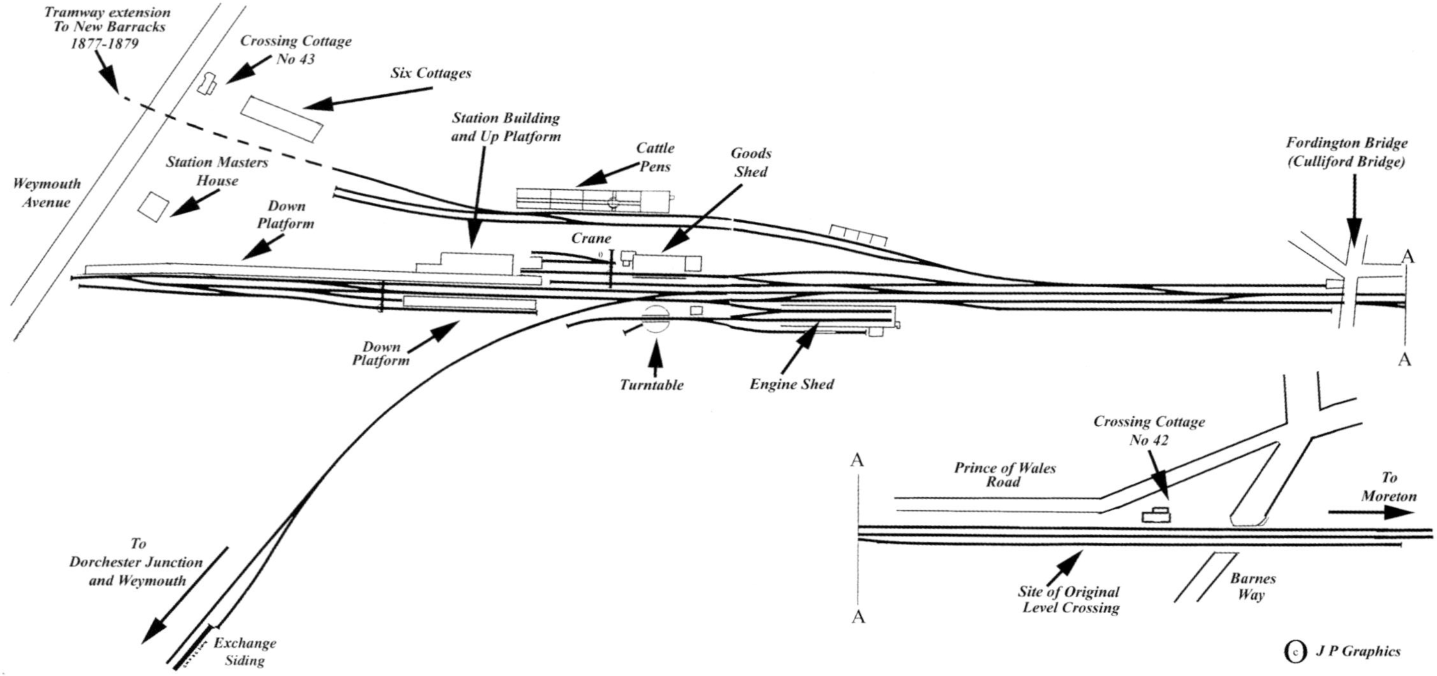

Fordington Bridge
(Culliford Bridge)

A

A

To
Moreton

Crossing Cottage
No 42

Prince of Wales
Road

Barnes
Way

Site of Original
Level Crossing

A

A

© J P Graphics

Goods
Shed

Engine Shed

Cattle
Pens

Crane

Turntable

Station Building
and Up Platform

Six Cottages

Crossing Cottage
No 43

Station Masters
House

Down
Platform

Down
Platform

Tramway extension
To New Barracks
1877-1879

Weymouth
Avenue

To
Dorchester Junction
and Weymouth

Exchange
Siding

DORCHESTER GENERAL ARRANGEMENT DRAWING 1868-1878

Chapter Six

Expansion, Shipping Services and Branch Lines

With the complete line open traffic quickly increased, excursions that previously began or terminated at Dorchester were extended to Weymouth. On 29th June, 1857 an excursion from the town calling at all principal stations to London departed at 6.20 am arriving in the capital at 12.30 pm, passengers returning from London at 3 45 pm the following day at a cost of 12s. first class or 8s. in covered carriages. Further excursions were reported in the local press: early in September one train was reported as conveying around a thousand passengers to Weymouth from various stations, whilst another excursion departed for London and when joined with other carriages at Dorchester the train consisted of 28 coaches hauled by two engines.

Regular passengers were not overlooked, the requirements for an early train from Dorchester to Weymouth was attended to by attaching carriages to a previous light engine movement departing at 7.15 am, although it was still a long wait for any passengers that had arrived at 3 am aboard the mail train!

The extension of the line also saw the LSWR renew their interest in the port, sending two of their captains to Weymouth to plan the return of shipping services; having the necessary Parliamentary powers and vessels available few difficulties were encountered. The GWR, however, was in a different position having no powers to operate steamships, and having just completed the Wilts, Somerset & Weymouth Railway at considerable expense it had given little thought to a Channel Islands service.

In the Islands there was dissatisfaction with the monopoly enjoyed by both Southampton and the LSWR. This resulted in a retired Jersey mail packet master canvassing at Weymouth during November 1856 and, with the support of several influential local people and several Directors of the GWR, the Weymouth & Channel Islands Steam Packet Company was formed. As an independent company matters could move more quickly than the involvement an Act of Parliament would entail if the GWR wished to operate its own service.

The LSWR commenced its service on Monday 13th April, 1857 when the PS *Express* sailed in unfavourable weather, only seven passengers making the crossing, which took 10 hours! The Steam Packet company in a race against time chartered two vessels *Aquila* and *Cygnus*, the former sailing from Weymouth and the latter from Jersey on 17th April to start the service. Thus Weymouth was established as a railway-connected channel port, albeit the harbour lacked many of the basic facilities for both passengers and ships alike.

Although there were various agreements governing the running of the trains between Dorchester and Weymouth, there was already disagreement between the two companies over the shipping services. There had been proposed inter-availability of tickets, but the LSWR then announced that its fares between London and Guernsey and Jersey via Weymouth would be 35s. first class and 25s. second class. As the fares from Southampton were only 31s. and 21s. the GWR protested but the LSWR refused to raise the Southampton fares.

THE
LYMINGTON RAILWAY
IS
NOW OPEN
FOR
PASSENGER TRAFFIC
AND UNTIL FURTHER NOTICE
The Trains will Run as follows:--

	ON WEEK DAYS.							ON SUNDAYS.		
	1&2 class.	1&2 class.	1,2,&3 cl.	1&2 class.	1&2 class.	1&2 class.	1&2 class.	1,2,&3 cl.	1&2 class.	1 &2 class.
	A.M.	A.M.	A.M.	A.M.	P.M.	P.M.	P.M.	A.M.	P.M.	P.M.
Leave LYMINGTON	7 15	10 10	10 10	10 55	1 50	5 50	8 0	7 45	2 10	4 5
Arrive BROCKENHURST	7 30	10 25	10 25	11 10	2 5	6 5	8 15	8 0	2 25	4 20
„ SOUTHAMPTON ..	8 40	11 20	11 20		2 50	7 0		9 10		5 30
„ DORCHESTER	10 25			1 15	3 55	7 55	10 5	11 0	4 35	
„ LONDON	11 0	2 30	5 0		5 50	9 55		12 50		9 0

	1&2 class.	1&2 class.	1,2,&3 cl.	1&2 class.	1&2 class.	1&2 class.	1&2 class.	1,2,&3 cl.	1&2 class.	1&2 class.
	A.M.	A.M.	A.M.	A.M.	A.M.	P.M.	P.M.	A.M.	A.M.	P.M.
Leave LONDON			6 0	8 0	11 0	3 0	5 0	11 0	10 15	
„ DORCHESTER	6 25	8 40			12 25	4 50		6 25		1 45
„ SOUTHAMPTON ..	6 30		10 30	10 30	1 30	5 30	7 45	7 0	1 45	
„ BROCKENHURST	8 0	10 34	11 20	11 20	2 15	6 25	8 25	8 30	2 37	4 30
Arrive LYMINGTON	8 15	10 50	11 35	11 35	2 30	6 40	8 40	8 45	2 52	4 45

The Omnibuses between Lymington and Brockenhurst will Cease Running after this date. Omnibuses will Run to and from the Lymington Station.

By Order,

ARCH^{D.} SCOTT,

Waterloo Bridge Station, July 12th, 1858.

Traffic Manager.

WATSON, PRINTER, GALPINE'S LIBRARY, LYMINGTON.

A poster advertising the opening of the Lymington branch in July 1858.

However, when it was announced that the Steam Packet company was going to charge 31s. and 21s. the LSWR was forced to fall into line, but the inter-availability scheme was abandoned.

In the face of many difficulties, including the fact that both passengers and goods had to be transported by horse drawn conveyances between Weymouth station and the Quay, the service continued. In November 1857 the Steam Packet company acquired the two hired vessels, and despite their precarious financial position purchased a third vessel the *Brighton* in July 1858 to commence a service to Cherbourg in the September. However, with unsatisfactory returns that service ceased the following June.

The LSWR continued with its sailings employing at various times the steamers *Express*, *South Western* and *Wonder*, but not without difficulties. When Brunel's *Great Eastern* was lying in Portland Harbour open to visitors the *South Western*, whilst running an excursion, struck a hulk lying alongside the great vessel requiring the *South Western* to need substantial repairs. This however paled into insignificance on 20th September, 1859 when the *Express* on departure from Jersey struck rocks at Corbiere; although run ashore in an attempt so save her, she broke up and became a total loss. The service continued using the *South Western* and the *Wonder* until suspended on 12th December, 1859 when *Wonder* made the final crossing. Both vessels returning to Southampton and the service was never revived, thus ending the direct involvement of the LSWR in the cross-channel services from Weymouth.

During that period the entire line, apart from the short double track section between Southampton and Redbridge, had been single with passing loops at the stations, traffic being controlled by the electric telegraph. It must be admitted that the permanent way was not of the highest quality, and in 1854 it was necessary to lay additional sleepers in many places because it was found that the originals were too widely spaced to maintain stability. The Board of Trade had insisted on the provision of double track throughout, but nothing was done until 1857 when the first two sections - Redbridge to Beaulieu Road, and Brockenhurst to Christchurch Road (Holmsley) - were widened, the double line being brought into use on 1st August that year. The section from Ringwood to Wimborne was inspected on 21st September: the rails consisting of 21 ft lengths on laid on sleepers of larch and Scottish fir placed three feet apart. The missing links from Beaulieu Road to Brockenhurst and Christchurch Road (Holmsley) to Ringwood were completed on 1st September, 1858.

At the eastern end of the line the only extension that was proceeded with from the second Act of Parliament was the branch to Eling Wharf, leaving the main line by a training connection off the down side at Totton. It opened in 1851 serving jetties owned by Sir John Barker Mill at the top of Southampton Water.

A branch line to Lymington had again came to the fore in August 1853 with local support in Lymington and the local MP anxious to rush a Bill through during the 1854 session. Whereas with the local company branch lines had been an attraction, albeit none were ever built, a branch line to the LSWR was a small consideration in the larger picture, resulting in the shareholders not reaching agreement. It was left to local initiative to construct the line resulting in the Lymington Railway Bill receiving the Royal Assent on 7th July, 1856.

Brockenhurst station looking west taken before the improvements of the 1880s, in the centre background can be seen the original goods shed and to the left the down platform arrangements. The main station buildings have been improved including the provision of a canopy; a disc signal can be seen to the right of this interesting picture. *Author's Collection*

The original Wareham station situated on the east side of the level crossing photographed pre-1885. Looking towards Dorchester the small engine shed for the Engineer's engine can be seen beyond the gates, with the up side waiting shelter in the right foreground. *Author's Collection*

The branch was to leave the main line one mile west of Brockenhurst at Latchmere Pond and proceed four miles to terminate at the Town Quay. Work on construction proceeded rapidly with the Board of Trade inspection being held on 11th May, 1858. As there were no turning facilities the inspecting officer required an undertaking that only tank engines would operate the branch. The LSWR, who had entered into an agreement to work the line for 50 per cent of the gross receipts, required additional work on the line before it could open to traffic. Excluding Hamworthy, the first branch off the original Southampton & Dorchester line opened for traffic on 12th July, 1858. Even then only a temporary wooden terminus was constructed at Lymington, the present permanent structure not opening until 8th September. A primitive wooden platform was opened at Shirley Holmes on 10th October, 1860 to serve the distant villages of Baldre and Sway.

From the earliest days there were constant improvements to both the stations and trackwork to provide a more efficient service as traffic increased. A letter from Mr Fryer of Wimborne suggested that passenger trains should stop at West Moors siding when signalled to do so. It is assumed that the West Moors siding referred to was in fact a passing loop known as Leonard's Bridge situated between Ringwood and Wimborne, which appears to have been abandoned when the section was doubled. Poole (Hamworthy) station came in for mention on several occasions; it was recommended that a 5 ton crane be erected at the station, followed by a suggestion to improve the platforms and erect a goods shed. In October 1857 repairs to the approach road were suggested and in the December it was decided to illuminate the station with gas lighting.

In July 1858 it was recommended that Brockenhurst be extended to accommodate the Lymington branch traffic, and a new siding should be laid behind the down platform. Increased accommodation for goods traffic at Ringwood was recommended in the November, however, an offer from a Mr Ayles to rent a refreshment room at the station should the company erect one was declined, the Board deciding one was not required at that time. The following year the small wayside station at Moreton required its up siding lengthening to hold an additional six wagons.

Wareham was also the focus of attention during 1859; there being several complaints concerning the lack of passenger accommodation at the station, it was decided to improve accommodation and provide shelter for passengers. In September the station master requested a 5 ton crane, the committee deciding that the travelling crane be tried first. In the October Mr Scott, the traffic manager, recommended that the down platform be lengthened and additional accommodation for goods traffic provided.

During 1848 a factory to process shale from the Kimmeridge area had been established near the site of the present Wareham station. Taken over by Messrs Wonostrocht & Company in 1858 they planned to expand the business and it was decided to lengthen a siding to handle the traffic. Unfortunately the shale oil industry failed to flourish and within a few years Messrs Wonostrocht and other local concerns closed down. Ironically, 100 years later the discovery of oil at Kimmeridge was to bring a new prosperity to the area.

At the February 1858 Board meeting Mr Scott recommended that he should be authorized to arrange with the GWR for the laying of a broad gauge siding

Bullied light pacific No. 34009 *Lyme Regis* takes the Northam curve with a Waterloo-Weymouth express on 5th August, 1966. The engine is passing the spot where the junction to Southampton Terminus from Tunnel Junction commenced, and the sub station for the forthcoming electrification has already been constructed on the left. *Author's Collection*

at Dorchester to enable the easy transfer of goods. By May it had been agreed to lay down parallel broad and standard gauge sidings at the joint expense of both companies. However, progress was slow, and it was not until 23rd April, 1859 that the *Southern Times* reported:

> The broad and narrow gauge junction is now being completed up to the goods station of the South Western Railway by which the transshipment of goods to and from the Great Western Railway will be greatly facilitated.

Dorchester station was not without its problems. In September 1858 it was recommended that the arrival shed should be boarded up to shelter passengers in the like manner as the down shed, and in the December it was decided that the ends of the shed over the departure platform should be closed in so as to afford better protection to passengers from the weather. In June 1859 Mr Scott recommended that the columns which supported the passenger shed should be altered so as to clear the carriage doors when open, and the following January the Revd Ellicot complained of there being no gentlemen's waiting room at the station, the committee considering another waiting room was not necessary.

If Dorchester station was a cause for concern the situation at Southampton was more pressing. From Monday 2nd August, 1858 Blechynden station was renamed Southampton West and on the same date Northam curve opened, this allowing direct running off the London line onto the Southampton & Dorchester eliminating the reversal required at Southampton Docks (Terminus) (then known as Southampton Docks). At first a majority of passenger trains still proceeded via the terminus station which at that time was the principal station in the town. The curvature of the new spur was extremely sharp requiring a speed restriction of 7 mph, this being raised to 15 mph in 1907.

However, the station was a serious problem, it being reported to the Board in the same month that 'something of a temporary nature must immediately be erected at Bletchenden to protect passengers from rain and wind'. The following August it was noted that the station required additional accommodation, and in October Mr Scott submitted a report on the necessity of immediately improving the station to protect the interests of the company.

The GWR, having reached Salisbury in 1857, were looking towards Southampton where the prospect of traffic could be obtained from the developing docks. Thus a nominally independent company with GWR backing, the Andover Canal Railway, was formed to construct a line from Andover to Redbridge utilising parts of the former canal. Following the passing of the Bill through Parliament in July 1858, an extension scheme entitled the Southampton, Andover & Wiltshire Railway was conceived to provide extensions at the northern end to join the GWR and a line constructed to the seaward side of the existing Southampton & Dorchester Railway between Redbridge and Southampton Royal Pier. Early in 1860 the Admiralty objected to the latter proposal, as it could be detrimental to the future development of the docks.

The LSWR had vigorously opposed both schemes and put forward a Bill to improve the foreshore between Southampton and Millbrook, the *Hampshire Advertiser* for 15th January, 1859 stating:

The covered up platform at Dorchester photographed in the 1890s; in later years the side screens were removed, a condition in which the structure remained until its complete removal just prior to World War II. *Author's Collection*

Southampton Town & Docks station (originally Southampton Docks, later Southampton Terminus) the original extent of the LSWR line from London. It played an important part in the working of the Southampton & Dorchester line as up until its closure in 1966 a number of local services to both Salisbury and Bournemouth and MSWJR trains commenced and terminated there. In the background the magnificent South Western Hotel towers above the station. Had one of the original Southampton & Dorchester plans been carried out the line would have proceeded past this station along the foreshore to Millbrook. *G.A. Pryer Collection*

Now, who in Southampton could have supposed, by the title of the Bill that such works as enclosing a portion of the mud-lands were contemplated? Yet this is the scheme brought out by the London South Western Company to prevent the extension of the Andover and Redbridge Railway from Redbridge to Southampton. Verily there are some awful pilots at the helm of the South Western. Is Southampton to be made the continual dupe of their artifices? Not much longer, we think.

Financial difficulties for the Andover & Redbridge company during 1861 caused it and the GWR to promote a Bill in December 1861 to lease the entire project to the GWR which would construct a mixed gauge line. In retaliation the LSWR proposed a Bristol & South Western Junction Railway, at which point Parliament imposed a settlement where both companies agreed not to promote new lines in each other's territories, but to promote facilities for through traffic, in particular between the North and the South Coast. Amalgamation of the Andover & Redbridge with the LSWR was authorized in an Act of 29th June, 1863 to construct a standard gauge line between Andover and Redbridge, opening on 6th March, 1865, although it was not until 1883 that a through route to the Midlands was completed.

Returning to the Southampton & Dorchester, whilst most stations along the line were struggling to cope with the traffic on offer, Beaulieu Road was not a success. From the beginning the income hardly paid the wages of the staff, and as early as June 1848 the Directors were considering its future. The station had been the result of the requirements of the Commissioners of Woods & Forests, no doubt as a result of the route the railway took through the New Forest. As the Commissioners refused the Directors' request to close the station it was decided in June 1849 that only Parliamentary trains would stop there.

In September 1859 it was again decided to close the station leaving the platform for the use of the Duke of Buccleuch. However, amid local protests the station remained open. Early in January 1860 the company solicitor Mr Bircham having been unable to find any obligation upon the company to keep the station open, the Board recommended its closure, the platforms would remain so that trains might occasionally stop when required by the Duke. Closure took place on 1st March, 1860. The lack of trade had almost caused the closure of Redbridge station in June 1859, local opposition having saved it. A mile further up the line towards Southampton the inhabitants of Millbrook were pressing for a station, resulting in the Directors on 12th September, 1861 deciding that work should without delay commence on a small wooden structure. In fact work proceeded rapidly, the completed station opening on 1st November. Later a short siding was provided from a trailing connection on the up side of the station.

In contrast to the difficulties at the Southampton end of the line, Dorchester was host to the prestigious Bath & West show at the end of May 1860. The LSWR provided accommodation for the movement of exhibits along with associated equipment and the provision of additional trains as did the GWR, the latter running almost an hourly service between Weymouth and Dorchester during the event.

An unfortunate accident at Wareham in May 1860 highlighted the dangers of footplate work in an age before any form of mechanical lubricator was fitted to engines. Shortly after a down train hauled by 2-2-2 *Apollo* left the station, driver

Millbrook station looking towards Southampton photographed around 1880, clearly showing the level crossing and the original signal box. Standing to the left by the signal box is Mr H. Anderson, appointed station master at Millbrook in 1852 at the age of seventeen. Retiring from Fleet station in 1911 he was still enjoying his retirement in 1936 aged 84. *Southern Railway Magazine*

Eaton became concerned about the lubrication of one of the bearings of the driving axle and climbed along the engine framing to attend to the matter. It appears that Eaton struck the sidewall of Worgret bridge and was knocked to the ground and fatally injured. The fireman stopped the train and with the guard recovered the body then reversed the train back to Wareham station. Both the *Weymouth, Portland & Dorchester Telegram* and the *Dorset County Chronicle* gave full accounts of the incident, the latter not sparing the gory details, also remarking on the fact that from the time the train had first called at the station until it again departed after depositing the body was just over 20 minutes!

Accidents were not restricted to railway staff; a report in the *Poole and South Western Herald* during November 1865 details the death of one of two horses at Wareham station about to haul wagons on the up line to Sandford Pottery siding being struck by a down train entering the station. It is clear from the report that the use of horses to haul wagons along the main line, albeit only a short distance, was permissible at that date.

During the summer of 1860 a substantial pottery had been completed at Sandford served by a private siding. Late in 1861 the LSWR proposed a short branch from Wareham to Creech Heath where many of the ball clay pits were situated. These proposals came in for strong opposition from the inhabitants of Wareham who feared that their ancient town walls would be breached by the route of the line. Surprisingly, the landowners of the heath were also against any intrusion into their style of working the clay, which they considered adequate, resulting in the Bill being withdrawn from Parliament in early 1862.

Later the same year the Isle of Purbeck Railway Company was formed at Wareham. Swanage by then had started to develop as a holiday result, paddle steamers were calling at the pier from both Weymouth and Bournemouth and the town was ripe for expansion. The scheme, with the support of the LSWR, was similar to the previous scheme of 1847, the Bill receiving the Royal Assent in July 1863. Clauses had been inserted to protect the town walls by constructing a separate station south of the town and facilities for goods traffic

An early view of Sandford Pottery near Wareham, showing a wagon on the private siding which served the site from its opening. *Author's Collection*

at wharves on the River Frome. However, further disagreements concerning the town walls and lack of financial support meant that the powers eventually lapsed in 1868.

The Board of Trade again pressed the company into action on the subject of doubling the line, the remainder of the line to Dorchester not being completed until August 1863. The section between Wimborne and Wool was inspected on 1st May, on this section the rails being double-ended weighing 75 lb. per foot and 22 ft long. Several points were raised by the Inspector that needed attention: the signal box at the junction with the Somerset & Dorset at Wimborne required both a clock and fireplace, whilst the signal at Lytchett level crossing required raising. The distant signals at both Wareham and Wool which had both been worked from points at the ends of the loops should now be controlled from the platforms and the facing points that formed the loops should be removed. Whilst this work was carried out many of the original small wooden bridges were either abolished and replaced by embankments or rebuilt as brick arches, and the station platforms, which had proved much too short for efficient working, were extended to the still modest length of 250 feet.

Significant developments were also taking place at the Weymouth end of the line where the lack of direct railway communication with the quay was a major operating problem and did little to enhance the quality of the shipping service. Ironically, the original plans for the Wilts, Somerset & Weymouth Railway had incorporated a branch or tramway to Weymouth Quay, as had the Southampton & Dorchester company's Moreton-Weymouth scheme of 1846. The dire financial circumstances of the former and the withdrawal of the latter removed all chances of its inclusion in immediate plans. The matter was also raised locally shortly before the opening of the line to Weymouth in January 1857.

However, there the matter rested until March 1861 when Mr J.A. Devenish, a Director of the Steam Packet company, devised a scheme for a harbour tramway. During the same period there were various proposals for a branch railway to the Isle of Portland from where the export of stone was of major importance. In 1861 two schemes were put forward for branch lines to Portland, the second of which included a tramway to Weymouth Harbour. Devenish and his supporters aligned themselves to the latter scheme, which resulted in the Weymouth & Portland Railway Bill receiving the Royal Assent on 30th June, 1862. At this point the LSWR became involved as it had been agreed with the Board of Trade, and included in the Bill, that both the tramway and Portland branch would be constructed to mixed gauge and on completion would be managed, maintained and worked by a joint committee of the GWR and LSWR, to which companies they would be leased in perpetuity at a fixed rent of £5,000.

Construction of both lines commenced in late 1862 and was completed by May 1864. Unfortunately, the Board of Trade inspection revealed deficiencies in the two viaducts on the Portland branch and with the signalling arrangements at the junction just outside Weymouth station. Added to these minor difficulties it would appear that the GWR and LSWR had not devised a satisfactory method of working trains between the junction and the station. Two suggestions made by the Inspector were to change over the positions of the goods yard and passenger stations, or alternatively construct separate accommodation for Portland trains to the west of the goods yard, but he admitted that either scheme would be inconvenient and expensive.

By October 1864 the affair was becoming a farce, the reason for the delay being a disagreement over accommodation for Portland trains at Weymouth station, with a dispute over the interpretation of the Act to which both the GWR and LSWR had agreed. The Weymouth & Portland company considered it was not obliged to provide a separate station at Weymouth and considered the existing station suitable for the accommodation of Portland traffic.

Bordering on overtones of the 1855 situation between Weymouth and Dorchester, the Weymouth & Portland company desperately approached the Board of Trade with the novel suggestion to open the line if the GWR would give an undertaking to operate the broad gauge only! This was refused on the grounds that, as the line was mixed gauge, sanction could only be given for the working of the entire line. The dispute eventually went to arbitration, which ruled in favour of the Weymouth & Portland company; however, the three companies continued to argue over the exact details of the arrangements. Finally the Portland branch opened to goods traffic on 9th October, 1865 with passenger traffic commencing on the 16th of the same month. The Harbour Tramway, although not involved in the dispute and only a goods line, was not subject to Board of Trade inspection, but by reason of it being an integral part of the Weymouth & Portland Railway could not open to traffic until the disputes had been resolved. The tramway was unique, not exactly a branch line, or just a siding and apart from a few chains at the station end it ran entirely over Corporation property. With many operating peculiarities it had its own rule book, and its uniqueness has given it a special place in railway history. However, as with the Portland branch, its operation and development are outside the remit of this publication, except for their bearing on main line events and dealt with in context.

The day to day activities of the railway are illustrated by two short items in the *Southern Times* during 1866. In the Poole column for 21st April a request was made to the Electric and International Telegraph Company requesting that their office be moved from Hamworthy railway station into the town of Poole, a move the company declined. In the issue for 30th June the Dorchester column stated that the LSWR had issued notice of its intention of resuming the 'bathing train' forthwith. Persons therefore desirous of having a sea bath would be accommodated with return tickets to Weymouth for single fares, leaving Dorchester at 7.15 am and returning by the train at 8.50 am. Although no comment was made by the paper, allowing for travelling from Dorchester and walking to and from the sands, then observing the propriety of the day, the time allowed to indulge in anything other than a quick dip was limited!

The annual camp at Lulworth of the Dorset Volunteers, the equivalent of today's Territorial Army, had become established by 1866; in the July of that year the *Southern Times* fully describing the event gave an insight to the transport arrangements. Whilst local detachments such as Wareham simply marched to camp, others arrived by train at Wool station where much of their equipment had arrived earlier. A number of others travelled by normal service trains, for example, those from Poole travelled as far as Poole Junction (Hamworthy Junction) by the 11.30 am down train, then transferred to a special train from Templecombe that carried contingents from Gillingham, Stalbridge, Sturminster Newton, Blandford and Wimborne.

The Sherborne detachment marched to Yetminster where they boarded a GWR train that then picked up Bridport troops at Maiden Newton, and others at Dorchester. Following arrival at Weymouth they marched to the pier to embark with the Weymouth detachment aboard the paddle steamer *Premier* to land at Lulworth Cove. The paddle steamer *Mayflower* brought the 3rd Hants (Lymington) Corps complete with band and around 100 visitors from Lymington for a day visit. Indeed, reports suggest the event was something of a jamboree rather than serious training, with many visitors and sightseers arriving by paddle steamer at Lulworth Cove or train at Wool station.

However, in November the same paper gives a very clear account of improvements to the previous very basic arrangements at Dorchester Junction with the provision of an interlocked signal box. The edition for 3rd November states:

A very great and important improvement has been made at the junction near Dorchester, where the Great Western and South Western systems converge to run by the mixed gauge down to Weymouth. Formerly all the points and signals were worked on the old system, but now a kind of observatory has been erected at the fork of the junction, from which a clear view can be obtained up and down the lines, and here, by a series of bars and pulleys, are concentrated the 'locking and signaling gear', so that by a system of leverage the whole apparatus for working the junction is brought under the control of one man, thus not only saving labour, but also securing greater safety by the avoidance of any mistake between two signalman. The correctness of the system is further ensured by an arrangement connected with the levers which work the points, whereby the signals cannot be made to say 'all right' until the points themselves are

The opening of the Portland branch in October 1865, although a joint operation with the GWR marked a further extension to the Southampton & Dorchester line, especially with the stone traffic available for the London market. Photographed at Portland station in the late 1860s is 2-4-0 well-tank No. 143 *Nelson*. *Author's Collection*

Wool station and staff photographed on 1st March, 1914, at which stage the station was in its original condition without a canopy or footbridge. At the end of the platform looking towards Dorchester are the crossing gates, signal box and tall down starting signal with repeater arm *Author's Collection*

properly adjusted for the passage of the coming train. The whole arrangements appear excellent, and it is surprising at what a distance up and down the line the signals and points can be worked from the observatory.

Further developments took place in the Weymouth area during 1871 when a station was opened at Upwey on 21st June, situated by an underbridge on the north side of a lane (now known as Old Station Road) leading to Bincombe. At first the small wooden structure was only served by the GWR, with four trains stopping each way daily and three on Sundays. It was not until February 1872 that LSWR trains commenced to use the station when four trains each way and two on Sundays stopped 'by signal' (request).

In preparation for the Bath & West show which was held at Dorchester in June 1872 the *Southern Times* reported in the previous February of 'extensive alterations and additions being made to the sidings, platforms and works at the LSWR station'.

A report of an unfortunate fatal accident at the station during May gave a brief account of the working of the down train which arrived at 9.50 pm. The shunter explained that whilst standing in the lower platform [*sic*] the engine was exchanged for another to take the train on to Weymouth, after which the train backed out onto the down main line. There were also references to the pointman, inferring that points were still ground operated.

Originally ballast for track maintenance was obtained locally from pits at Totton, Ringwood, Sandford and Woodsford. Extension of these sites was applied for in the 1873 South-Western Railway (General) Act 1873 which made references to various locations on the Southampton & Dorchester line: Ringwood, a site near Bournemouth station on the Ringwood, Christchurch, and Bournemouth Railway, Keysworth ballast pit near Wareham, and land lying on each side of the company's Woodsford Ballast pit near Moreton, and of their siding leading from that pit, which was extended at that time. By October 1884 the leases were running out on both the Sandford and Woodsford sites, the company Engineer recommending that negotiations be entered into with Miss Drax and Lord Illchester, the owners of the respective pits, for an extension of time for which the company had the right to extract ballast. The Engineer reported back in July 1885 that he had agreed with Lord Illchester to take ballast from his land for a further three years at the same rent of £67 11s. 3d. per annum on similar conditions to the previous agreement. However, the use of locally produced ballast fell into disuse when a high-grade material could be obtained from Meldon Quarry in Devon by the turn of the century.

Improvements were required at Wimborne, no doubt in view of the extra traffic created with the opening of the Poole & Bournemouth Railway. In November 1873 approval was given to the erection of a new signal box at the station and the following June it was recommended that the down platform be lengthened and that gentlemen's waiting rooms should be placed on both down and up platforms.

Having lost the battle of the gauges, from the 1860s the GWR slowly began to convert its lines to standard gauge. The entire Wilts, Somerset & Weymouth was converted during June 1874. At 11 pm on Thursday 18th June the last broad gauge train departed from Weymouth, and following a major engineering task

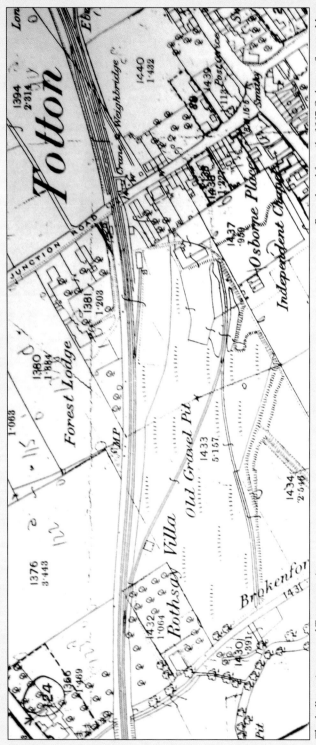

Reproduced from the 1867 Ordnance Survey Map

The ballast pits west of Totton station.

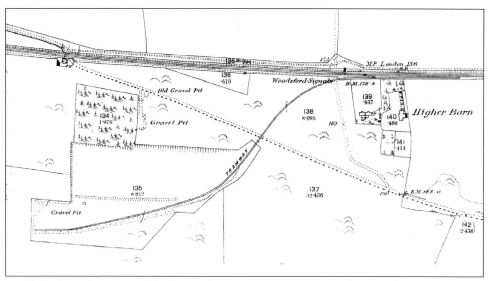

The ballast siding at Woodsford, west of Moreton. Crossing No. 38 is shown on the main line to the right of the drawing, the dotted line running from the crossing across the drawing is the present road between West Stafford and Crossways. At the time of writing the ballast pit is part of Warmwell Quarry.   *Reproduced from the 1889 Ordnance Survey Map*

The site of the original Upwey station 1871-1886 looking towards Weymouth. The up side station buildings stood on the right with the down platform on the left in front of the photographer.   *Author*

the entire Weymouth line reopened for traffic on Monday 22nd. However, as the Dorchester-Weymouth section was mixed gauge the LSWR maintained its service and the GWR sent standard gauge rolling stock via Reading and Basingstoke then over the LSWR to Weymouth to enable the service to recommence on the Monday. The broad gauge rails between Dorchester and Weymouth and along the Portland branch and the Weymouth Harbour Tramway were removed shortly afterwards.

The joint working of the Dorchester-Weymouth section was administered by a joint committee. Apart from the original disagreements over the working of the Portland branch, matters appeared to run smoothly naturally, both companies being keen to obtain the best financial result out of any agreement. To list all various toll arrangements over the years would be uninteresting and unbalance this work. However, the arrangements during the 1870s give a flavour of the general arrangements and are worth setting out following a meeting at Paddington on 19th February, 1879.

It was agreed to recommend the following arrangement for the settlement of the accounts from 1st January 1870 to December 31st 1878 continuing thereafter subject to six months notice from either Company.

A. The tolls to be paid up to the 31st December 1878 on the principle of Captain Galton's award and in the mode as agreed upon under that award.

B. The payment for interest on the cost incurred in providing additional rails etc. which under the award was in respect of the line between Weymouth and Dorchester £1,028 per annum, to be paid at that rate from 1st January 1870 up to 30th June 1874 when the broad gauge rail was taken up.

C. No payment to be made by the South Western to the Great Western Company after 30th June 1874.

D. The payment for the cost of providing additional rails etc. which under the award was to be in respect of the 7½ miles east of Dorchester £451 3s. 0d. per annum to be paid from 1st January 1870 up to 30th June 1874.

E. No payments to be made by the Great Western Company to the South Western Company after 30th June 1874.

The arrangements under C and E to be in perpetuity.

F. The payment under the award for the maintenance and working of the junction at Dorchester and the payment for rent of stations at Weymouth and Upwey and for maintenance taxes, Working expenses inclusive of staff employed thereat and in respect of the London South Western user of the station and also inclusive of the payment in respect of the Portland line traffic to be £2,100 per annum.

G. The claim of the Great Western Company for interest on the payments to be made in respect of the Weymouth and Dorchester line under Captain Galton's award or otherwise on the settlement of those accounts up to the 31st December 1878 to be withdrawn.

Most interestingly, clause 'D' was mentioned, although it would appear that the third rail was removed when the section to Dorchester was doubled, and no records appear to survive of a broad gauge train ever using the track, one of the remaining mysteries of the Southampton & Dorchester Railway!

Chapter Seven

The Dorset Central, Somerset & Dorset and Poole & Bournemouth Railways

With the main line to Dorchester established it was only a matter of time before further developments took place. In 1856 there occurred an event that seemed insignificant at the time but which was destined to exert great influence not only upon the existing Southampton & Dorchester line, but upon the future railways of the Poole and Bournemouth area generally. This was the passing of an Act of Parliament for a line, 10¼ miles in length, from a point near Wimborne station to the market town of Blandford under the rather magnificent title of the Dorset Central Railway with a capital of £100,000. It was to be a standard gauge single line following the Stour valley, not dissimilar to the branch envisaged in the original Southampton & Dorchester plan of 1846.

In fact, the Stour valley had long held appeal for railway promoters, partly because the broad gauge of the GWR created difficulties for North-South freight consignments which would be overcome by a standard gauge link between the Midland Railway and LSWR, but also because it was thought desirable at the time to provide a coast-to-coast route between the Bristol and the English Channels. In the days of sail the passage around Land's End was often hazardous - and at best uncertain - making a land route seem very attractive! Ideed, there had been proposals for such a route from the earliest days, it being raised again in 1844 with a scheme for the British and Bristol Channels Junction Railway taking a route from Poole to Bridgwater. Although the scheme was never proceeded with, it had an affinity to the original Somerset & Dorset line, as did an 1852 scheme for a 'South Midland Union Railway'. This would not only have fulfilled the first of these purposes, but also tapped the traffic of the developing Somerset coalfield by providing a line joining the existing Midland Railway at Mangotsfield and running thence via Keynsham, Radstock, Blandford and the Stour Valley to Poole Harbour. It would, no doubt, also feature a connection with the LSWR, but in the years immediately following the Railway Mania the capital requirement of £1 million discouraged investors and the scheme was dropped.

The contract for the construction of the Dorset Central was awarded to Waring Bros of London, the first sod being cut on 13th November, 1856 at Blandford St Mary by Lady Smith of the Down House. The ceremony was reported to have cost £224 13s. 2d. - £71 of which went on wine representing a very significant sum in those days - and an ornamental wheelbarrow and spade (both now housed in the National Railway Museum, York) were made especially for the occasion. Indeed, the celebrations seem somewhat over scale for a 10 mile branch line, but then it was obvious from the start that the company had ambitions reaching well beyond the Stour Valley, and that, once again, the lure of a through coast-to-coast route was proving strong. A northward drive and connections to other railways were greatly encouraged by the fact that the Dorset Central Chairman, H. Danby Seymour, was also Chairman of the Salisbury & Yeovil Railway (then under construction) and a

Director of the Somerset Central Railway which - by 1856 - had succeeded in opening a broad gauge line between Highbridge (where it connected with the Bristol and Exeter) and Glastonbury, but had further extensions - including one from Glastonbury to Cole (near Bruton, where another connection was to be made with the broad gauge) - already authorized. Furthermore, one of the Directors was Ivor Bertie Guest of Canford Manor, Wimborne, who held shares in the LSWR and whose father, the Welsh ironmaster Sir John Guest, had been involved with the earlier South Midland Union scheme and clearly had an interest in establishing a North-South route.

The full extent of the enterprise became apparent when, on 10th August, 1857, the Dorset Central obtained another Act of Parliament for an extension up the valley from Blandford to a spot near Bruton, the capital of the company being increased by £300,000 for this 24 mile line. In the meantime the Somerset Central had not only decided to end its association with the Bristol & Exeter Railway, building the Cole extension to standard gauge, but had opened another extension from Highbridge to the Bristol Channel at Burnham-on-Sea, thus bringing the 'coast-to-coast' dream one step closer to reality. However, the B&E lease did not expire until the end of August 1861 so mixed gauge track had to be laid on the Cole extension initially, although the junction with the Wilts, Somerset & Weymouth line near Bruton that would have been useful to broad gauge trains was never completed.

Construction of the Dorset Central proceeded rapidly; the line left the Southampton & Dorchester line at Wimborne Junction, 23 chains south of Wimborne station, and ran to a temporary terminus at Blandford St Mary - a mile short of the town proper - with intermediate stations at Bailey Gate and Spetisbury. A majority of the work was completed by the late summer of 1859. Only one section gave trouble - a stretch near Merley where the alluvial deposits, soft clay and gravel of the valley became waterlogged by heavy rain, delaying completion until September 1860. The *Southern Times* then reported an experimental trip was made by an engine with first and second class carriages and several trucks from Wimborne cutting at Oakley to Blandford St Mary. The same paper on 13th October stated,

> A little delay has been occasioned in the opening of the first section of this railway from Wimborne to Blandford, in consequence of the Government Inspector requiring a large sized turntable to be laid down at the Wimborne end of the line.

The line was officially opened on Wednesday 1st November, 1860 when a special train, double-headed by two LSWR tank engines, left Poole (Hamworthy) terminus at 12 noon for Blandford. At Wimborne it awaited the arrival of a train from Waterloo to allow LSWR officials to join the party before setting off again at 12.55 pm. The leading engine was recorded as being the 2-4-0 well tank *Minerva,* but nothing is known of the other locomotive.

Adverts appearing in the local Press of the time gave the unmistakeable impression that the new line was owned and operated by the LSWR, and to a certain extent this was true as they staffed and managed the line on behalf of the Dorset Central. They also provided motive power and rolling stock under a five year agreement by which they received 50 per cent of the annual gross receipts,

SOUTH-WESTERN RAILWAY.
*OPENING OF THE WIMBORNE AND
BLANDFORD LINE.*
THE BLANDFORD LINE will be OPEN for
PASSENGER and GOODS' TRAFFIC on
THURSDAY, 1st NOVEMBER.
For Trains, see the Time Tables published at all
Stations.

Notice published in the *Southern Times* in November 1860 advertising the opening of the Dorset Central Railway line between Wimborne and Blandford, clearly giving the impression that it was a South Western Railway line whereas in truth the latter only operated it on behalf of the Dorset Central.

or 60 per cent whilst revenue remained at less than £600 per mile, with the safeguard that payment to the LSWR would never be less £360 per mile! The initial service consisted of five trains each way on weekdays and two on Sundays, all of which had to be worked by tank engines as there were no turning facilities at the Blandford terminus.

Amalgamation between the Dorset Central and Somerset Central to form the famous - if poverty-stricken - Somerset & Dorset Railway took place on 1st September, 1862. The two concerns had made physical connection with each other at Cole in February that year - although the line between Blandford and Templecombe was still incomplete and the only access to this isolated section of Dorset Central property was over the connecting spur from the Salisbury and Yeovil line at Templecombe! The missing section was eventually opened on 31st August, 1863, and a fortnight later - on 14th September - the Somerset & Dorset took over the working of the whole line and commenced through services between Burnham-on-Sea and Poole (Hamworthy). The LSWR no longer worked traffic to Blandford, but a new agreement allowed the use of LSWR engines on through trains between Wimborne and Poole (Hamworthy) whilst Somerset & Dorset guards remained in charge of the trains, the LSWR receiving appropriate payment for the five miles involved in this 'joint' operation.

Although, on the face of it, the whole thing had started as nothing more momentous than a branch line to Blandford, the subsequent development of this line was to have far-reaching affects upon the railways of the South West, in general, and those of Poole and Bournemouth in particular. Indeed, it would not be overstating the case to say that the growth of Bournemouth as a resort for the masses (a development that was anathema to the original planners of the town) was largely the result of Somerset & Dorset enterprise - especially after the opening of the Bath Extension in 1874 gave direct access to the area from the industrial North and Midlands. Furthermore, it was chiefly because of the Somerset & Dorset that Poole not only survived as a seaport but subsequently expanded as such, for the LSWR was wedded to Southampton and the GWR to Weymouth, so neither of the major companies had any interest in fostering maritime activities in the district.

From this point forward the story of the Poole/Bournemouth area becomes complex, but before becoming more deeply involved with it we should pause to examine an interesting traffic development that resulted from the amalgamation of the Somerset Central and Dorset Central railways. As already mentioned, a coast-to-coast line of railway had long been considered an economic necessity. But by the time it was provided sail was being ousted by steam on the high seas and this, with improved methods of navigation, was encouraging vessels to continue to ply between South Wales and the south coast of England via Land's End and rail traffic proved disappointing. There was, however, a brave attempt to establish a through service between South Wales and France which involved steam ship from Cardiff to Burnham-on-Sea and train from Burnham to Poole (Hamworthy) - with, of course, a reversal at Wimborne. Poole (Hamworthy) station, situated as it was near to the quay wall, was ideally suited as an embarkation point for the Continent, and a six hour crossing to Cherbourg compared favourably with the time occupied in sea crossings by other routes of the period. There were, of course, connecting rail services to Paris and other Continental connections.

The service had its origins in an agreement of 1864 between the Somerset & Dorset and the Chemin de Fer de l'Ouest of France which operated the railway between Paris and Cherbourg. In the spring of the following year the Somerset & Dorset examined the paddle steamer *Albion* to assess her suitability. She was a single-decked vessel, 165 feet in length and weighing 306 tons gross, built in 1860 for the Glasgow and Stranraer Steam Packet Company. After that company was taken over by Messrs M. Langlands & Son, she was taken out of service and passed into the hands of a shipbroker, Captain P.L. Henderson of Liverpool, in April 1865. The original intention had been to purchase a vessel, but for reasons now unknown (possibly lack of funds), *Albion* was chartered, entering service for the railway company in May 1865.

Although the shipping service and its connections to various places in South Wales and along the Midland Railway main line towards Birmingham was widely advertised little is known about the activities of the ship itself. Certainly the route was far from direct for places in the Midlands, as the Bath Extension lay in the future and the journey involved running down the B&E from Bristol to Highbridge before setting out across the Somerset Levels. Sailings left Poole (Hamworthy) Quay on Monday and Thursday nights at 11.45 pm having connected with the 8.50 pm train from Burnham-on-Sea. Cherbourg was reached shortly after 7 am and first class passengers were whisked off to arrive in Paris at 5 pm. Second and third class passengers were not so lucky, being obliged to use slower train services across France and not arriving in the capital until 10.20 pm.

As two very elderly paddle steamers were employed on the Bristol Channel connection with Wales there was nothing either 'Swift' or 'Delightful' about a trip from Cardiff to Paris by this route! However, the company endeavoured to stimulate interest by offering two-day excursion options (out Monday, back Wednesday), but the service was not a commercial success and was discontinued in February 1867. The same month, the vessel's owner, Captain Henderson, sold her to a firm in Hayle, Cornwall, from where she operated a service to Bristol for about a year before returning into the possession of Langlands.

Following the departure of *Albion* from Poole a nominally independent body under the title of the Poole and Cherbourg Steam Packet Company was formed to restore the service, acquiring the paddle steamer *Spicy* of 250 gross tons for the purpose, but this too failed in 1868. It must have seemed to many that Poole simply was not destined to succeed as a cross-Channel port!

In the May of 1868 a weekly excursion was offered from Poole to Burnham-on-Sea at the cost of 1s. 6d. The *Poole Pilot* in reporting the event was a little sceptical about the attractions of Burnham but remarked: 'If a long ride for a little money is desired it is here available'.

Much has been published elsewhere concerning the Somerset & Dorset and it is not proposed to repeat it in this work as the Somerset & Dorset will surface again and again as our story unfolds - such was its effect on the history of the main line. Suffice it to say for now that any agreements into which the LSWR had entered with the Somerset & Dorset came at a high price as various competitive schemes were fended off. For example, on 3rd July, 1860 when applying for its Extension of Time Act to complete the Cole extension, the Dorset Central also deposited a Bill for its own line between Wimborne and Poole and - in view of the Borough's dissatisfaction with their existing station at Hamworthy - they were able to support it with a petition signed by 1,400 local residents. Naturally the LSWR fiercely opposed this line, and there followed a round of urgent talks between the two companies during which the Dorset Central made the rather impractical suggestion of extending the existing branch from the Hamworthy terminus to a more central station in Poole by means of a bridge spanning the harbour. In the end it was rather vaguely agreed that, in return for the Dorset Central withdrawing its proposal, the LSWR would provide better accommodation for Poole traffic, but a report by Gaselee (a member of the Traffic Committee) suggested carrying out only minor improvements to the existing station. In fact very little was done and the only positive result was the introduction in May 1860 of through coaches to Hamworthy from Waterloo avoiding a change of train at Poole Junction (Hamworthy Junction), followed by the doubling of the entire Hamworthy branch during 1864.

The Dorset Central's plan had envisaged a line from Wimborne, via Broadstone and a well-sited station in Poole, to a terminus situated near the present Branksome station, and there was much displeasure locally when it was dropped in favour of the rather weak agreement already described. Its failure brought forth a rash of schemes over the next three years, all of which managed to solicit a fair level of public support. In the Parliamentary session of 1860/61 several alternatives were on offer, including the Wimborne & Poole Railway - a nominally independent concern allied to the Dorset Central and more or less repeating the proposal previously made by that company; the Poole Railway - a purely local creation similar in many respects to the Wimborne & Poole but with the addition of a branch to serve Poole Quay; and a much grander Salisbury, Poole & Dorset Junction Railway. As the latter promised to do more to open up the district, it proved to be the most popular. It consisted of a line connecting with the LSWR's Bishopstoke - Salisbury line at Alderbury to reach

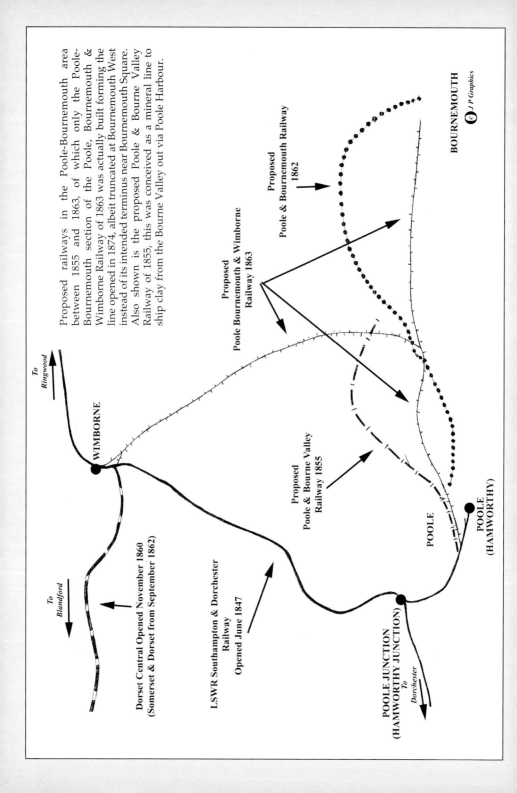

Proposed railways in the Poole-Bournemouth area between 1855 and 1863, of which only the Poole-Bournemouth section of the Poole, Bournemouth & Wimborne Railway of 1863 was actually built forming the line opened in 1874, albeit truncated at Bournemouth West instead of its intended terminus near Bournemouth Square. Also shown is the proposed Poole & Bourne Valley Railway of 1855, this was conceived as a mineral line to ship clay from the Bourne Valley out via Poole Harbour.

To Ringwood

WIMBORNE

To Blandford

Dorset Central Opened November 1860 (Somerset & Dorset from September 1862)

LSWR Southampton & Dorchester Railway Opened June 1847

Proposed Poole & Bourne Valley Railway 1855

Proposed Poole Bournemouth & Wimborne Railway 1863

Proposed Poole & Bournemouth Railway 1862

BOURNEMOUTH

POOLE

POOLE (HAMWORTHY)

POOLE JUNCTION (HAMWORTHY JUNCTION)

To Dorchester

© *J P Graphics*

West Moors by way of Fordingbridge. At West Moors a spur would connect with the Southampton & Dorchester line and the southward route would divide into two – one arm turning south-easterly to join the Ringwood and Christchurch line (then under construction) and the other heading due south into the heart of Poole. Despite the popularity of this scheme it was soon in financial difficulties that resulted in all the lines south of West Moors being dropped. When the company eventually received the Royal Assent on 16th July, 1861 its reduced ambitions were recognised by a change of name to the Salisbury & Dorset Junction Railway with powers for only the Alderbury-West Moors section.

Construction of the 18½ mile line commenced in February 1864 and, following difficulties with contractors and later the Board of Trade over poor construction, eventually opened on 20th December, 1866 with a service of four trains each way daily between Salisbury and Wimborne. The station at the line's junction with the Southampton & Dorchester at West Moors, which was provided as a begrudging afterthought by the LSWR, was not opened until 1st August, 1867.

The opening of the Salisbury & Dorset line offered a second route for LSWR passengers to Dorset, both the new line and the route via Southampton and Ringwood offering a service between Waterloo and Weymouth that varied from between six hours to just over four hours, although a few journeys via Salisbury with a change of train could offer a quicker service. In December 1877 passengers departing from Waterloo at 9.45 am arrived in Weymouth at 4.12 pm via Southampton and Ringwood, although it was possible to depart Waterloo an hour later changing at Salisbury and still change onto the earlier departure at Wimborne for a 4.12 pm arrival in Weymouth. During 1880 two journeys via Salisbury could be achieved in four hours 20 minutes and four hours 32 minutes respectively.

West Moors station looking east with a train departing towards Ringwood. Although at the time of the photograph West Moors was a small rural community substantial goods, agricultural and horticultural traffic was carried from the surrounding countryside. The station building itself, which contained the station master's house, had originally been a single storey structure.

The citizens of Poole continued to complain about their railway facilities, the upshot being the emergence in 1862 of the curious Poole & Bournemouth Railway - an isolated line with no connections to any of the existing rail system. It is perhaps not surprising that this failed to make progress!

The following year saw the publication of two more schemes that never reached the Parliamentary arena. One of these, and possibly the most satisfactory to date, was the Poole, Bournemouth & Wimborne Railway, which envisaged making junctions with both the Southampton & Dorchester and Dorset Central lines at Wimborne and, after running southwards for a short distance splitting into two. One arm went to a terminus in Bournemouth and the other formed a loop line through Poole to rejoin the Southampton & Dorchester at Poole Junction (Hamworthy Junction). Although this gave Poole what it had always wanted - a through station on a main line - it failed to meet the requirements of Poole Council and was withdrawn at the planning stage.

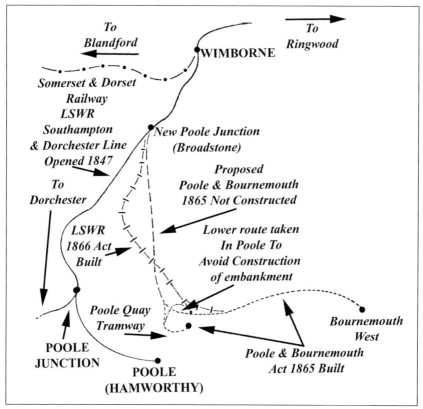

The indecisive planning of the railway at Poole still has repercussions to the present day with the selected route and the resultant level crossings. These would have been avoided had the more northerly route north of the town and the present Poole Park been chosen.

The other scheme was a re-working of the earlier Dorset Central scheme and followed much the same route as the projected Wimborne & Poole Railway, for the Dorset Central was far from satisfied with the outcome of the 1860 agreement and now considered the LSWR to be in breach of it! By this time an air of desperation was abroad, Poole itself was expanding at a rate, which deemed better facilities than the cramped terminus on Hamworthy Quay. The port was in danger of losing business to Southampton and even Weymouth, whilst neighbouring Bournemouth was growing apace without any rail connection whatsoever. However, not everybody in Bournemouth was anxious to encourage railways, some of the more genteel residents fearing that they could lower the tone of the resort by bringing in hordes of excursionists. This fear may have been partly justified, but such reactionary attitudes had to give way as the town continued to expand. It became clear that eventually Bournemouth would have to be placed on the main railway map. Furthermore, by 1864 the Dorset Central had joined forces with the Somerset Central to become the Somerset & Dorset Railway, and the additional traffic arising from the establishment of this through route strained the limited accommodation available at the Poole (Hamworthy) terminus to the utmost.

These factors combined to bring about the formation of an independent company - (another) Poole & Bournemouth Railway - which was to follow much the same route as the earlier Dorset Central proposals. The Act of Parliament authorizing construction received the Royal Assent on 26th May, 1865, although the section between Broadstone and Poole was withdrawn at the Committee stage and only that between Poole and Bournemouth was actually authorized. Capital was set at £90,000 in 9,000 shares of £10, with further borrowing powers of £30,000.

Although this company was nominally independent, it was no accident that it shared the same offices in Victoria Street, London as the Somerset & Dorset Railway, and also had some of the same officers. Charles Waring, a Director of the Somerset & Dorset, was Chairman of the Poole & Bournemouth, and the Secretary of the new company, Robert Read, had previously been Secretary to both the Somerset Central and the Dorset Central railways, and continued to hold the post with the amalgamated concern. Soon after the passing of the Act, Waring was elected as Liberal Member of Parliament for Poole, his success at the ballot box having been virtually assured by his enthusiastic support for the new railway scheme and his promises of further expansion in the future.

However, it soon became apparent that many of his statements in that direction had been solely made to secure his election, and once he had taken his seat he showed little inclination to carry out the work. At that time the contracting firm of Waring Bros, in which Charles was a partner, was heavily committed with railway construction elsewhere, including the Solway Junction Railway in Dumfriesshire, the Bristol Port & Pier Railway, several sections of the London Underground, and various projects abroad, and had little interest in adding further to its burden. Furthermore, the perceived involvement of the Somerset & Dorset brought the whole scheme under a cloud, as by the following year that company was in such a financial muddle that it could not possibly contribute towards any new works.

The LSWR had objected to the scheme from the outset on the grounds that the line as planned would not connect with the Ringwood, Christchurch & Bournemouth Railway, then under construction on the eastern side of the town, but would terminate on the western fringe of Bournemouth leaving passengers to make their own way between the two stations. This was indeed a weak point of the line, but to be fair to its promoters, the Bournemouth Commissioners had not been enthusiastic about a railway crossing the town, and there remained a vociferous minority who wanted to keep railways out all together. In fact, the LSWR now found itself in a somewhat odd position. Although far from keen about the Poole & Bournemouth line, it realised that Waring was a force to be reckoned with and that it lay within his power to break the LSWR's monopoly in the district. It was also worried by the threats of invaders, for the Somerset & Dorset was in receivership and could fall into the hands of any company willing to rescue them from disaster, and the Midland Railway had expressed an interest in the Salisbury & Dorset Junction line. These considerations resulted in the company reaching an agreement with Waring whereby they would seek authority to build the Wimborne-Poole section themselves and withdraw all objections to the Bournemouth section, which would remain Warning's responsibility.

At this stage the LSWR intended to take the line north of the centre of Poole town, but the Corporation objected to this route because it would cut through a recreation ground and involve a steep incline to reach the quay. Despite all the planning and discussion no work was started on either line, and when Waring returned to the Borough in 1868 to defend his Parliamentary seat he found that the electorate had turned against him and he was resoundingly defeated. The following year he wrote to the LSWR assuring them that he still intended to build his section of the line, and adding that their agreement of 1866 provided for his company to have the contract to construct the Wimborne-Poole section. Meanwhile the LSWR had decided to reduce the length of its line by moving the junction from Wimborne to a site later known as Broadstone, and the company replied that Waring would be given the contract for this revised route at a cost to be calculated by the company's own engineer, provided he would give a firm undertaking within 10 days to complete the Poole-Bournemouth section within three years. Waring's reply cannot have been satisfactory, for in August 1869 a local contractor, James Taylor of Poole, was awarded the contract for the Broadstone-Poole section. By February 1870 work on the formation and bridges was reported to be well in hand, about one-third of the earthworks being complete. The *Southern Times* reported that in Poole,

> The railway works to the north of the town are progressing favourably. The permanent rails have been laid from Mr Green's field to the archway at Tatnam, which is fast approaching completion.

In July that year local residents again protested about the formation of an embankment across the north side of the town, and in September the Press commented that all construction work on the line had apparently come to a halt. The LSWR apologised for the delay, adding that it still expected to have the line open for public traffic by the end of June 1872.

On 8th February, 1871 the Mayor of Poole led a deputation to London to meet the LSWR Board, the intention being to pressurise the company into adopting a route closer to the Quay and the main business area and to complete it as soon as possible. The formation was then complete from Broadstone to the point where any such deviation would have to commence, and it was therefore urgent to press their case before any more construction work was done. The LSWR pointed out that they were not prosecuting the work with any vigour because lack of progress on the Poole-Bournemouth line, the responsibility of Waring, rendered it useless. But their answer to the request for a deviation was evasive, and the townspeople were still trying to obtain a satisfactory settlement of this matter in April.

Running true to form, Waring continued to be inactive in his part of the scheme, and it now seemed clear that the only way forward was for the LSWR to purchase the Poole & Bournemouth outright. This was sanctioned under the company's General Powers Act dated 24th July, 1871. Meanwhile it had been decided to divert the line in accordance with the wishes of the Mayor and Corporation, and in mid-August 1872 the local Press was able to report that work on the line had restarted. By the end of September it was not only stated that the approach to Poole was in 'active progress', but also that work on the Bournemouth section had actually commenced and that the tramway to the quay was being put in hand.

Poole at the time of the line's construction, workmen are completing the brickwork to the footbridge crossing the line in the High Street. In the distance Poole station and the stationmaster's house appear complete and the original signal box is under construction. Today only the footbridge bearing the inscription 'Ransome & Rapier London 1872' survives amongst the ever changing Poole scene. *Poole Museum Service*

The single track of the original Poole & Bournemouth railway photographed from the High Street footbridge, a rare view of the original Poole signal box at the Towngate Street Crossing next to the station can be seen. Photographed before 1880 from which date it was replaced by a new structure to the west of the station. *G.A. Pryer Collection*

Almost as if to rub salt into the wound over the delay in completing the line, on Saturday 27th July, 1872 the workmen of the Somerset & Dorset Railway carriage works at Highbridge partaking of their annual treat accompanied by families and friends had to travel to Hamworthy, from where they boarded the paddle steamer *Royal Albert*. This took them to Bournemouth where they spent the day before returning via the same route.

Nobody can ever pretend that any of Poole's three stations have ever been well placed or indeed elegant in design. A letter published in the *Poole and South Western Herald* in July 1872 signed 'grumbler with a cause' had definite views on the original structure:

> I have visited the so intended Poole station of the South Western Company, and anything more discreditable to the company and town I can hardly imagine. I wish some public-spirited person would employ a photographer to take a view from the front door of the shed called a station. I will answer for it there are no houses in the lower part of the town presenting so miserable and tumbledown an appearance as those near the station. The photograph should be exhibited in the shop headed by 'a first impression of Poole, as collected at the station of the South Western Company'.
>
> Can anyone but an engineer imagine why the station had not been made to abut on the Parade? It would at all events have presented a larger line of straight approach.
>
> The Town Council would have done better service to have looked after this footbridge (which will only be used by boys) and a corner behind Mr Soul's house. I cannot conceive any thing simpler than a covered station would have been just behind Mr White's old shop.
>
> It is a fact, however, that railway engineers seldom scheme a station adapted to any given locality. They would be much wiser in their generation if they called in the aid of a good practical railway porter having knowledge of the locality.

On 4th November the section between Broadstone and Poole was sufficiently completed to allow an engineer's inspection train to pass over it, and hopes ran high that services to the new station would start without delay. But although the line had been sited according to the wishes of the local authority and contrary to the plans originally proposed by the LSWR, not everybody was happy about it. The situation of two level crossings in the heart of the town and immediately on the Bournemouth side of Poole station brought forth much adverse comment, one resident writing to the press:

> I don't know who the designer was nor who carried out the plans, but a more one eyed, one sided, crablike, crooked, patched-up concern I have never seen! The gates... have just fallen down from the clouds!

If this correspondent was displeased with the crossings, he also shared the opinion of many that the station itself - situated on a sharp curve - was dangerous. It would have been quite impossible to build bridges over the line, with the necessary approach ramps, without demolishing a large part of Poole town centre, so the level crossings were the price that the town had to pay for the centrally-situated station it had always wanted. However, the Corporation managed to salvage something from the inconvenience they had brought upon their own borough by making an agreement with the LSWR that all trains would call at Poole station. It was hoped that the guaranteed excellence of the service would go some way towards compensating people for the nuisance of the gates.

The single track section between New Poole Junction (later Broadstone) and Poole was inspected on behalf of the Board of Trade by Col Yolland during November 1872. However, all was not to the Inspector's satisfaction, he insisted on the following improvements before sanction for opening could be given. Additional fencing was required at an occupation crossing; at New Poole Junction (Broadstone) sheds to shelter passengers were required on the platforms of the down branch and the up main line. At Poole the level crossing gates at the High Street required to be locked in conjunction with both the up and down signals, and a safety siding with the points interlocked with the signals needed to be placed near the down line at the station. The LSWR also agreed to operate the single line between New Poole Junction (Broadstone) and the new Poole station

Broadstone Junction viewed from the north in July 1960 with the original Southampton & Dorchester line in the foreground, and the 1872 lines to Poole and Bournemouth West to the left. A changing point for many passengers until the completion of the Bournemouth Direct line and Holes Bay curve, the footbridge was a substantial structure.

H.C. Casserley

Broadstone station looking eastwards viewed from York Road around the turn of the century. A train pulls away in the Bournemouth direction, by this time a number of residences had become established such as the ivy clad villa in the foreground.   *Author's Collection*

'T9' class 4-4-0 No. 30307 heads a Salisbury-Bournemouth West train away from Broadstone during 1957 taking the Poole & Bournemouth line opened to Poole in 1872. To the left is the original Southampton & Dorchester line to Hamworthy Junction. The building development on the right has been relentless since Broadstone was established as a junction with the opening of the railway to Poole.   *C.L. Caddy/J.W.T. House Collection*

Broadstone Junction viewed from the Poole & Bournemouth Railway platforms; in the centre is the signal box and the convergence of the Somerset & Dorset and the Southampton & Dorchester lines.   *H.C. Casserley*

under the Train Staff system and the Absolute Block system. These requirements carried out, the line opened for traffic on 2nd December, 1872. To start with only Somerset & Dorset trains used the new station, departing at 8.10, 10.55 am, 1.30 and 5.30 pm, with arrivals at 9.58 am, 12.06, 2.06, 4.02, 6.06 and 9.23 pm. Trains of the LSWR continued to use the original terminus at Hamworthy, as it was thought that another Act was required before their trains could be diverted.

Although Poole at last had a central railway station, the facilities appear to be lacking at this early stage. A notice in the local press on 1st January, 1874 giving details of train alterations also stated,

On and after 1st January, 1874 the new Poole station will be open for general merchandise and parcel traffic between Poole and all South Western stations to the eastward of Wimborne, but inclusive of Wimborne. Mineral and special class goods will not be conveyed to or from the new Poole station. Unless general merchandise be specially addressed or consigned to Longfleet station, Poole, it will be conveyed to Hamworthy station.

These arrangements failed to please Poole Council who complained of the passenger service in general and in particular the fact that trains over the Salisbury & Dorset line terminated at Wimborne and not Poole. A complaint to the LSWR brought forth the reply that 'it is not intended to run trains from the new station to Salisbury via the Salisbury & Dorset Railway until the Poole and Bournemouth line has been completed'. On the subject of goods traffic it was stated: 'Until the Tramway to the town quay has been completed it is not considered to be necessary or advisable to convey mineral and special class goods traffic to and from the new station as a general rule'. There was also difficulty in sending goods towards Dorchester, again in reply 'the company did not contemplate taking goods from the new station westwards at present'.

In a letter of reply from the LSWR to Poole Corporation concerning complaints about the new railway arrangements, the LSWR stated:

Their intention always had been, so soon as the Poole & Bournemouth Railway was completed, to run all, or nearly all, of their trains in connection with the Somerset & Dorset and Salisbury & Dorset lines, via the new line. The Directors cannot, until the opening of the Bournemouth line, foresee what may be necessary, or advisable, to be done as to the connections with their main line trains, but in order to provide whatever accommodation

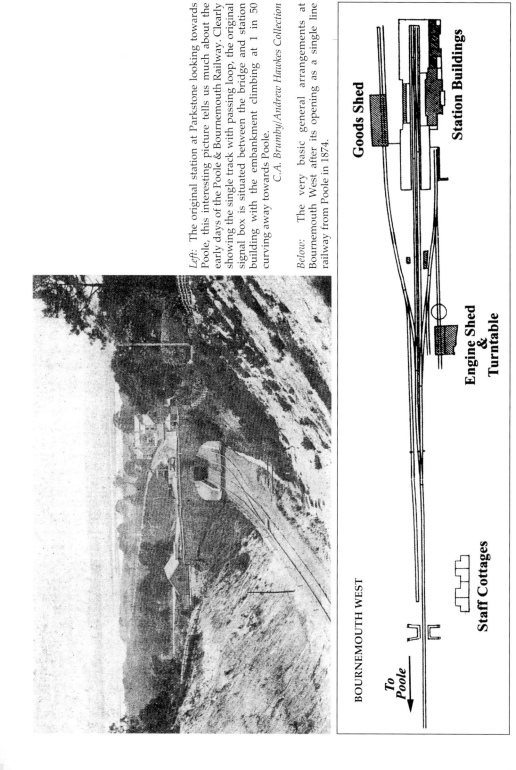

Left: The original station at Parkstone looking towards Poole, this interesting picture tells us much about the early days of the Poole & Bournemouth Railway. Clearly showing the single track with passing loop, the original signal box is situated between the bridge and station building with the embankment climbing at 1 in 50 curving away towards Poole.

C.A. Brumby/Andrew Hawkes Collection

Below: The very basic general arrangements at Bournemouth West after its opening as a single line railway from Poole in 1874.

Goods Shed

Station Buildings

Engine Shed & Turntable

Staff Cottages

BOURNEMOUTH WEST

To Poole

may at any time become necessary, they have at considerable expense, and without obligation, so to do, erected an interchange station at the new Poole Junction, to be enabled, when the proper time comes, to interchange traffic between their main, Southampton & Dorchester line and the new line, via Poole and Bournemouth should that be found advisable.

At the present time and until the Poole and Bournemouth line has been opened, it would be very inconvenient to the public, and unadvisable in every way to disturb the old established connection with the main line trains via the old Junction; but in the case of the fast train to London where a connection by the old Junction does not exist, a connection a connection has been maintained by the new line via Wimborne.

The Directors will be guided in the working of the new line by experience and circumstances, but they cannot undertake to make any material change in the existing train arrangements until the opening of the Poole and Bournemouth line.

Concluding with the complaints concerning the level crossing gates, the Secretary stated that 'they had been constructed in such a mode as to receive the approval of the Board of Trade'!

Meanwhile work went ahead with the extension to Bournemouth. In sharp contrast to the initial section from Broadstone to Poole which had only needed light earthworks, this section involved some heavy engineering including a causeway section across an inlet of Poole Harbour, high embankments and deep cuttings in the neighbourhood of Parkstone. From the end of the causeway there was a continuous climb, part of which was 1 in 60 through to Branksome. Six underbridges carried the line over public roads and four overbridges carried roads over the railway. An Act authorizing an extension of time to complete the works had been obtained in 1870, but by this time Waring had lost interest altogether and he sub-let the contract to Messrs Brassey & Ogilvie for £29,175 5s. Despite this action and the fact that this firm of contractors had a good reputation for getting on with their work, nothing was done for a while and a further period of time had to be authorized by Parliament on 22nd June, 1872. Thereafter better progress was made, and by April 1874 the Directors were sufficiently confident to arrange a Board of Trade inspection for 25th May, Colonel Hutchinson being appointed inspecting officer. This proved a little over ambitious, for on 8th May Mr Read, Managing Director of the Poole & Bournemouth company, sent a panic telegram to Hutchinson begging him to postpone inspection on the grounds that 'The signal works are not so forward as had been supposed'. However, in general work on the 4¼ mile line from Poole was complete apart from a few outbuildings at Bournemouth West, otherwise all the station buildings and bridges, which were constructed by T.C. Kerridge, were complete.

The Colonel eventually visited the line on 27th May, 1874. He found a single line laid with rail 74 lb. per linear yard secured to cross sleepers by fang bolts and dog spikes. Signal boxes were provided at Parkstone - where there was a crossing loop - and at the terminus at Bournemouth West, traffic being controlled by train staff and ticket under absolute block regulations. The signalling equipment was supplied by Messrs Saxby & Farmer, well-known contractors in that field - although they supplied very little to the lines associated with the LSWR who used mostly Stevens' signals and fittings. A turntable was provided at Bournemouth West, but at Wimborne (from where all trains started) the company was empowered to make use of that belonging to the Somerset & Dorset company. Hutchinson pronounced himself satisfied with the line in general, his only criticism being that Parkstone lacked station name boards and a clock in the signal box. With these minor defects rectified, 15 years after the proposals had first been made, the line opened without ceremony on Monday 15th June, 1874.

The *Bournemouth Visitors Directory* reported that:

> On Monday last the carriages of every train between Poole and Bournemouth were crowded and large numbers of persons assembled near the Poole, Parkstone and Bournemouth railway stations to witness the arrival and departure of the trains. The passenger traffic on the line was very much greater than any person could have supposed. All the trains were densely crowded, and some persons were unable to get seats in the carriages in the morning and evening trains. It was stated that upward of 1,100 persons went to Bournemouth from Poole. Through traffic was also very great.

Mr W.J. Mears, son of Mr Mears the traffic manager of the Southampton & Dorchester line, was appointed station agent at Bournemouth West, Mr White-Horn at Parkstone and Mr Joseph Potter at Poole. The opening train service consisted of a mixture of Somerset & Dorset and LSWR trains giving nine trains daily between Wimborne and Bournemouth and eight in the opposite direction. However, this was to change the following month.

The LSWR worked the line from the outset for a fixed annual rental of £2,500 payable in two half-yearly instalments of £1,125, and the Somerset & Dorset was granted running rights. However, the full potential of the new line was not obtainable until the opening of the Somerset & Dorset extension over the Mendips from Evercreech to Bath, thus giving a connection to the Midland Railway. Unfortunately this was delayed until 13th July. In anticipation of this event the Somerset & Dorset had in May opened a receiving office for parcels and light goods and a general enquiry office in Bournemouth at 2 Tower Buildings, Commercial Road.

UP.	Somerset and Dorset	South Western	Somerset and Dorset	South Western	Somerset and Dorset	South Western	Somerset and Dorset	Somerset and Dorset
	A.M.	A.M.	A.M.	P.M.	P.M.	P.M.	P.M.	P.M.
Bournemouth (West) ... dep.	7 55	9 10	10 30	1 0	1 15	5 15	5 30	6 50
Parkstone	8 4	9 19	10 39	1 8	1 24	5 24	5 39	6 59
Poole	8 10	9 25	10 45	1 15	1 30	5 30	5 45	7 5
Poole Junction	8 20	9 35	10 55	1 25	1 40	5 40	5 55	7 15
Wimborne ...arr.	8 26	9 42	11 1	1 32	1 46	5 46	6 1	7 21

DOWN.	Somerset and Dorset	Somerset and Dorset	South Western	Somerset and Dorset	South Western	Somerset and Dorset	Somerset and Dorset	South Western	Somerset and Dorset
	A.M.	A.M.	P.M.	P.M.	P.M.	P.M.	P.M.	P.M.	P.M.
Winborne ...dp.	9 49	11 36	12 15	1 54	3 43	54 6	9 7	9 9	9
Poole Junction,,	9 55	11 42	12 21	2 0	3 10 4	0 6	15 7	16 9	15
Poole	10 6	11 53	12 32	2 11	3 21 4	10 6	26 7	26 9	26
Parkstone	10 12	11 59	12 38	2 17	3 27 4	16 6	32 7	32 9	32
Bournemouth (West) ... arr	10 21	12 8	12 47	2 26	3 36 4	25 6	41 7	41 9	41

From inquiries we have made we learn that the fares between Wimborne and Bournemouth will be 2s. first class, 1s. 6d. second class, and 9½d. third class. The fares between Poole and Bournemouth will be 10 . first class, 8d. second class, and 4d. third class, and between Parkstone and Bournemouth the fares will be 6d. first class, 5d. second class, and 2 d third class. The fares between Bath and Bournemouth will be 14s. first class, 10s. second class, ane 6s. 1d. third class.

Right: Timetable published in the *Bournemouth Visitors Directory* for 13th June, 1874 with details of local fares for the opening of the Poole & Bournemouth Railway the following week.

Chapter Eight

The Ringwood, Christchurch & Bournemouth Railway

Concurrent with the developments in the Poole area, moves were afoot to provide a railway to Christchurch and the rapidly developing Bournemouth from the east. By the mid-1850s Christchurch had developed into a market town with an expanding population. However, owing to the route taken by the Southampton & Dorchester Railway it was some seven miles from the nearest railway station at Holmsley, then named Christchurch Road. Situated on the turnpike road from Southampton, the station was at that time served by eight trains daily to and from London, a coach owned by a Mr Humbey providing a link between the station, Christchurch and Bournemouth. Alternatively there was a coach service to Salisbury from Ringwood connecting with trains arriving to and from Christchurch Road station. The only other conveyance for the inhabitants were carriers' carts that travelled up and down the Avon valley.

The inhabitants of Christchurch, having been left off the railway map and with Bournemouth to the west developing, decided the time had arrived to rectify the situation. On 3rd September, 1856 the Mayor of Christchurch, William Ferrey, presided over a meeting he had called in the Town Hall. This meeting was well attended by the local gentry and inhabitants of the area; it was proposed that a railway be built down the Avon valley from the Southampton & Dorchester line at Ringwood to the Christchurch and Bournemouth area. At the meeting was George Townsend, a solicitor with offices both in Salisbury and London, who was solicitor to the recently formed Salisbury & Yeovil Railway. When the Mayor asked him to explain the object of the meeting, it was clear to see that some preliminary work had been carried out. The Earl of Malmesbury who owned a considerable amount of land in the area had been approached and was in agreement with the scheme. Engineer William Collett Homersham had made a survey, his suggestion being that the line divided into two at Avon Cross Way, one line going direct to Christchurch the other to Bournemouth ending at a site between the present Cooper Dean roundabout and Holdenhurst Road. It was proposed by Admiral Walcott that the line went to Christchurch then on to Bournemouth, giving Christchurch direct access to Bournemouth, Mr Aldridge seconded this resolution. Mr Kingdon the clerk to the Bournemouth Commissioners told the meeting of the interest shown by a great number of Bournemouth people in the project, the meeting agreeing that ways of proceeding with the scheme be sought carried it unanimously.

A contractor, Mr J.R. Davidson, estimated that the cost of the 11½ mile line, built for double track but only laid for single line, would be £100,000 and he himself would be prepared to lease and work the line for 10 years, and had the confidence to guarantee a dividend of 5 per cent. Lord Malmesbury told the meeting that the line would pass through three miles of his woods, to which he had no objection, and that all those present should do all in their power to support the scheme; also letters had been received from Sir George Gervis and other local men of influence all supporting the scheme.

The solicitor of the proposed railway gave public notice on 5th November, 1856 of the intention to put a Bill before Parliament incorporating a company to be known as the Ringwood, Christchurch & Bournemouth Railway to construct,

A Railway commencing in the parish of Ringwood by a junction with the line of the London & South Western Railway at a point about 8 chains east of the hundred and six mile post from London on the same railway and terminating in the parish of Christchurch on a piece of land part of Portfield situated to the east of Barrack Road, Christchurch, near a house called Half-Way House. A Railway commencing in the parish of Christchurch by a junction with the above described intended railway at a point about 15 chains northward of the described Christchurch Town thereof, and terminating at or near a point on a road from Bournemouth to Great Dean and Holdenhurst about 16 chains north-east of the intersection of that road by a boundary line between the parishes of Christchurch and Holdenhurst.

The Prospectus for the company stated that the contractors had agreed to have the line constructed for a cost of £100,000 within a year of the passing of the Act, and that they would both lease and work the railway having invested £25,000 in the scheme. The Mayor of Christchurch called a public meeting on 17th December, to discuss the furtherance of the scheme; having deposited the plans for the line on 29th November a committee was formed to canvas for subscriptions to shares in the line. On 18th February, 1857 the Bill received its second reading in Parliament, although there had been a vast amount of verbal support for the railway, financial support was not so forthcoming as had been expected. On 9th June the promoters had to withdraw the Bill, but they hoped that within a year to proceed again having no desire to abandon the scheme.

A meeting was held at Christchurch on 21st October, 1858 consisting of shareholders of the previous scheme. The Mayor Mr J. Drewitt introduced Captain Moorsom, who had been Engineer of the Southampton & Dorchester Railway, to those assembled. Moorsom told them that in general he supported the earlier plans with alterations made to save expense. Building a line from Christchurch Road station was suggested by one person, to which Moorsom replied that the area had been examined earlier as a route for the Southampton & Dorchester Railway and not considered feasible. For an outlay of between £40,000 and £45,000 Moorsom considered a line could be built and produce a dividend to

The seal of the Ringwood, Christchurch and Bournemouth Railway Company, depicting the arms of the Earl of Malmesbury.

the shareholders by constructing it from Ringwood to Christchurch only, the section to Bournemouth being considered at a later date. As to raising the capital required, Moorsom told the meeting that if £10,000 could be subscribed locally, he had friends in London who would be willing to provide the remainder.

The new Prospectus of the Ringwood, Christchurch & Bournemouth Railway Company was issued on 22nd January, 1859. Named Directors were William Rose, John Chapman, Robert Russell, and Edward Sleet Elliott, with R.D. Sharpe of Christchurch, and T. Kingdom of Bournemouth as local solicitors. Chapman was Deputy Chairman of the Salisbury & Yeovil Railway Company and Townsend was their solicitor, having been one of the founding members of the 1856 scheme. Messrs Brassey & Ogilvie who were also involved in the construction of the Salisbury & Yeovil were introduced (as builders) to the revised Christchurch scheme by Moorsom, Brassey being prepared to invest the balance of the capital if the local inhabitants and landowners were to take up 1,000 shares and supply the necessary land.

During April the *Christchurch Times* reported of shares being taken up by more people than in the previous scheme, but added a note that although many people wanted a railway they hoped that others would provide it for them. Subscriptions closed on 30th May and by the end of July the Bill had passed the committee stage in Parliament. The Ringwood, Christchurch & Bournemouth Railway Act received the Royal Assent on 8th August, 1859, the capital of the company being £45,000 consisting of 4,500 shares of £10 each, and borrowing powers of £15,000.

Lord Malmesbury sold 22 acres of land at the Ringwood end of the line for its construction which later contained four level crossings with gates to allow access to premises nearby. One of these was at Avon Cottage, the Act stipulating that a lodge and siding be built at the site, and that the occupier of Avon Cottage have the right to stop any ordinary train to either pick up or set down passengers. There was also the question of Common Lands that had to be crossed at both Avon and Sopley Commons, where, following meetings with local committees, £71 18s. and £21 11s. 6d. respectively was paid for the extinguishment of Common Rights, a further £146 being paid for compensation for rights at Christchurch. The company's registered offices were in Leadenhall Street London EC and the first meeting of the Board of Directors was held there on 16th August, 1859, when Chapman was elected Chairman, Moorsom was officially appointed Engineer to the company, and Henry Notman, Secretary, a position he also held with the Salisbury & Yeovil Railway. It was reported that £10,230 worth of shares had been subscribed to. Messrs Bassey & Ogilvie who were to construct the line sent a memorandum to the meeting in which they undertook to complete the railway for £53,000, £11,000 in cash, £15,000 in debentures and £27,000 in shares in the company.

It was also decided that the arms of Lord Malmesbury be adopted as the company seal, subject to permission being obtained. On 28th February, 1860 it was reported that the seal incorporating the Malmesbury Arms had been prepared, and that the LSWR had been offered the option of working the completed line. Although there was delay in commencing works owing to disagreement with the LSWR over the junction arrangements near Ringwood, the Directors had entered into negotiations with landowners and in many cases had succeeded in purchasing the necessary land on favourable terms, and the Engineer was instructed to mark out the route of the line.

Avon Lodge Halt looking towards Ringwood around the turn of the century. A tank engine shunts a wagon at the private siding provided for the Earl of Malmesbury at this then remote site. Today although the branch line has long gone the Lodge building still survives surrounded by other property in a rather select estate.   *C.G. Maggs Collection*

Two gentlemen reflect on the passing scene at Avon Lodge Halt. Behind them is the waiting room, to the right the crossing keeper's cottage.   *John Alsop Collection*

The first half-yearly meeting of the company was held at 7 Delahay Street, London, on 29th February. However, as there was not a quorum, the meeting was adjourned until 1st March when again there was not a quorum and it appears the meeting was abandoned. Despite this lack of enthusiasm, on 12th April it was reported the contractors were due to commence work the following week.

Moorsom reported to a meeting held at the Kings Arms Hotel, Christchurch, on 14th July that nearly a third of the earthworks had been completed and work on the station buildings was about to commence. By the end of October he reported that half the earthworks were complete and both cuttings and embankments were settling well, all bridges were built and about half the culverts completed. The junction embankment was now close to the LSWR line and the viaduct to form the junction was shortly to be commenced. Some £14,077 had been paid to the contractors and it was agreed by the shareholders that the borrowing powers be invoked up to the total of £15,000. The heavy rainfall during the summer had done little to assist the construction of the line; in August a landslide in a cutting at the Ringwood end of the line killed a navvy.

Problems concerning the junction at Ringwood were resolved in November. The LSWR, fearing delays to traffic on the recently doubled main line, agreed to construct a separate line alongside its own from the station to the point where the branch would diverge. The total cost of this work to the LSWR was £3,400, the Christchurch company only paying £780 and £100 per annum until the cost was cleared. During 1861 the contractors were issued with debenture bonds to the amount of £6,000 in part payment for work carried out, whilst in the January Moorsom was given 30 paid-up shares in payment for his work.

At the annual meeting held in October 1861 the Directors reported that the line would not be opened that year as a great many local shareholders were in arrears with their share calls. Although all the shares had been taken only about half were fully paid up; they had paid £1 per share upon subscribing, the other £9 of each £10 share being called as required not exceeding £2 at any one time and two months were to elapse before a further call. However, as was not uncommon in these cases, 'putting your money where your mouth is' has always proved painful, so much so that the company's solicitors were told to take proceedings against defaulters. Desperately short of funds to continue with the work Brassey & Ogilvie as part payment were given debentures to the value of £6,000 and the £300 owed to Moorsom was given as 30 paid up shares to that value, it being noted in the minutes that on occasions in the past Moorsom had been paid in shares. In the end, as final payment shares to the value of £35,000 were handed over to the contractors.

Work slowly proceeded along the line during 1862 as funds allowed, and at last on 13th November the 7¾ mile line opened, having cost £50,383 to construct. Despite all the initial enthusiasm for a railway it appears that Christchurch did little to celebrate the event, or at least the *Christchurch Times* had little to say over the matter. The edition for 15th November stated the following:

At last in spite of the prophecies of many croakers, our railway commenced on Thursday its passenger and goods traffic between here and Ringwood. We can do no more this week than to congratulate our fellow townsmen upon the fact to refer them to the timetables in our advertisement columns both as regards trains and omnibuses, and to say that we shall shortly refer to the advantages which as is already proved will be conferred by this branch railway upon the town generally. Most heartily do we wish success to this new undertaking.

The third track of the Christchurch branch running between Ringwood and its divergence point west of the River Avon is clearly shown in this view taken from a passing train.

Mark Yarwood, Great Western Trust Collection

Ringwood looking west from the footbridge in April 1966 showing Station Road crossing with Christchurch Street crossing and Ringwood West signal box in the distance. The width of the crossings allowed for the Christchurch branch to run parallel on the left, Minteys warehouse on the left was also originally served by a private siding. *South Western Circle Eyers Collection*

Trains.

L. & S. W. Railway.

Passenger Station—Stour Road.

Goods Station—Fairmile.

Station Master   Mr. Charles W. Durrant

The Railway Time Table is subject to alteration without notice and train departures and arrivals continually vary. For through journeys or connections it is advisable to obtain information at the Station booking office immediately prior to the journey. The following trains are usually to be relied on :

WEEK-DAYS.

Waterloo to Christchurch :—A.M. 5.40; 7.30; 11.30; P.M. 2.30; 7.30; 8.0; 10.0.

Christchurch to Waterloo :—A.M. 10.12; 12.10; 12.37; 1.38; 5.42; 8.59; 11.48.

SUNDAYS.

Christchurch to Waterloo :—A.M. 9.3; P.M. 1.15; 4.33; 7.22; 11.48.

Waterloo to Christchurch :—A.M. 10.0; P.M. 2.0; 5.0; 7.0; 10.0.

Notice published in the local press at the opening of the Ringwood-Christchurch branch in November 1862 gives a very poor impression of the service provided.

However, in the same edition more column inches were given to a boiler explosion at Paddington station, and to a description of a section of the Metropolitan Railway! The original train service only consisted of three trains in each direction daily, the first train departing from Christchurch at 9.30 am followed by a train at 1.20 pm and the last train of the day departing at 5.30 pm. The service of trains in the reverse direction was even worse, the first one arriving at Christchurch at 12.20 pm, the next at 2.55 pm and the final one at 6.55 pm - all arrivals and departures connecting with a horse bus service from Bournemouth.

Traffic was not as good as had been expected, up until the end of December £192 2s. 7d. had been taken in passenger receipts and only £31 2s. 10d. in goods traffic. With working expenses to the LSWR of 55 per cent and a Government duty of 5 per cent on passenger fares (unless they were third class at not more than 1d. per mile), there was only £93 2s. 3d. left.

The line itself was of a lightweight nature; it took a winding course seeking the higher ground of the Avon flood plain, thus creating many curves and changes of gradient. An article in the *South Western Gazette* for 7th April, 1888 describes the situation; one which could be applied to many cheaply constructed lines:

The enterprising landowners of the neighbourhood who decided to connect the town with the South Western Company's system via Ringwood were wisely decided not to waste their funds in grand engineering works but whilst benefiting the district, to secure a fair return on their investment. Accordingly, under the direction of one well versed in the construction of Indian Railways, they laid their line out to avoid all serious tunnels, bridges, cuttings and embankments. To do this, however, involved curves of the most

Hurn a remote outpost on the Dorset-Hampshire border, a view taken after the removal of the down loop in August 1927. A few milk churns stand on the platform, but poor patronage caused the closure of the line to all traffic in September 1935.

Mark Yarwood/Great Western Trust Collection

The original Christchurch station photographed in October 1963, closed since the opening of the Direct line in 1888, which is seen curving in from the right. The remaining short spur of the original Ringwood curves away past the goods shed to the left. The wartime tank traps in the foreground are now a national monument.   *C.L. Caddy*

exceptional nature and visitors to Bournemouth must frequently have been surprised to find their train forming a graceful semicircle, suggestive of a speedy union between the engine and the tailguard's van.

Owing to the nature of the line, with gradients as severe as 1 in 80 and 1 in 66 and curves of 18 and 15 chains and one as tight as 9 chains, a speed limit of 25 mph and 15 mph on the sharpest curves was imposed, the single line being signalled on the train staff and ticket system. The branch engine was housed in a small engine shed situated at Christchurch. The station buildings at both Hurn and Christchurch followed Moorsom's earlier style used on the Southampton & Dorchester line, whilst Avon Lodge Halt was of individual design, to a standard superior to many country estate lodges. Following the opening of the branch Christchurch Road station on the main line was renamed Holmsley.

A special meeting of shareholders was held on 18th May, 1863 to consider the promotion of a Bill through Parliament to extend the railway to Bournemouth. There were also proposals to seek amalgamation with the LSWR. The Christchurch & Bournemouth Railway Act received the Royal Assent on 13th July, 1863 allowing for the construction of 3 miles 44 chains of railway, the Act also allowing additional capital of £30,000 with £10,000 borrowing powers for the project. Meanwhile financial matters had to be dealt with in April 1864. Mr Ogilvie stated that the line had been open for over a year and he was ready to come to a financial settlement with the company under the contract. This resulted in the handing over to Mr Ogilvie of 2,700 and 800 shares making together 3,500 (or £35,000 when they were sold) in exchange for a final discharge and release from all claims by Mr Ogilvie, who it was stated was the largest shareholder.

The financial state of the railway made depressing reading over a three-year period.

Traffic Receipts

13th November, 1862-30th June, 1863

	£	s.	d.
Passenger traffic	958	7	10
Goods traffic	205	7	11
	1,163	15	9
Deduct:			
Working expenses	641	1	8
Government duty	39	8	5
	679	10	1
net	484	5	8

Year ending 30th June, 1864

Passenger traffic	1,761	10	1
Goods traffic	332	15	6
	2,094	5	7
Deduct:			
Working expenses	1,151	17	1
Government duty	67	1	3
	1,218	18	4
net	875	7	3

Year ending 30th June, 1865

	£	s.	d.
Passenger traffic	2,082	13	2
Goods traffic	363	17	3
	2,446	10	5
Deduct:			
Working expenses	1,354	11	9
Government duty	79	5	10
	1,424	17	7
net	1,021	12	10

For the year ending 30th June, 1865 the total receipts had been £2,450 5s. and expenses £2,311 18s. leaving a net balance of £138 7s. 10d. and traffic was still below expectations. Despite having obtained an Act of Parliament no work had started on the extension, by the end of October Messrs Brassey & Ogilvie the contractors had moved equipment onto the site but had done little else.

A certain number of Bournemouth residents were still opposed to a railway, a rather distasteful rhyme being branded about at the time about the 'Presence of the Iron Road'. So much was the resistance that the railway had to be out of sight, 'Out by the brickfields' was the message from the Commissioners.

There were also changes taking place at management level, Notman the original Secretary had died as had Moorsom the Engineer. John Strapp, Engineer of the LSWR also became Engineer of the local company.

Following the retirement of John Chapman as company Chairman in March 1866, Sir Henry Drummond Wolff was appointed to the Board of Directors and immediately elected Chairman. Sir Henry who had just retired after a distinguished career in the diplomatic service had moved to the Bournemouth area and purchased land at Boscombe, where he built Boscombe Tower, Boscombe Spa Hotel and other property. He had become a Director of the Poole & Bournemouth Railway Company in June 1865; in 1868 he was elected Member of Parliament for Christchurch.

The financial collapse of bankers Overend & Gurney in the City on 11th May, 1866 did little to assist with any construction work. Brassey the appointed contractor for the line survived but lost heavily, like many schemes throughout the country very little money was being put forward and by October only £2,050 had been invested in the concern. Of this amount Sir George Gervis had subscribed £1,500, the remaining capital being put up in small amounts mainly by people 'in trade' and at a meeting held on 31st October the company solicitor was instructed to take the necessary preliminary steps allowing the sale of the line to the LSWR.

Work actually started on the construction of the line early in 1866, the Engineer reporting in October that several of the embankments had been formed and about 80,000 bricks, lime and sand had been deposited. Reporting to the 1867 annual meeting, the Engineer stated that 90,000 cubic yards out of a total of 118,000 cubic yards of material had been worked to form cuttings and embankments, and nearly all the fencing had been erected. The construction of the station at Bournemouth was about to commence, but to date there was no viaduct over the river Stour and all the permanent way had to be purchased. By

1st December, 1867 the account showed that £58,801 4s. 3d. had been raised using the Act of Parliament, at that time the only good news was the increase in goods traffic at Christchurch resulting in the Board agreeing during July 1868 to an extra siding being laid using second-hand materials at a cost of £66.

There were further difficulties in raising capital and in July 1868 a share call for £5 was made, followed by £2 in December and another £2 in the following June when a special meeting authorized borrowing up to the full limit of £10,000.The Directors announced on 29th October, 1868 that 'The work is now being vigorously pushed to completion'. However, in the next year very little was done towards completion of the line, and no work whatsoever on a bridge over the Stour, resulting in the Directors having to make the point with Ogilvie the contractor, Brassey by this time being in failing health. The Directors decided that they would make arrangements for the delivery of the ironwork for the bridge over the Stour. The postponement of the line's opening had also caused embarrassment to Sir Henry Drummond Wolff during his election speeches. A year later the line was still not complete, the Board of Directors, by now running out of excuses to the public, admitted that they were far from satisfied with the progress made. Eventually work came near to completion, and on 23rd February, 1870 a trial run was made with an engine and loaded wagon. Captain Tyler of the Board of Trade inspected the line on Tuesday 8th March and gave approval of the work carried out.

The opening of the Bournemouth extension took place on Monday 14th March, 1870. Flags were hung across Holdenhurst Road and a band played at the station. The railway had arrived, but it was not to everybody's liking and had been banished to the outskirts. Indeed, Bournemouth was a little sniffy about the Iron Horse, not everybody was anxious to encourage railways, some of the more genteel residents fearing that they could lower the tone of the resort by bringing in hordes of excursionists. This fear may have been partly justified, but such reactionary attitudes had to give way as the town continued to expand. It became clear that eventually Bournemouth would have to be placed on the main railway map.

However, Bournemouth did at last have railway communication and was 116 miles from Waterloo, the five trains daily to and from Ringwood providing connections.

Bournemouth-Ringwood timetable March 1870

Bournemouth	dep.	7.05 am	9.40 am	11.10 am	1.15 pm	5.30 pm
Christchurch		7.17	9.51	11.22	1.26	5.42
Herne		7.26	9.59	11.30	1.34	5.50
Ringwood	arr.	7.41	10.11	11.45	1.49	6.05
Ringwood	dep.	7.53	10.25	11.58	2.35	6.35
Herne		8.08	10.40	12.13 pm	2.50	6.50
Christchurch		8.17	10.49	12.23	2.59	6.59
Bournemouth	arr.	8.29	11.00	12.55	3.10	7.10

In April slight alterations were made to the timetable and an extra late train was provided departing from Bournemouth at 7.20 pm with a return working arriving back at 9.14 pm.

The report of the Directors on 30th June stated the following,

> ... that since the opening of the extension last March a marked increase has been apparent in the earnings of the railway. The length of the line from Ringwood to Christchurch is 7 miles 66 chains that of the extension from Christchurch to Bournemouth 3 miles 52 chains, making a total length of railway of 11½ miles. The amount available for dividend is £1,620, and a dividend of 2% declared, which will require £1,314 2s. 11d., the agreement with the LSWR has received the approval of the Board of Trade. The working cost is reduced to 50%.

In July of the same year the Directors doubled their fees to £200 per year and the Secretary's salary was raised to £150. A total of £40,000 had been raised for the building of the extension, out of this, £34,250 was subscribed in shares and bonds by Messrs Brassey & Ogilvie the contractors, who now all but owned the line!

Shortly after the line opened the residents of Pokesdown and Boscombe petitioned the LSWR for a station in their vicinity, the LSWR replying that they were waiting to view the situation after the traffic of the new line could be judged. A meeting took place on 5th November, 1870 between the LSWR Board and a deputation of Pokesdown residents led by Mr R.D. Sharpe, a local solicitor, requesting and pointing out the necessity of a station. At the meeting the Board ask what financial contribution the local people would make to the station. Drummond Wolff, Chairman of the Ringwood, Christchurch & Bournemouth company, told the local people that he had worked very hard for a station, which would also be convenient for his home. He suggested the deputation sent yet another petition through the Board of the Ringwood, Christchurch & Bournemouth company to the LSWR. That company's General Manager replied in a letter on 29th December explaining that if the Ringwood, Christchurch & Bournemouth company were to build a station, signalling, station house and other requirements, to the standards required by the LSWR Engineer, the trains would stop there, and this was only providing that the Ringwood, Christchurch & Bournemouth paid 50 per cent of the cost of working the new station. Ogilvie had turned down the idea of a temporary station to test the traffic potential.

In June 1872 following a meeting of Pokesdown residents the Ringwood, Christchurch & Bournemouth Directors themselves refused the station suggestion as the company had no capital and it was unlikely that powers to raise more capital would be arranged. It could never be said that the company were reckless with their finances or their shareholders' interests, the line was operated as cheaply as possible and the cost of construction kept down. The station at Bournemouth East was locally referred to as a 'veritable shanty' taking the form of little more than a collection of huts. The *Bournemouth Visitors Directory* on 25th April, 1870 said,

> The railway had been found to be of very great benefit to the town, but nevertheless the accommodation at the station was felt to be below the standard which the inhabitants had the right to expect.

With the increase in traffic the LSWR suggested to the local company that they erect a small wooden shed some 18 ft by 15 ft for the protection of passengers and luggage. The contractor Ogilvie said that he could not erect it, even if it was required for increased traffic, in the absence of Brassey through ill health; Ogilvie had no control over capital expenditure.

The facilities at Bournemouth were soon to prove incapable of handling the traffic on offer. Indeed, they were more akin to the facilities of a country branch terminus instead of a fast growing town. There was a shortage of siding space resulting in loaded wagons having to wait at Ringwood until space became available. In July 1872 the LSWR decided to enlarge the goods department, and a small extension of the goods office was authorized, an additional siding was also laid. However, it appears this was not exactly what the Board of Trade Inspector expected; in his report during December 1872 he stated:

> The term siding scarcely represents what is being done at this station, the single platform is to be extended eastwards and a line of rails of rails has been laid down on the north side of this platform to enable a second passenger train to be drawn into the station on this line while one is standing on the south side of the same platform ready to depart as soon as the incoming train has cleared the single line on which it has travelled from the junction with the main line at Ringwood station.

As this siding was to be used as an additional passenger platform the Inspector required additional signalling and interlocking work to be carried out. The Inspector also required additional signalling and interlocking on an additional siding being laid on the south side of the station. The report concluded by stating that,

> ...there appeared to be a difficulty of siding accommodation at this station for the goods traffic which has largely increased of late, which may possibly prevent the new siding from being at all times used for passenger trains.

A further Board of Trade inspection in July 1873 failed to satisfy the Inspector who requested additional interlocking between the points and signals, he also critisiced the lack of a signal box at the station stating:

> Instead of having the frame for the levers at the end of the platform I think it would be desirable and safer to establish a signal box between the first and second pair of facing points on the down line, and to concentrate the working of the points and levers in this signal box, rather than to work the points at such a distance and leaving the frame exposed.

Work was quickly put in hand resulting in a signal box complete with locking frame being brought into use on 10th January, 1874, and the Inspector was now satisfied with the arrangements at the station.

Despite these problems the financial results were an improvement on the earlier years, for the year ending 30th June, 1873 the gross receipts were £12,325 13s. 3d. as opposed to the year ending 30th June, 1869 (when the line terminated at Christchurch) when the gross receipts were £2,900 3s. 3d.

In March 1872 through coaches between Bournemouth and Waterloo commenced to run, departing from Bournemouth at 10.10 am arriving at Waterloo at 1.43 pm, the return working leaving Waterloo at 3.15 pm, arriving at Bournemouth at 6.44 pm. The running of these trains resulted in a court case: Mr Turner the occupier of Avon Cottage requested the train stop for him but the LSWR claimed it was not an ordinary train within the meaning of the 1859 Ringwood, Christchurch & Bournemouth Railway Act. The court case heard on 17th February, 1874 upheld the LSWR point of view.

On Christmas Eve 1872 the LSWR General Manager in a letter made a formal application for the purchase of the Ringwood, Christchurch & Bournemouth company, referring to the Poole & Bournemouth Railway then under construction, and to possible disputes that might arise. The Directors of his company considered it wise to come to an agreement to purchase the Ringwood, Christchurch & Bournemouth with effect from 1st January, 1874, the LSWR offering £100 nominal value 5 per cent preference stock in exchange for every £100 nominal value paid up shares in the Ringwood, Christchurch & Bournemouth. They would also acquire the debenture bonds and pay off a debt of £456 on the capital account.

At a special general meeting of the shareholders held on 30th October, 1873 to consider the proposals, it was noted that 5 per cent preference stock of the LSWR was being quoted at £112 to £114 so if accepted the immediate cash value was £113. The meeting agreed to the terms of the offer, the final general meeting of the company taking place on 27th June, 1874. Brassey & Ogilvie who owned shares worth £4,250, overnight had LSWR shares worth £38,702 10s., or cash if sold.

Thus from 1st January, 1874 the Ringwood, Christchurch & Bournemouth Railway officially became part of the LSWR. It had survived its early years mainly thanks to Messrs Brassey & Ogilvie who had both taken shares as opposed to financial payments, although for them the speculation eventually paid handsome dividends when later transferred into LSWR shares! The fortunes of the railway had also improved following the opening of the extension to Bournemouth. Historically what had started life as a minor branch line was to later play a major part in the Bournemouth railway network.

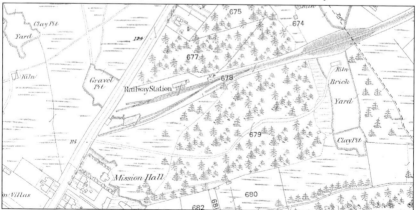

Bournemouth East station shown shortly after its opening, out of the sight of a much smaller Bournemouth. Today the surrounding area is covered with residential and business premises. The present Bournemouth Central station is built on the land across Holdenhurst Road, to the left of the original station.

Reproduced from the 1874 Ordnance Survey Map

Chapter Nine

General Progress 1877-1886:
The Southampton & Dorchester

The need for improvements at Wimborne caused the local agent Mr Gale to write to the Traffic Committee in October 1877 recommending that a transfer shed for goods traffic be constructed to keep the passenger platform clear of packages; but after having the plans prepared in December the matter was postponed. However, in May 1878 they did approve a plan to extend the platform canopy up to the refreshment room on the up platform at a cost of £130.

The deferred question of the transfer shed became somewhat overtaken by events when, during the early hours of 27th March, 1879, Wimborne goods shed was destroyed by fire, together with the adjacent stable which resulted in the death of the station horse. Fortunately, two or three wagons that were on the line near the shed were moved to a place of safety by those who were first on the scene. Plans for a new shed at an estimated cost of £1,750 were approved that August - with a transfer shed also to be erected later on the up side 'if found necessary'.

Finances were and still are a serious matter to any company, a perusal of records will quickly reveal that shareholders, Directors, and management took most seriously the revenue and other accounts. These included the expenses and income of the section between Dorchester and Weymouth, referred to in the minutes as the Weymouth and Dorchester Tolls, which were a regular source of disagreement.

Financial expenditure towards improvements was not easily granted unless a revenue return could be obtained. Although the operation of railways had vastly improved since the earliest days the working methods of the late 1870s still left much to be desired when compared with later standards. Many trains ran without any form of continuous brake and mixed trains of both passenger and goods vehicles were common - even on the main line! Two accidents within months of each other - both fortunately without loss of life - brought operating conditions on the Southampton & Dorchester lines at that period into sharp focus.

Doubtless because of the dreams of westward extension, Dorchester had been laid out as a through station orientated in that direction and consisted of a main platform divided into two parts for both up and down trains, resulting in the track layout being unusual and calls for some explanation. The up and down main lines ran into a terminal platform, the whole peculiar arrangement being under the control of a signal box situated 65 yards east of the station. The next signal box eastward was Chalk Siding which controlled the entrance to Mansfield Siding, a crossover road, and Chalk Sidings beyond Wareham Road bridge, the resultant Absolute Block section being less than a mile in length. The single line between the station and the Great Western Railway signal box at Dorchester Junction was worked by gong communication.

An interesting combination of buildings through the ages at Wimborne, centre stage is the goods shed built to replace the original structure, to the right a small building that probably pre-dates the goods shed. To the left a typical store on stilts to store agricultural requirements once a familiar sight at many stations, whilst in the foreground two concrete huts, in later years a noted feature of Southern architecture. *South Western Circle, Eyers Collection*

Part of the main platform of Dorchester, taken around the turn of the century; to the left of the grounded coach body stands the remaining part of the original arrival platform arrangements, which originally had a covered train shed joined to the remaining structure on the right. *G.A. Pryer Collection*

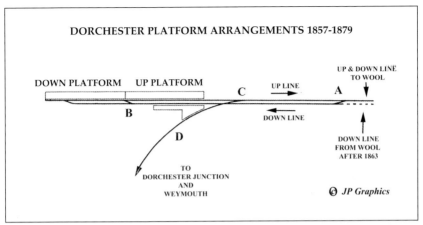

DORCHESTER PLATFORM ARRANGEMENTS 1857-1879

Diagram showing the arrangements for shunting both up and down trains at Dorchester before the construction of the new down platform.

Down trains continuing to Weymouth arrived passing points A (*see plan above*) on the down line and continued to points B where they crossed over into the down platform, which was basically an extension of the up platform. Then having completed their station work, they would reverse out over points B proceeding wrong road up the down line, owing to the fact there was no connection between the down line and the single line to Dorchester Junction. The train then regained the up line at points A, some 320 yds after leaving the down section of the platform, then proceeded forward along the up line to points C where it crossed onto the single line to Dorchester Junction (D).

It is not recorded whether such movements always took this rather complex route or if they pushed out via the up section of the platform if it was unoccupied. Up trains from Weymouth simply passed clear of point C and then backed into the up platform, and after completing their station work, proceeded up the main line. What (from the plan) appears to be a short down platform has been described as a second up platform, it was all very confusing!

The first accident to emphasize the oddities of the Dorchester layout took place on the evening of 6th November, 1877. The 2.10 pm Waterloo-Weymouth express, consisting of a tender engine, three carriages and a brake van at both ends, was approaching the station. At the same time the 5.45 pm up passenger and goods train from Weymouth, headed by a tank engine hauling nine goods wagons, three carriages, and two brake vans, was approaching on the single line section from Dorchester Junction. Unfortunately the latter train failed to stop at the branch home signal and struck the second carriage of the down express. This vehicle was knocked over onto its side and damaged and the third carriage was derailed with its leading end driven in. The force of the impact parted the couplings, allowing the engine, front brake van, and leading coach to continue into the platform, whilst the rear brake van broke away and ran 50 yards back down the track in the direction of Chalk Sidings.

Dorchester showing the train shed over the up platform in later years following the removal of the side screen. The area of platform behind the camera was the original down platform, trains arriving via the crossover in the foreground. The replacement curved down platform of 1879 can be seen in the background beyond the grounded vintage coach body.   *G. Beale Collection*

The engine of the up Weymouth train suffered damage to the left end of its buffer beam and left buffer and was derailed - as were two of the wagons. There were no complaints of injury from passengers on the up train, but seven passengers on the down express were injured - including the Mayor of Dorchester, Henry Lock, and the Town Clerk, Giles Symonds.

In his accident report Major Marindin of the Board of Trade concluded that the principal cause was that the driver of the up Weymouth train approached Dorchester Junction at excessive speed and then over-ran the signal, but blame also attached to the signalman at Dorchester station signal box for giving 'Line Clear' to the Junction signalman for the up train before the down express had cleared the pointwork and entered the station. Had he attended to his rules, the Junction signals would also have been against the Weymouth train and, in all probability, no accident would have occurred. It appeared to the Inspector that this signalman had imperfectly understood some verbal instruction regarding the necessity of getting the South Western trains off the Great Western Line as expeditiously as possible 'but he should have been bound by his printed rules, which are clear and precise'. Obviously both signalmen thought that running traffic promptly off the GWR was of more importance than maintaining their 'clearing points'!

Having briefly described the complex working arrangements at the station, the Major concluded his report with the following recommendations:

All this backing of trains on their wrong lines might be avoided if the South Western Dorchester station was made a through instead of a terminal station, which it ought not to continue to be, as nearly all the Down trains go through to Weymouth. If a station were erected east of the junction of the Weymouth branch, and this single branch were doubled, it would add very materially to the safety of the public using this line, for the main line would then be continued through to the Dorchester Junction and a dangerous single connecting line would disappear.

For some strange reason this sensible recommendation was never fully implemented, and Dorchester continued to be a difficult station to operate.

In the published copy of the Board of Trade report reference was made to the engine of the up Weymouth train being 'a bogie tank engine, 4-wheel coupled, with 4-wheeled trailing bogie, weighing 44 tons, with brakes on the driving and trailing wheels', but this must be a typographical error as the LSWR possessed no 0-4-4 tanks at that period. There is little doubt that the engine referred to was a member of the 4-4-0 'Metropolitan' class, of which Nos. 321 and 322 were allocated to Dorchester by early 1878.

Another accident featuring a mixed train occurred on 5th December, 1877, when the 8.20 am Wimborne to Bournemouth West train become derailed on the single line between Poole Junction (Broadstone) and Poole station, at a point north of what later became Holes Bay Junction. There the line ran along a 6 ft-high embankment across a small creek in the upper reaches of Poole Harbour.

The train consisted of an unspecified tank engine, six loaded wagons, two third class carriages, a brake van, one third class carriage, a second class carriage, a first class carriage, another brake van, and a third class carriage which formed the rear of the train - a mixed formation indeed! At a point approximately 1 mile 3½ furlongs west of Poole station an axle on the second wagon failed, causing the entire train with the exception of the engine and leading wagon to leave the rails. The second wagon plunged down the low embankment and landed upside down in the water with the third wagon on top of it; the fourth, fifth, and sixth vehicles were on their sides in the water, as were the two third class coaches, which followed. The leading brake van was partially overturned halfway down the embankment, the following third class carriage was tilted at an angle half on the embankment followed by the second class carriage in much the same position. A first class carriage came to rest at the top of the bank but totally derailed, as was the rear brake van, but the rear vehicle - the third class carriage - had only its leading wheels off the rails.

Fortunately the 10 or 12 passengers on the train were travelling in the three carriages in front of the rear brake van and escaped without injury. All the wagons were severely damaged, the leading carriage having the front end 'knocked out' whilst the following one was damaged, and the permanent way was disturbed over a length of 50 yards.

Major Marindin of the Board of Trade, on examining the second wagon, which was a 'private owner' vehicle belonging to the Radstock Coal & Wagon Company, stated that the body was old and the woodwork decayed in places. The axle was even worse! The report said that it was,

...difficult to understand how it can ever have run a mile without breaking, much more how it can have done so for three of four years. It had been broken before, and a new end had been welded, or attempted to be welded, on to it. This weld (which does not deserve the name of a weld) had adhered on the surface only, and imperfectly there, in no place deeper than an inch, and in most places for about a quarter of an inch at the outside.

He was severely critical of the fact that this flaw had not been noticed before, or indeed when the axle was fitted to the wagon, and remarked that whoever was responsible for fitting it was either grossly ignorant or guilty of total disregard for the safety of the public. He concluded:

Moreover, where these mixed trains are necessarily used, the passenger carriages should be in front and the goods wagons in rear, so that passengers in such trains may not be exposed to the risk of an accident such as the one now in question, arising from causes beyond the control of the Company.

On the 2nd December, 1877 the Traffic Committee read the report into the Dorchester collision and considered the alterations required to the layout. At a meeting held on 20th March, 1878 Mr Scott recommended that in co-operation with the GWR the line connecting to that company should be doubled at the joint expense of both companies, and a new 33-lever signal box provided at the station.

In his report of 17th October, 1878 Major General Hutchinson of the Board of Trade described the alterations taking place:

A single line about 700 yards long between this station and the Great Western Company's line from Weymouth is being doubled. When the alterations are completed it is the intention to cease running the Weymouth portion of a down train into the end of the Dorchester station, but to stop it at a new platform on the branch after it has been separated from the Dorchester portion of the train, which will then as at present be taken into the terminal platform.

With regards to an up Weymouth train it is proposed to bring it forward over the junction and then back it into the Dorchester portion of the train which will be standing in the up platform. Owing to local circumstances, there would be a difficulty in dealing otherwise with the up trains and providing two sets of trailing points (which will become facing ones for trains from Weymouth) are provided with locking bars and a signal, there appears to be no great objection to the mode of dealing with the up traffic. As regards the down traffic, it is necessary that a bridge or subway be provided for connecting the new down platform with the old up platform, otherwise the passengers will have to cross the lines of rails in order to reach the down trains for Weymouth.

The new down platform on the curve was brought into use on 5th May, 1879, but was far from a lavish structure. Furthermore, the only access to it from the station entrance was a boarded crossing, the very matter the Board of Trade Inspector had been concerned about!

At this point in history the pronouncements of the Board of Trade only counted as recommendations and the degree to which they were implemented depended entirely upon the conscience of the company concerned. It was immediately obvious that full compliance at Dorchester was going to be expensive, so the company was somewhat less than whole-hearted in approaching the problem.

The *Dorset County Chronicle* was quick to point out the dangers of this arrangement:

> Passengers will have to cross two lines of railway, in each instance the crossing being level. This cannot but cause danger, which it is always important to prevent as far as possible.

On 27th November, 1879 the same newspaper again drew attention to the dangers of this practice:

> Railway Circumlocution - It used to be a standing joke that GWR stood for Great Way Round, but from the arrangements at the South Western station, Dorchester, the inconveniences and difficulties of passenger traffic are by no means confined to the company which used to boast of the broad gauge. Our attention has been called to the very inconvenient and indeed dangerous arrangements at the station named. Finding the annoyance of having to 'go all the way round' after alighting at the new platform or siding complaint was justly made by travellers, whose convenience was eventually consulted by making a doorway in the middle of the partition dividing the platforms. But this puerile attempt to remedy the evil of having to cross no less than four lines is more annoying than ever. Why the beautiful simplicity of stopping trains at stations accessible without endangering life and limb is not observed at Dorchester has long been a mystery. These remarks apply more especially to the 6.5 pm down express which lands its passengers at the new platform and they have to cross in the dark no less than four lines of metals. The present arrangements are excellent for providing work for the coroner, and it is on that ground alone we give further publicity to the complaints in question.

From the cryptic references in minute books it is clear that the LSWR did not wish to spend large amounts of money at Dorchester, but they were unable to ignore completely the question of access to the new down platform! In August 1881 the minutes recorded that:

> ...The arrival shed to be taken down, platform on the down line side to be used as the arrival platform. A covered footbridge to be made to communicate with the platform on the Weymouth line. This arrangement to be carried out.

In November the plan for improving Dorchester station was approved at a cost of £3,638.

Despite the positive tone of this entry nothing happened immediately - but there was a change made to the plans, for in February 1882 a letter from the Town Clerk of Dorchester made reference to the subway at Dorchester station when suggesting the construction of a new station, but the company agreed to adhere to the former resolution. It is evident that - for some reason - a subway had been substituted for the proposed footbridge, although nothing appears in the minutes to the effect! However, the *Dorset County Chronicle* reporting on the annual inspection of the line by officers of the LSWR in July 1882, stated that they were received in the town by Mr Holliday, district superintendent and station master, and made a thorough inspection of Dorchester station, after which they expressed themselves well pleased with the alterations recently executed.

Above: Dorchester South viewed from Maumbury Rings photographed pre-1897 the goods shed is shown without its second extension. The 1883 engine shed extension to the extreme right is still in a clean condition and the up platform train shed still retains its side screens again in a clean condition.

Author's Collection

Right: An early 20th century view looking into the train shed at Dorchester with the down platform of 1879 to the left. In front of the left side of the train shed is the covering over the subway steps that led to the long disused left-hand platform under the building.

G.A. Pryer Collection

Some other work was done at Dorchester at around this time. In July 1878 sanction was granted to build an additional room onto the lodge cottage at Dorchester station at a cost of £40, and in May 1879 the road bridge over the railway at Fordington Fields (Wareham Road Bridge) was replaced by a more substantial structure.

In September 1882 it was decided that the goods shed required enlargement and plans were duly prepared. In December there was a recommendation that a further eight cottages for staff be built - and that they be in a row rather than in pairs as was the usual practice - but the March 1883 meeting rescinded this and decided to erect only four cottages!

Meanwhile, developments in the town of Dorchester had an influence on the railway. The Government decided to construct a new military barracks on a site in Poundbury (off the Bridport road), the contract being awarded to Messrs Bull & Sons of Southampton. Construction commenced in April 1877 and the following month Messrs Bull made an application to the Urban Sanitary Authority to lay a standard gauge tramway from the LSWR station yard across Weymouth Road, through the new Fair and Market Ground, thence along Cornwall Road and across the Bridport Road to the building site. Permission was granted subject to removal of the line on the completion of the works - except that the section between the station entrance and the fair and market ground be left if so required by the Council 'for their use and benefit'.

Work on the construction of the tramway commenced in the first week of June, the siding in the LSWR yard that had been laid for extra traffic in 1872 being extended to the Weymouth Road. The passage of time has left us very few details of this tramway - apart from the frequent public complaints about the state of the road! The main part of the barracks was completed by March 1879 and removal of the track commenced on 19th July, after which it was reported that about 100 feet a day was being lifted. In September the Borough council raised the matter of allowing the rails into the market to remain - provided that the LSWR would consent to that course as regarded the station yard - but the following month the railway company replied that they would not allow it. Thus the Dorchester Tramway was consigned to history. The following month it was announced that Messrs Bull had obtained the contract to construct the new Eldridge Pope brewery. This being adjacent to the LSWR station a siding was laid to deliver materials to the site, it remaining upon completion to serve as a private siding for the brewery.

By 1883 the original two-road engine shed at Dorchester had become inadequate - especially as the road nearest to the main line was the only means of access to the shed yard and was therefore unsuitable as a stabling point for engines - and a two-road extension, constructed of timber, was added to the south side of the original structure. As it was customary at that period for down trains to change engines at Dorchester for their onward journey to Weymouth, a connection was provided from the shed sidings to the down line at the Dorchester Junction end of the down platform. The points were operated from a ground frame and it was brought into use in July 1883. For some obscure reason it was known as 'Came Siding' - although the hamlet of 'Winterbourne Came' was a mile away south of Dorchester!

Above: Dorchester shed photographed in 1938 where little had changed over the years, the 1883 extension stands in contrast to the 1847 brick structure. An engine stands on the turntable at the extreme right, above which can be seen the engine crew dormitory and railway cottages.　　*R.K. Blencowe Collection*

Right: Superimposed on a later street map of the town is the route of the tramway from Dorchester station to the construction site at Dorchester Barracks between 1877 and 1879.

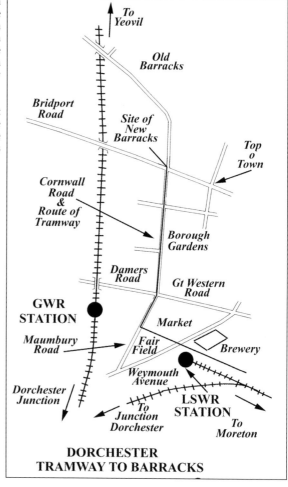

To
Yeovil

Old
Barracks

Bridport
Road

Site of
New
Barracks

Top
o
Town

Cornwall
Road
&
Route of
Tramway

Borough
Gardens

Damers
Road

Gt Western
Road

GWR
STATION

Market

Maumbury
Road

Fair
Field

Brewery

Weymouth
Avenue

Dorchester
Junction

To
Junction
Dorchester

LSWR
STATION

To
Moreton

**DORCHESTER
TRAMWAY TO BARRACKS**

Moreton, a typical small station set in the Dorset countryside; over the years it had received a number of extensions both to house the occupants and cater for increased traffic. Although situated a distance from the village of Moreton it handled a considerable trade from the surrounding villages and had sidings serving both a brick works and a sand pit.   *C.L. Caddy*

Moreton signal box, to the left of the gates stands the original crossing keeper's cottage, which served for many years as a goods store. Behind stand the later railway cottages erected for staff.
    K. Hastie Collection

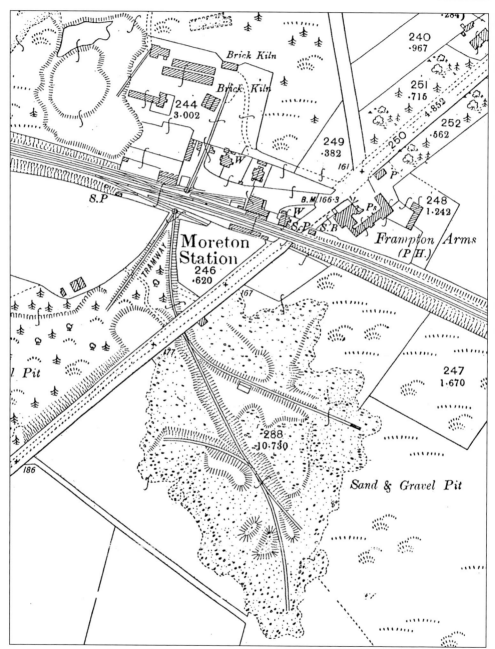

Moreton station showing the tramway running to the brickworks north of the station, and the tramways into the sandpits to the south passing under the B3390 road.

Reproduced from the 1889 Ordnance Survey Map

Dorchester was not the only station where there was a reluctance to incur the expense of improvements, for in September 1881 it was decided that work on a wharf at Hamworthy was not required 'at the present time'. Poole was another station that received improvements only in small doses. Whereas up to June 1880 a signal box situated alongside Towngate Street crossing had controlled all movements at the station assisted by a ground frame at the High Street crossing, these arrangements were improved no doubt with the future doubling of the line in view. A new signal box was constructed at the west end of the station and High Street crossing upgraded to a signal box whilst Towngate Street crossing was controlled by a ground frame.

The handling area of the goods shed had been enlarged by filling in the cart loading bays and providing a canopy as protection to the openings in the wall, but the passenger station was still lacking in certain basic facilities. During 1882 there was correspondence between the Town Clerk of Poole and the company on the subject of the accommodation available to passengers at the station. The discomfort occasioned by the want of a waiting room on the down platform had been frequently emphasized, but the LSWR was of the opinion that such a luxury was hardly necessary as it would only be of use to passengers travelling to Parkstone and Bournemouth West for whom the existing canopy was considered sufficient. Doubtless in an attempt to silence the critics on the council, a plan was prepared in August 1892 for both a waiting room and an extension to the down platform canopy at a total cost of £246. After further consideration this was whittled down to a canopy extension of two bays only and a shelving of everything else - including the waiting room! Following this even another spate of letters from the Town Clerk failed to have any impact until December, when it was finally agreed that a small general waiting room be erected.

Despite the problems at Poole, there appears to have been little quibbling in September 1881 when it was suggested that a shelter screen against the elements be constructed at the end of the down platform at Parkstone. Indeed, by the following April this had become an extension of the roofing and a screen at a cost of £105! (It must be remembered that, prior to the opening of the Holes Bay curve, the down direction on the Poole & Bournemouth Railway was towards Bournemouth West and the up direction towards Broadstone.)

In many cases it took considerable time for relatively simple additions to be carried out, the words declined, refused and deferred often appearing in Committee minutes. However, the Southampton & Dorchester was but a small part of the LSWR system all of which required improvements and decisions were often made bearing in mind the income and traffic requirements on that section of line and the influence of the local community.

As early as 1874 a memorial requesting a waiting room at Wool station was declined although approved two years later. It was not until 1881 that approval was given to construct a waiting room there in the end bays of the up side waiting shelter. In August 1882 approval was given for the lengthening of both platforms at Wareham by 100 ft, and the following month it was agreed to extend the up siding at Moreton by 250 ft.

Before leaving the Dorset area a quick look at the 1881 census for Moreton reveals some interesting facts. The station master was Uriah Sansom aged 73,

The curve between the High Street Crossing and Poole station photographed between 1880 and 1897 in which year Poole 'A' signal box was erected on the site of the High Street crossing keeper's hut in the left foreground. *Poole Museum Service*

The up side shelter at Wool photographed in later years, the right-hand end having been converted into a waiting room. This design of curved-fronted shelter was repeated at a number of stations on the Southampton & Dorchester line. In later years the curved frontage was simplified and the entire shelter replaced with the rebuilding of the station; the present up side accommodation is of the bus shelter variety. *G.A. Pryer Collection*

his wife Harriett was a mere 48 and their daughter Sophia was only 5 years of age.

The three station cottages were occupied by the following staff and their families: Francis Cox, 54, signalman; William Bishop, 47, platelayer; John Lane, 47, porter; the latter family also had a lodger, Henry Holmes, 18, telegraph clerk. A check of the records reveals that this was the Henry Holmes who later became superintendent of the line.

A further look into the career of station master Sansom reveals the conditions of the period. A local man, he had been recommended to the LSWR by the local Squire, and commenced as a porter at Moreton in October 1847 at 18s. per week. In May 1848 the record of the baptism of his sixth child Sophia describes him as 'gateman at railway station'. During 1850 he was appointed station agent at 24s. per week with house. However, tragedy was to strike the family in the October and November with the death of three of his children within four weeks. Firstly Sophia aged 2, who suffered from debility from birth, passed away, followed by Elizabeth aged 11 and Uriah aged 9 of Scarlatina (Scarlet Fever) within days of each other, then Sidney aged 2 died the following March of Croup.

It is not recorded where the family lived before moving into the station house, be it the crossing cottage (No. 36) or another cottage, but poor living conditions, overcrowding and the lack of modern medicine were some of the reasons for the high mortality rate, particularly in children.

Two years later a further child also named Uriah was born and, in 1856, a daughter Frances completed the family. The previous year Sansom had been placed on the salaried staff at £70 per annum, increased to £75 in July 1856 and to £80 in July 1863. Early in the same month further misfortune befell the family when their eldest child David aged 28, residing in Lambeth, London with a wife and two young daughters and employed as a guard on the LSWR, received fatal injuries after striking his head when leaning out of a carriage window. To heap more misery on this unfortunate family Sansom's wife, Sophia passed away in late July 1867 aged 55.

The 1871 census reveals that Sansom had remarried, the household now consisting of himself, wife Harriett and stepson John Legg age 13. A further daughter Sophia was born early in 1876. In the April of the same year Sansom received his final salary increase to £90 (the same salary his successor was receiving 29 years later). Sansom retired in February 1882 on £60 per year from the pension fund, a sum that gave him 23s. per week, itself well above the average wage of the time, and in today's world who can obtain a two-thirds final pay pension! After a lifetime of hard work and personal tragedy he passed away at Greenhill Cottages Fordington, Dorchester on 14th October the same year aged 75.

Improvements were also taking place at the eastern end of the line. For a number of years the LSWR had received supplies of sleepers, rail, chairs, fishplates and other materials at Eling Wharf. However, in 1880 a site situated between Redbridge station and the water was acquired from William Sharland, formerly a timber yard it was to become the company's rail and sleeper depot. Within a year of taking over the site large tanks were constructed to allow sleepers to be soaked in creosote. Already Redbridge was changing from a

A general view of Brockenhurst looking towards Southampton following the alterations made during the 1880s. Note the older rolling stock, still employed on local services, standing in the Lymington branch bay.   *Author's Collection*

The scene at Brockenhurst on 8th April, 1899, 'T9' class No. 702 passes with the 12 15 pm Waterloo-Bournemouth, this train contained a Pullman car and the first stop was Christchurch. 'O2' class 0-4-4 tank No. 194 stands in the bay on the left. Also of interest is the block train of four-wheelers on the extreme right.   *Author's Collection*

storage site into a works, a site they shared with an oil cake mill, a vitriol works, and between 1897 and 1922 a gunpowder factory. All these premises over a period of time became absorbed into the railway works.

Other improvements at Redbridge saw the station master have a new office erected for his use in 1882, and the following year alterations and extensions to sidings at the station were approved at an estimated cost of £378. A new viaduct across the River Test west of Redbridge station was authorized in April 1881, and erected by Messrs Perry & Son, being brought into use on 1st June, 1883. The structure consisted of 30 spans, the piers being cast-iron screw piles in groups of four, with the deck carried on wrought-iron girders.

Brockenhurst, a small wayside station in the New Forest, was about to be awakened from its slumbers. Although it had enjoyed some importance since becoming the junction for Lymington in 1859, the station was little changed. During tours of inspection by LSWR Directors during the 1870s suggestions for various improvements were made, however, as with suggestions for work to be carried out at many stations, its financing and other considerations often resulted in little being done.

It was not until powers to extend the Lymington branch to the new pier were granted in August 1881 that improvements to Brockenhurst were seriously considered. This resulted in improvements which included a footbridge, a bay platform for branch trains provided on the down side and the original signal box situated on the up platform was replaced by a new structure containing a 20-lever Stevens' frame to the west of the station. These new facilities came into use in July 1883 ahead of the Lymington extension to the pier, which opened on 1st May, 1884

Doubling of the Andover and Redbridge line was also taking place during 1883, the section between Romsey and Redbridge being completed in February 1884. Although this had no direct influence on the Southampton & Dorchester line, it contributed towards more efficient working in the Southampton area. At the same time a private siding into a gunpowder works on the down side at Redbridge was commissioned, connection with the main line being through a slip connection operated from a 7-lever ground frame at the east end of the station.

A study of the company's minute books will reveal the numerous requests and suggestions from both corporate bodies and individuals constantly received, the most frequent being for improved services or cheaper fares. One such request came in January 1884 from the Mayor of Weymouth requesting improvements in the through train service between Waterloo and Weymouth, the company agreeing to provide new fast trains by extension of the 9 am up express from Bournemouth and the 4.55 pm down express from Waterloo from 1st April.

A further request came from the residents of Dorchester in March when they asked that third class return tickets from Dorchester to Weymouth be issued at the fare of 1s., a matter that had to be referred to the GWR. However, a swift refusal came to a suggestion from a Mr Skelton requesting a reduction of fares and season ticket rates between Lyndhurst Road and Southampton. A second request was received from the same gentleman in October proposing that a bridge be constructed over the railway near Lyndhurst Road station which would allow the closure of two crossings. A report from the Engineer put the

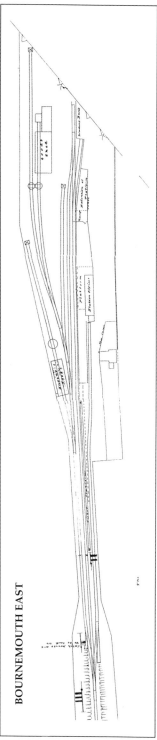

BOURNEMOUTH EAST

Bournemouth East, a plan of the arrangements in 1873 following improvements but before the erection of a signal box.

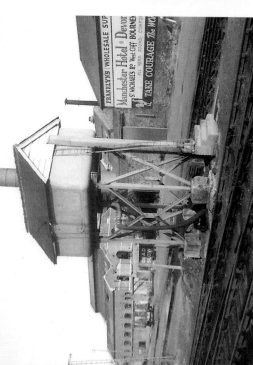

A small water tank in Bournemouth Central goods yard, thought to be part of the original Bournemouth East arrangements. However, its original provenance cannot be proved.

L. Tavender

This small building situated in Bournemouth Central goods yard is believed to be the top section of the original Bournemouth East signal box of 1874.

L. Tavender

Redbridge station looking west *circa* 1910. Adams 'T6' class 4-4-0 No. 683 approaches with an up stopping train. Above the down side shelter can be seen the signals for the junction, the lower signals on the right protecting the Redbridge-Andover line.   *G.A. Pryer Collection*

Engineer's Department engine No. 13 *Rich* standing outside the small engine shed at Wareham, this was situated on the up side west of the level crossing on the site of the present station. *Rich* was employed on permanent way work and the haulage of ballast from both Woodsford and Keysworth pits. Built in March 1866 by Robert Stephenson & Company it ran as No. 227 for the locomotive department until transferred to the Engineer in August 1875 and finally withdrawn in November 1890.   *Author's Collection*

Wareham new station looking east, in the background can be seen one of the original crossing keeper's cottages of 1847 and beyond the footbridge the original station buildings.

Author's Collection

The up side platform of Wareham new station; constructed to the standard design of the LSWR of the period it has changed little in the following 76 years.

South Western Circle, Eyers Collection

cost at an estimated £816, the proposal being declined, it taking a further 48 years before a bridge was eventually constructed.

Following a number of requests in July 1884, the company made a concession in the interest of the many workmen living in the Poole area but employed at Bournemouth who were paying 8*d*. for an ordinary third class return. They could thereafter purchase a weekly ticket for 2*s*. 6*d*. which effected a saving of 1*s*. 6*d*. a week using the 5.40 am train from Poole and available on any return train.

During the 1880s the status of the 'Old Road' was to change as developments took place in the Bournemouth area which was to drastically change the operating structure of the Southampton-Dorchester line. Owing to the fact that many of these developments took place within a short time or were concurrent with each other, they have been separated in this text for brevity and ease of reading.

Firstly, the long awaited branch to Swanage became a reality in 1885, the Swanage Railway Bill receiving the Royal Assent on 8th July, 1881 to construct a 10 mile 7 chain line from Worgret, west of Wareham to Swanage. Work on construction commenced in June 1883 and was completed early in May 1885 and, following inspection, was open to traffic on 20th May with a service of five trains daily running from Wareham station. The agreement between the Swanage company and the LSWR was that, for a year after the line's completion, the LSWR should work and maintain it as part of its main system, with an option to purchase it if so desired. In August 1885 the Swanage company asked the LSWR if the latter would be willing to purchase the line and its liabilities of £2,914, this resulting in the branch being acquired by Act of Parliament of 25th June, 1886.

Originally it had been planned to lay a third set of rails between Worgret and Wareham allowing the branch trains independent access to Wareham station. However, a conventional junction was installed at Worgret, the branch trains travelling 1 m. 74 ch. over the main line to and from Wareham. The decision to lay the junction was taken in December 1884 and approval also given to lay additional sidings at Wareham station.

The original Southampton & Dorchester Railway station at Wareham stood on the east side of the level crossing and followed the general pattern of many stations on the line with a vaguely Tudor-style station house and office on the down platform, with a simple waiting shelter with an arched front on the up side. Indeed the accommodation was barely suitable for the previous traffic of the district. A letter from the Civil Engineer Mr Jacomb to the Operating Committee on 11th May, 1885 called attention to Major Marindin's report of inspection of the Swanage Railway and his requirements for improvements at Wareham station in conjunction with the working of the branch. It was decided that plans for a new station be prepared. These plans were completed by October 1885, two were submitted, plan A cost £2,266 and plan B £1,755, it being recommended that plan A be carried out.

Work on the new structure, situated to the west side of the level crossing, did not commence until late 1886. Consisting of two main platforms and two bay platforms, one each side for Swanage trains, the main building on the down side was built in a elaborate Flemish/Queen Anne style similar to that used at other LSWR locations during that period, but more decorative than most, including fine stone window surrounds and a carved LSWR crest in the gable. The roof was of red tiles not the slate found at most other stations, and although the up platform sported only a waiting room there was a generous canopy.

The layout was controlled by a new signal box Wareham West, situated at the west end on the up side. The original signal box situated between the end of the old down platform and the crossing gates was closed, a new ground frame, Wareham Crossing, situated between the crossing gates and the new down platform taking its place to work the gates, whilst a further ground frame, Wareham East , worked the east end of the goods yard.

To allow construction of the new station the engine shed situated on the up side of the line, used to house the engineer's locomotive, was removed. After the opening of the new station the platforms of the old station were demolished, the building remaining as the station master's house for many years. The two original crossing keepers' cottages to the west of the level crossing also remained, as did the goods yard and goods shed. The original entrance to the goods shed, which had been at right angles to the running line and reached via a wagon turntable, was altered to a conventional entrance in line with the running line and passing through the second arch at the north end of the shed, these alterations having been carried out earlier with the lengthening of the platforms of the old station which had been sanctioned in August 1882.

The original timber viaduct at Rockley, a tidal inlet of Poole Harbour west of Hamworthy Junction, was replaced in 1885; it had served well only requiring some strengthening in 1850 costing £100. However, its replacement was a protracted affair drawn out over seven years. In September 1877 the appropriate committee was instructed to prepare plans. As the new structure was to be built alongside the original to the north side, the scheme was included in the 1882 LSWR Act to divert the line for 71 chains. As this required the use of a small portion of Crown land, the Harbour Department of the Board of Trade required 10s. in compensation. A postal order for the due amount was paid in October 1883, the £6,000 project having been approved by the LSWR Board the previous month. Inspected by Major Marindin on 27th May, 1885 and brought into use on Sunday 31st, the structure consisted of seven 20 ft 6 in. spans, each pier consisting of cast-iron piles below low water level and wrought iron above, as was the superstructure which was provided with iron handrails, a distinctive feature of LSWR bridges of that period.

Although railways were very reliable the forces of nature could at times cause disruption, one example during this period being on Boxing Day Sunday 26th December, 1886 when a terrific gale and snowstorm brought chaos throughout the South of England. Damage on the Southampton & Dorchester line was substantial, the up mail train encountering difficulties between Woodsford signal box and Moreton where upon arrival the engine was found to be 'liberally covered' by telegraph wires which had been blown down. After station staff had assisted the crew in freeing the wires the train proceeded as far as Wimborne where it was detained overnight owing to a washout of the track near West Moors. The following day the bridge over the River Frome east of Wool was severely damaged by flood water and a section of the line submerged, causing suspension of traffic until the bridge (which was an original structure of 1847) had been replaced, this being completed in the space of five days.

Chapter Ten

The Great Awakening

During the 1880s the importance of Bournemouth was growing rapidly. The census of 1881 shows 15,800 persons resident in the Town – a figure that could probably be increased by some 25 per cent if hotel dwellers with permanent addresses elsewhere were taken into account. The area controlled by the Commissioners had been enlarged, but despite much about the place that was progressive there remained some hardcore reaction to the railways. Most people now accepted them as a necessity – but there was an unwillingness to allow them too near to the centre of the resort! However, those who did appreciate the value of an efficient transport system spent much time complaining, either directly to the railway company or through letters in the Press, about the inadequate facilities provided at both the East and West stations.

Back in 1878 the inhabitants of the developing Pokesdown area had petitioned the LSWR for a station without result, but the Board was willing to recognize that their facilities in Bournemouth were in need of improvement and looked at ways of enlarging the East station, together with a line linking it to the West station. But by the following year the idea had been dismissed in the short term as the company had more pressing interests at Southampton.

It is difficult to judge at this distance in time whether the LSWR simply allowed itself to be distracted by events elsewhere or if it was complacent over the needs of a quickly-expanding Borough. But whatever the answer, the Town Fathers were becoming impatient with the railway. To them it was absurd that such a large and important place should be served only by two dead-end branch lines, neither of which offered direct or speedy communication with London or any other large centres of population. It is therefore hardly surprising that any opportunity to break out of the LSWR circle was welcomed, and on 11th November, 1878 a public meeting considered the virtues of a West Moors Railway - in fact a reworking of an earlier proposal.

The revised scheme envisaged a line from a junction with the Salisbury & Dorset Railway near West Moors to a terminus in Bournemouth at a cost estimated at £60,000. The promoters thought that it could be worked jointly by the LSWR and GWR, although exactly where the latter company would have gained access was not explained, as they came no closer to it than Salisbury!

The meeting was clearly promising, for a few days later - on 16th November - it was publicly announced that a Bill would be sought for the 'Bournemouth Direct Railway'. This would begin in the parish of West Parley by a junction with the Salisbury & Dorset Railway about 40 chains from the junction of that railway with the LSWR and terminate in Bournemouth on the north side of Branksome Wood Road, 240 yards north-west of Richmond Hill.

Not everyone was impressed. There was those who apparently retained some loyalty towards the LSWR and were of the opinion that a direct line between Brockenhurst and Christchurch would serve their purpose better, for despite

159

the notion that the West Moors line would open up the district to competition
from the GWR, this could only happen if running powers were granted to that
company south of Salisbury and the LSWR were likely to contest this -
especially in the light of the operational difficulties of the single track Salisbury
& Dorset Junction! Furthermore, the route from London to Bournemouth was
even longer via Salisbury than it was by the existing lines! It is hardly surprising
that nothing more was heard of this project.

Perhaps alarmed that the people of Bournemouth were beginning to
consider alternatives, the LSWR held discussions with the Bournemouth
Commissioners in January 1879 about possible improvements to Bournemouth
East station. The Commissioners considered that there should be separate
arrival and departure platforms with a covered area, but at the same time
hopes of a direct line between East and West stations were dashed for the
immediate future.

Meanwhile to the east events were unfolding that had the potential to destroy
the LSWR's monopoly of both Southampton and Bournemouth. During the
mid-1870s plans for a Didcot, Newbury & Southampton Railway (DN&SR)
were conceived. At the time the Corporation and many citizens of Southampton
were not satisfied with the service provided by their one and only railway, the
LSWR. So with the possibility of a rival the town was prepared to offer
inducements to secure its establishment, and as early as 1876 reserved land at
what later became Queens Park for possible railway use.

In August 1879 work commenced on the construction of the northern section
of the line, an independent company with GWR support, which was to join the
LSWR near Micheldever and reach Southampton by exercising running
powers. As work progressed the DN&SR moved the site of the intended
junction southward to Winchester, although at that stage no agreement had
been reached with the LSWR about any connection. Within a month of work
commencing the business interests in Southampton, desirous both of breaking
the LSWR monopoly and obtaining a direct route to the Midlands and North,
invited the DN&SR to extend its line to the port, offering land and financial
support.

The LSWR immediately went on the defensive with plans to construct a line
from Hurstbourne (on the Basingstoke-Salisbury line) to join the Andover &
Redbridge Railway near Chilbolton, at a place subsequently called Fullerton
Junction, and double the line thence to Redbridge. It suggested to the
impoverished DN&SR that a short spur at Whitchurch would give them access
to Southampton by this route and save them the cost of building several miles
of single track across the empty downland. On the face of it this was a helpful
and sensible idea, but the GWR could sense a route of their own into the Port
and urged the minor company to reject it. Both companies were now planning
new stations in Southampton at the end of Bargate Street, but the House of
Commons Committee examining the railway Bills threw them out! The LSWR
then offered the use of a joint station at Southampton and enlargement of
Winchester station and running powers from Micheldever, these overtures
being rejected by the DN&SR. When the latter's Bill received the Royal Assent
in August 1882 it was authorized to construct 33½ miles of railway from

Burghclere which would have approached Southampton from the north and after passing through Shirley, where a station and marshalling yard was planned, would have crossed the Southampton & Dorchester line on a bridge in the confined space between Southampton West station and Southampton tunnel. The terminus would be on land below Bargate Street near the Royal Pier, where a substantial area of mudflats was to be reclaimed, a new pier constructed and a line laid for goods traffic to and from the docks, together with a solid embankment and esplanade extending from the Town Quay to Millbrook.

The matter was brought before a House of Commons Committee in April 1882 where the LSWR produced a model of the 35 acres of mudflats they proposed to transform into a handsome promenade. If required there would be slipways for yachts and boats, extensive quays, and a tidal basin where, by dredging, they would get water at all times of the tide. A station would be provided opposite Bargate Street, which would be for both goods and passengers, and a station at the pier.

Outside the embankment there would be a roadway 60 ft wide, which would be approachable from the Western Shore roads by subways and there would also be a level crossing. A road would join Blechynden Terrace in one direction and West Park Road in the other with a bridge over the line dispensing with the level crossing at Blechynden station, and a large portion of the reclaimed land would be formed into ornamental ground.

Despite the LSWR's impressive plan the Didcot Newbury & Southampton Bill passed through Parliament. Unfortunately, owing to financial restraints the Southampton section and other proposed extensions were abandoned, the completed line joining the LSWR at Shawford Junction, west of Winchester. Originally planned to approach Southampton through the suburb of Shirley, Didcot Road, Newbury Road and Stratton Road (originally named Station Road) are the only tangible reminders of a railway that never was. The proposed site for the station became St James Park, and that for the marshalling yard became 'The Dell', for many years the home of Southampton football club. Between the Dell and Commercial Road there is still a section of unused embankment, whilst the mudflats remained for many years until the construction of the Pirelli factory, Mayflower Park and the Western Docks. One can only speculate as to what the outcome would have eventually been had either the Didcot or LSWR schemes proceeded!

Further west at Bournemouth there was frustration at the lack of improvements by the LSWR. Discussions between influential townspeople and the LSWR Board combined with threats of GWR intrusion brought results, and in June 1882 LSWR engineers surveyed a direct route between Brockenhurst and Christchurch, the results of which were available on 22nd July. The haste for this was the DN&SR Bill, which would receive the Royal Assent on 10th August allowing the construction of a line to Southampton.

Despite the recent burst of activity by the LSWR, the Bournemouth Commissioners were still seeking alternatives. Having approached the GWR enquiring if they were prepared to provide a direct link to Bournemouth from the Didcot line, the GWR referred them to the Didcot company. So, on 9th

The plans of the Didcot, Newbury & Southampton Railway in 1882 included a line crossing the LSWR west of Southampton West station on a bridge before proceeding across reclaimed mudflats near Western Shore Road to an independent station with a further line proceeding towards Royal Pier.

August, 1882, they communicated with the Didcot Board to ask them if they would extend their line from Southampton to Bournemouth. At the stroke of a pen Bournemouth had entered the arena of railway politics and commenced the dangerous game of playing one company against the other, a situation that was to create much controversy in the next year. In addition other schemes were being canvassed in the local press.

On Thursday 2nd November, 1882 the committee recently appointed at a public meeting of inhabitants for promoting the extension of the Didcot, Newbury & Southampton Railway to Bournemouth, held a meeting where it was stated that a survey was being carried out of the district and that the proposed line would be some eight to ten miles shorter than the existing route. It was also intended to extend the line form Bournemouth to Poole, where a commodious station and waterside premises would be erected.

A Council meeting at Poole revealed that the Railway Committee had interviewed the solicitor of the Didcot company who submitted a scheme for a new railway extending from the authorized line at Shirley to Bournemouth with running powers over the LSWR company's line to the present Poole station. The solicitor also intimated that should the company be successful in obtaining a Bill, they would subsequently apply for powers to construct an independent station at Poole.

In generalPoole Council were in agreement with the proposals, although there was dissension from one councillor who thought that having just approached the LSWR for improvements to the station, they should play into the hands of another company. To this the Mayor replied, 'The Bournemouth Commissioners did the same thing', adding that anything in the way of competition would be favourable to the town.

The Didcot company planned its line to cross the New Forest via Lyndhurst and Burley, and approach Bournemouth through Dean Park where the station would be situated. It was to cross the valley on a high viaduct before curving westward to join the Poole-Bournemouth railway, over which running powers would be sought to reach Poole.

Wishing to strengthen its existing operation against attack, the LSWR took over the Poole & Bournemouth company on 31st October, 1882 and then hastily revised its existing plans. Apart from the new line between Brockenhurst and Christchurch, the existing railway between Christchurch and Bournemouth would be doubled, the original Bournemouth East station would become part of an enlarged goods yard, the main line passing under Holdenhurst Road to a new Bournemouth East station. From this point a new line would then proceed to Bourne Valley before curving south on a high viaduct to join the Poole-Bournemouth line on its approach to Bournemouth West station. A new Central station was proposed to be sited just short of Branksome Wood Road (now named St Stephens Road); this would be a terminus with curves leading to both east and west.

Immediately there was a clash of factions as various influential residents supported either the Didcot or LSWR schemes. And there was the brittle subject of having railways in the town at all, especially the placing of a station in Branksome Wood Road which raised further arguments despite the intention

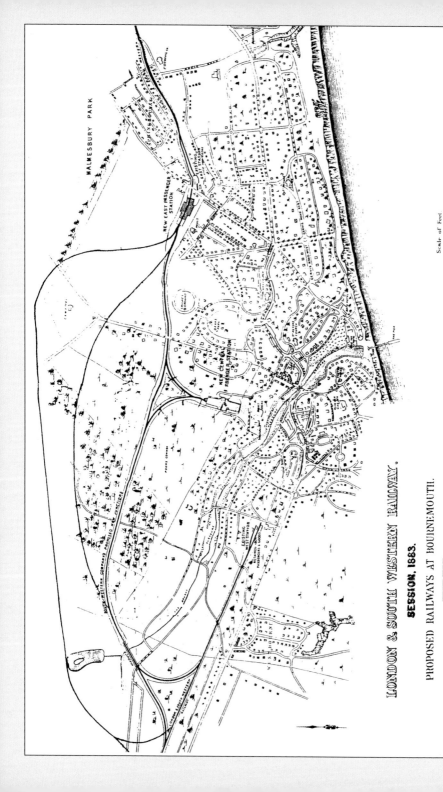

LONDON & SOUTH WESTERN RAILWAY.

SESSION, 1883.

PROPOSED RAILWAYS AT BOURNEMOUTH.

Scale of Feet

The outline map for the extension railway at Bournemouth to connect both the East and West stations as shown on the plans submitted by the LSWR for the 1883 session of Parliament. Of the three routes the centre one running just south of Bournemouth Cemetery was passed.

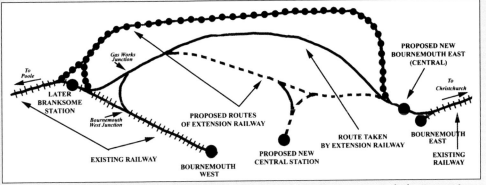

General outline plans of the proposed railways for Bournemouth to connect both the East and West stations put forward by the LSWR in the 1883 session of Parliament. Of the three routes the centre one running just south of Bournemouth Cemetery was passed by Parliament.

The principal railways in West Hampshire and district in 1893. The dotted line shows the proposed extensions of the Didcot, Newbury & Southampton Railway to Southampton and Bournemouth around 1882. The threat of these incursions caused the LSWR to focus its attention on improvements in the Bournemouth area. Had the DNSR plans proceeded the railway history of the area could well have been very different.

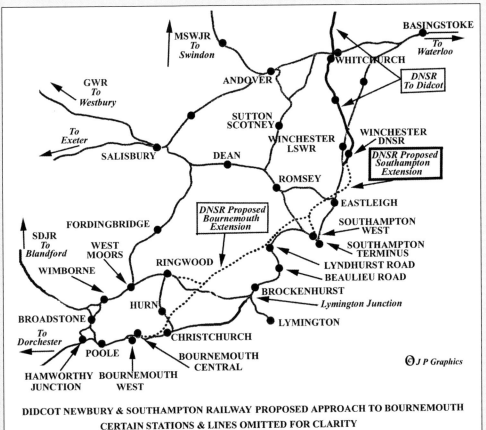

DIDCOT NEWBURY & SOUTHAMPTON RAILWAY PROPOSED APPROACH TO BOURNEMOUTH

CERTAIN STATIONS & LINES OMITTED FOR CLARITY

that it would be masked from view. The preamble of the LSWR 1883 Act described it thus:

A new central station for passenger traffic only, it is proposed to be constructed in the open space by the Poors Common (now a natural dell) and well set back from the Branksome Wood Road. The offices will be at the southern end of the station, thus shutting out the view of the railway. The station will be designed with every regard to the comfort of visitors and residents, ample shelter being provided; and carriages will drive under cover to the departure and arrival platforms, so that passengers may pass between the trains and their carriages under complete protection from weather. There will be an entrance at the front from Branksome Wood Road leading to the terrace, which will be roofed over, and from thence there is access to the departure and arrival sides of the station.

The building will be designed with due regard to architectural effect, and have the appearance rather of a winter garden than a railway station. The front of the building will be two hundred feet from the Branksome Wood Road, and that space being used for ornamental purposes; the grounds adjoining the station would become a source of attraction to residents and visitors.

Having taken over the Poole & Bournemouth company the L&SWR was looking towards a line joining the two stations that would have taken the route of the present Wessex Way, which involved building a railway through one of the most select parts of the town, this being agreed on 12th October, 1882. However, this caused objections from the Bournemouth Commissioners and many residents. There would appear to have been two sets of values applied at this

A contemporary drawing of the 1883 proposed Central Station in Branksome Wood Road for the LSWR; designed in the Gothic Revival style so popular with the Victorians.

Courtesy Lawrence Popplewell

point, as when the Didcot company had proposed a station sited near Horseshoe Common (just off Old Christchurch Road) which the Commissioners had been assured was a vital part of the whole project, they had readily agreed to it!

Various meetings were held in January and February 1883 demanding that the new station be sited to the north of the town beyond the cemetery and past the existing limit of building. It was made quite clear to the LSWR that the town would not be dictated to using the threat of support to any Didcot scheme as a defence. With the LSWR on the defensive the inhabitants of Bournemouth were using the Didcot company as their trump card to obtain the best options, however, the LSWR could not delay for too long. Poole, which in their opinion had never been served well by the LSWR, suggested to them that they were prepared to support any scheme that Poole would benefit from!

Whilst the various options were being discussed the circumstances of the Didcot company had changed. The construction of the original line was becoming a protracted affair, only the northern section between Didcot and Newbury having been completed. Capital became difficult to raise and construction had not yet commenced on the southern section, added to which relationships with the GWR were not so close as the Didcot Board had imagined. There was widespread opposition to the route of the Bournemouth extension through the New Forest, including that from the all powerful Commissioners of Woods & Forests, and perhaps not obtaining the amount of support required at Bournemouth, the Didcot company decided on 6th February, 1883 not to proceed with the Bournemouth extension in the present Parliamentary session.

The Didcot company was not alone in its desire to reach Southampton, the shadow of the once-attempted Manchester & Southampton scheme still existed in a quest to obtain a direct route northwards from the port. In 1873 the Swindon, Marlborough & Andover Railway (SM&AR) obtained powers to construct a line, which would join the LSWR Basingstoke-Salisbury line with a junction at Abbots Ann, west of Andover. Following construction services commenced running between Swindon and Andover Junction on 5th February, 1883. The northern section of the line commenced construction under the name of the Swindon & Cheltenham Extension Railway, the two companies amalgamating in August 1884 to form the Midland & South Western Junction Railway (M&SWJR). Eventually after many difficulties the line opened to through traffic in August 1891.

Albeit not a first class route there was now a direct line northwards with access to the GWR at Swindon and both the GWR and Midland Railway at Cheltenham. Under its 1883 Act the M&SWJR had obtained running powers over the LSWR between Andover Junction and Southampton Docks (Terminus) via the Andover & Redbridge Railway.

In 1881 the Swindon, Marlborough & Andover Railway promoted its Isle of Wight Extension Railway, receiving the Royal Assent on 10th August, 1882, there were plans to construct a westward-facing curve at Redbridge and a 12 mile 49 chain branch from Totton down the south shore of Southampton Water to Stone Point on the shore at Stonewood Bay, opposite Cowes. This part was a separate undertaking of the SM&AR called 'The Southern Section'.

Discussions with the LSWR over the proposed line were not encouraging, the latter requiring a sizable proportion of the revenue to carry the local traffic and have a great degree of control over the line. The SM&AR obtained a further Act in 1883 authorizing the construction of a 470 yds-long deep-water pier at Stone Point. No capital was raised or construction commenced on the Stone Point Railway; by this time the financial affairs of the parent company were in a perilous state followed by bankruptcy. In December 1885 a Prospectus was circulated to form the South Hampshire Extension Railway and Pier, there were also plans for a hotel at Stone Point and it was anticipated that ships would call at the pier. However, other routes to the Isle of Wight were well established and the commercial prospects of additional facilities were over-stated; despite the South Hampshire Railway and Pier Act being obtained in June 1886 no development took place and a further Act five years later abandoned the scheme.

Around the same period a further scheme to promote an independent line in the Bournemouth area arose when in November 1884 Parliamentary notices appeared for Christchurch Harbour Improvements, and the Wimborne & Christchurch Railway. These were ambitious plans for a railway joining the Somerset & Dorset line near Corfe Mullen then passing over the Southampton & Dorchester Railway east of Wimborne station before proceeding towards Christchurch and passing over the Ringwood-Bournemouth East branch between the present Pokesdown station and Christchurch.

At this point two spurs would link the new line to the existing line in both directions. Upon reaching the south side of Christchurch a branch to Christchurch Harbour and along its south bank to Hengistbury Head was planned. The harbour would have been enlarged and a large dock constructed at Longfield, Hengistbury Head, the harbour entrance being protected by 1,000 yds-long breakwaters, the complete railway being 12 miles 1 furlong 75 chains in length.

What particular shipping interest would have used these docks was never explained and despite hopes of gaining running powers over the Somerset & Dorset and the LSWR, there appears to have been no direct benefit to Bournemouth. The scheme faded away and proved to be the last attempt to usurp the monopoly of the LSWR in the Bournemouth area.

Returning to the affairs at Bournemouth the LSWR, fearing a future revival of the Didcot scheme, or indeed, any other, was determined to press ahead with the direct line and a connecting line between the two stations. When the Bill began its passage through Parliament on 1st February, 1883 the siting of the new central station and the route of the connecting line were still the main points of disagreement with the Bournemouth Commissioners and were the subject of a number of meetings in the town.

The LSWR had clearly underestimated the power and influence of the Bournemouth residents who were not prepared to have their town desecrated or devalued by the railway. It was made quite clear to the LSWR that they did not wish to have a central station in Branksome Wood Road with all the detriment it would cause to the surrounding area, but they agreed to a new station in the brickfield to the west side of Holdenhurst Road adjacent to the existing East station. So Bournemouth lost its chance of a central station, leaving

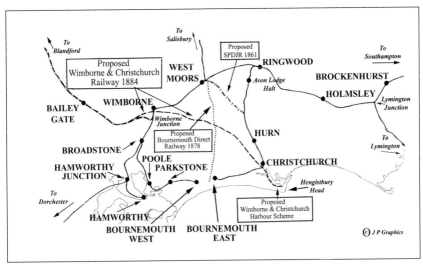

Outline map of three proposed developments between 1861 and 1884 affecting the Bournemouth area: the Salisbury, Poole & Dorset Junction Railway of 1861, the Bournemouth Direct Railway of 1878, an extension of the Salisbury & Dorset Junction Railway, and the Wimborne & Christchurch Railway and Harbour Scheme of 1884.

present day railusers with a goodly walk to the shops and the sea front.

No doubt in fear that time was running out if the Bill did not obtain its second reading it would be rejected in that Parliamentary session, on 14th March, 1883 Archibald Scott the LSWR General Manager in a letter to the Bournemouth Commissioners agreed to the site of the new station as requested, although the LSWR still disagreed as to the route of the connecting line. This resulted in a further meeting in the town attended by 700 people followed by discussions with the LSWR. The townspeople demanded the line pass to the north of the cemetery at a point beyond what was marked as land for future development. In a town where status and property value was of particular concern the railway had to be discreet!

Finally on 4th April agreement was reached by all but a few of the parties involved when the route was decided. It did not pass to the north of the cemetery but skirted it 80 yards to the south in a short 69 yds-long tunnel under the Wimborne Road, then continued at about 200 yds from the northern edge of Poor's Common (the present Meyrick Park) past Decoy Pond then south of the gasworks before turning south over a viaduct to join the Poole-Bournemouth West line. At last sense had prevailed and Bournemouth was about to obtain the railway accommodation it deserved. However, having appeased the inhabitants of Bournemouth, early in August the residents of Hordle petitioned the company requesting that the new station to be constructed at Sway should be situated at Vags Lane, a suggestion that was declined.

The Bournemouth Direct Railway Act received the Royal Assent on 20th August, 1883. In reality the Act covered four schemes in the Bournemouth area:

1. The Bournemouth Direct Railway, Lymington Junction-Christchurch with upgrading of the existing line between Christchurch and Bournemouth East.
2. The Bournemouth Extension Railway between Bournemouth East and Bournemouth West..
3. The Corfe Mullen-Poole Junction (Broadstone) cut-off.
4. The West Moors Junction Railway.

The latter scheme was for a 2 furlong 8.7 chain curve off the Salisbury & Dorset Junction Railway at West Moors, curving east to join the Southampton & Dorchester Railway, allowing direct running towards Ringwood; this curve was never constructed.

The Corfe Mullen-Broadstone cut-off constructed, by Messrs H. Lovett of Wolverhampton, was officially known as the Poole & Bournemouth Junction Railway. Although only 2¾ miles long, it ended the need for all Somerset & Dorset trains to reverse at Wimborne and the occupation of the 2½ mile section of the Southampton & Dorchester line between Wimborne and New Poole Junction (Broadstone), which at that time carried all the traffic to and from Bournemouth West, Dorchester and Weymouth.

The Board of Trade sanctioned its opening for passenger traffic in November 1885 (also quoted as 14th December, 1885). However, according to the working timetable only one goods train per day in each direction used the line until the following year when four fast passenger trains each day used the facility after its official opening to passenger traffic on 1st November, 1886. Although earthworks had been provided for double track only a single line of rails was ever laid.

POOLE & BOURNEMOUTH JUNCTION RAILWAY.

DIRECT ROUTE

TO BOURNEMOUTH.

This Line will be OPENED for Passenger Traffic on
NOVEMBER 1st, *and several of the Trains between Bourne-mouth and Bath, the Midland Counties, and North of England and vice versa will be accelerated.*

Advertisement for the opening of the Corfe Mullen cut-off displayed in the public timetable for November 1886.

Chapter Eleven

The Direct Line and Improvements in the Bournemouth Area

The contract for the Direct Line's construction was awarded to Messrs Kellett & Bentley. The *Bournemouth Visitors Directory* for 24th November, 1883 reported that 'The ceremony of cutting the first sod of the new Bournemouth Direct Railway has been delayed for a short time'. However, work commenced in August 1884, but they soon became aware of the difficulties of the project and progress was extremely slow and by October little had been achieved. Despite meetings between the LSWR and the contractors little progress was made during the next year including problems with the foundations of the bridge over the River Stour at Christchurch. At the beginning of July 1885 the contractors failed, bringing misery to the navvies at Christchurch who starved until the vicar and missionaries raised money to feed them.

Work recommenced on 20th July with a more reputable contractor, Joseph Fairbank, who was well acquainted with major projects. Unfortunately, on 29th June, 1886 Joseph Firbank died aged 67, the contract being continued by his son Joseph T. Firbank. In the following May, Jacomb the LSWR Engineer also died, the work being placed under the supervision of W.H. Galbraith a consulting engineer to the company.

Although the plans for the station buildings along the line were completed by December 1885, and in January 1886 plans for alterations, additional lines and a new station at Christchurch were approved, along the route of the new line many serious difficulties had to be overcome. There had been geological problems with the original Southampton & Dorchester line in the New Forest area, these were to prove even more difficult on the new line. Preliminary borings that had shown gravel and sand were misleading, as it was discovered sections of the work passed through beds of Barton clay and marl which under wet conditions could rapidly become slippery and prone to movement to a treacherous degree. There was the difficulty that the works were at right angles to the natural drainage courses of the New Forest as water tables and streams moved towards the sea.

Situated to the west of Sway station was Sway embankment, over half a mile long and 60 ft high, the construction of which had caused problems for the previous contractor. The nature of the clay when tipped was so slippery that the profile of the embankment had to be modified to make it stable. This meant the embankment being built up in tiers resulting in the base of the embankment, which should have been 200 ft wide, being extended out to 400 ft in places. Even with a larger area to distribute the weight slips still took place and stone-filled trenches were inserted to assist drainage.

Despite all these difficulties the *Salisbury & Winchester Journal* for 12th June, 1886 gave an optimistic account of the proceedings, stating:

> Great progress has been made at the Sway end of the line, in spite of difficulties that had to be contended with through the remarkably wet winter and spring, which caused immense slips in the cuttings. Thanks to the energy and ability displayed by Mr Charles

Right: Joseph Fairbank the contractor who undertook the construction of the Bournemouth Direct Railway. Destined not to live to see the difficult work completed, he passed away on 29th June, 1886 aged 67 years.   *Author's Collection*

Below: BR Standard No. 76063 breasts the summit of Sway bank with an up local train. The cuttings and embankments on this section caused many problems during construction, note the twin-arched bridge in the background a feature of the Direct Line. On the horizon to the left is Sway tower, a Victorian folly.   *J. Read*

Young, these difficulties were successfully overcome, and the bridges from Latchmoor to Sway are so far completed that the laying of the permanent way has begun. On Tuesday morning an event of some importance to the inhabitants of Sway and neighbourhood occurred, when Mr James Kidgell of Pilley, laid the first brick of the handsome new station which the LSWR Company are erecting, and which is being pushed forward with all dispatch.

In the late spring of 1887 when the works were almost completed and it was anticipated that the line would shortly be opened, the treacherous clay gave further problems. Heavy rain caused saturation resulting in some cuttings being flooded to a depth of several feet, the force of the water destroying the wings of two brick bridges. A number of cuttings experienced drainage problems, which resulted in the movement of soil causing weeks of work to be undone within hours as embankments and cuttings slipped away. An estimated 130,000 tons of chalk and 16,000 tons of stone had to be added to assist stability and drainage.

The *South Western Gazette* reporting the problem stated,

In a few hours, sides of cuttings, with slopes of three to one, and which were regarded as finished, slipped - in one case for nearly one hundred yards - and levels have had to be altered and heavy trenches of chalk put in to allow a free drainage.

It was stated that there were more problems for the LSWR engineers than Chat Moss had for George Stephenson!

There were also problems with the construction of the bridge over the River Avon on the approach to Christchurch. After digging through 10 feet of sand piles had to be driven a further 15 feet before a solid base could be established. The bridge itself, 300 ft-long, consisted of five iron spans, three 60 ft long and two 40 ft in length. Further problems arose following heavy rain and flooding in the water meadows which formed a flood plain either side of the bridge. After a three month delay the 2½ miles of embankment were constructed requiring a further 600,000 cubic yards of material.

Whilst the Direct Line was under construction other parts of the scheme were proceeding. The most impressive project was the construction of the new Bournemouth East station (later Bournemouth Central). As agreed with the Bournemouth Commissioners it was built in a hollow and as promised with the original Branksome Wood Road plan it was disguised to look like a Winter Garden. Designed by William Jacomb the LSWR Civil Engineer and constructed by Messrs Perry & Company of Bow, it eventually cost £50,000. Construction commenced in April 1884.

To reach the site of the new station, the extension of the existing railway had to curve away and run along the back of the existing Bournemouth East station buildings, at the same time dropping down a gradient to pass under Holdenhurst Road in a 48 yard twin-bore tunnel. Here a compromise had been reached, the road being raised several feet to obtain the correct levels. This also involved the removal of the three-road engine shed and turntable as these were sited on the new alignment. To facilate the servicing of engines whilst these alterations were taking place a temporary two-road shed was erected to the east of the original structure.

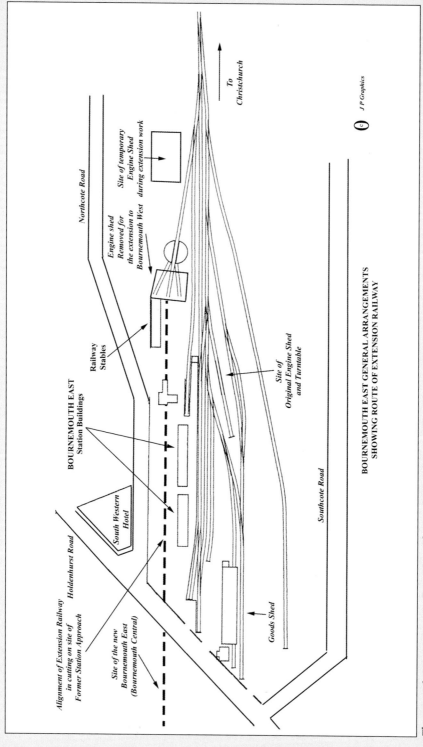

The general arrangements at Bournemouth East during the mid-1880s showing the alignment of the new line in a cutting to pass under Holdenhurst Road to the new station.

Within the figure:

To Christchurch

J P Graphics

Site of temporary Engine Shed during extension work

Northcote Road

Engine shed Removed for the extension to Bournemouth West

Railway Stables

BOURNEMOUTH EAST
Station Buildings

Site of Original Engine Shed and Turntable

South Western Hotel

Southcote Road

Goods Shed

Alignment of Extension Railway in cutting on site of Former Station Approach

Holdenhurst Road

Site of the new Bournemouth East (Bournemouth Central)

BOURNEMOUTH EAST GENERAL ARRANGEMENTS
SHOWING ROUTE OF EXTENSION RAILWAY

The alterations required to extend the line from Bournemouth East to Bournemouth Central are clearly shown. Adams 'T6' class 4-4-0 No. 684 climbs the 1/150 from Bournemouth Central over the site of the original Bournemouth East engine shed. The higher level to the far left was the site of the passenger station which in its final days backed onto the cutting formed to pass the line under Holdenhurst Road which can be seen in the distance. No. 684 built in March 1896 was withdrawn in April 1940 having travelled a recorded 1,397,151 miles.   *Author's Collection*

Apart from sections of the goods shed very little of the former Bournemouth East station survived the construction of the new line. The stables standing in the passenger station approach survived and in later years served as the motor lorry repair depot. Viewed from the goods yard the cutting of the new line is between the photographer and the stables.   *K. Hastie*

Bournemouth Central goods depot, the two bays to the left are the original buildings of Bournemouth Goods shed, the third bay on the right was added following the closure of Bournemouth East station with the extension of the line to Bournemouth Central.

Lawrence Popplewell

This Ordnance Survey map shows the rapid development of the Holdenhurst Road area in the later years of the 19th century. The present Bournemouth Central is marked as Bournemouth East, whilst the former Bournemouth East is shown as a goods yard to the right.

Reproduced from the 1897 Ordnance Survey Map

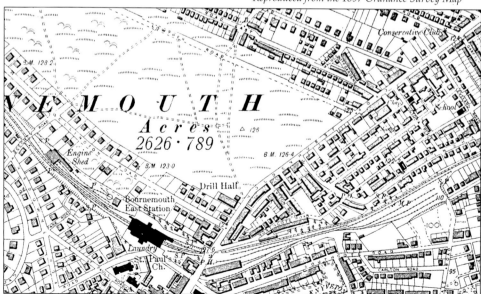

Preliminary work taking place in late 1884 on the site for the new Bournemouth East station (Bournemouth Central), clearly showing one of Messrs Mowlem's steam excavators behind which on a higher level are two contractors' saddle tank locomotives and wagons. In the background is St Paul's church in its original form with a steeple and short nave, the building to the right of the church was a steam laundry.   *Bournemouth Library Collection*

The west end of Bournemouth Central station viewed from the tower of St Paul's church in 1888. At the time only the original engine shed seen on the top right had been constructed, in the foreground is the laundry and other development was only beginning to spread to this area, then the northern extent of the town.   *J. Boudreau Collection*

Bournemouth Central viewed from the east end just after the turn of the century clearly showing the massive structure of the station. Note the workmen on the track, their white shirts the Edwardian answer to the high visibility vest. A close look at the engine reveals that the driver has climbed into the frames to 'oil up' before departure of this up train. The engine is No. 715 a Drummond 'T9' class 4-4-0 was built in June 1899 and finally withdrawn from service in July 1961 and like the station a tribute to solid Victorian engineering.   *Bournemouth Library Collection*

Passengers wait the arrival of an up train under the magnificent span roof of Bournemouth Central; luggage to be loaded and spare stock standing on the centre sidings add to this quintessential Edwardian railway scene.   *Author's Collection*

The exterior of the down side of Bournemouth Central station photographed prior to 1914. The elegant sidewalls that support the massive roof of this now listed building are clearly shown. The covered porte cochère for carriages was removed in later years. Today the approach road is shared with the entrance to a bus interchange and the car park of a supermarket.

Beattie 4-4-0 No. 0353 heads away from Bournemouth Central westwards at the turn of the century. To the left can be seen part of the original engine shed, and to the right Bournemouth Central West signal box, with a train occupying the original down bay platform.

Author's Collection

A view taken from the down platform of the first engine shed erected at Bournemouth Central in May 1902. It is reputed that much of the material used in its construction was recycled from the shed at Bournemouth East, whatever the facts of the matter the building would fail miserably in a design contest. In the foreground Beattie '348' class 4-4-0 No. 0353 having been rebuilt in April 1890 with an Adams boiler and cab.   *Author's Collection*

The original engine shed at Bournemouth Central viewed from the turntable area. Although replaced by a new structure to the west end of the yard, the building remained standing until the early 1920s.   *Author's Collection*

The new station was impressive, although no particular style of architecture was copied; it was 'built in the grand style' yet functional and served well. Of brick construction, the glazed roof 350 ft long and 95 ft wide was carried 40 ft above on massive iron girders each weighing 17½ tons. The two main platforms were 25 ft wide, the down platform being 770 ft long (one of the longest in the country). On the up side there was a covered carriage dock siding, the platform section being approached from the main platform through semi-circular brick arches. An open horse dock siding was placed behind the London end of the down platform, access between platforms being provided by means of a subway. Substantial office and other accommodation was provided on both up and down sides, there also being covered carriage arrangements at the entrances.

Between the up and down platform roads there was an up through line and a down siding, the entire station being controlled from two signal boxes, East box at the London end with 22 working levers, and West box at the Branksome end with 31 working levers, both situated on the down side. Opened without ceremony on Monday 20th July, 1885 the new station could not be worked to its full potential, the line to Christchurch was still single and the new 3 mile 64 chain line westwards towards Bournemouth West was far from complete. Indeed, for a short period the new station was without a doubt the most ostentatious branch terminus in the country!

Having built a first class station the LSWR authorities were less disposed to invest in improved locomotive facilities. For the opening of the new station it would appear that the former three-road shed from the old Bournemouth East, or at least parts of it, was re-erected and served by a new 50 ft turntable supplied by Eastwood Swingler, these arrangements being placed behind the up platform at the south end of the site.

There was clearly a requirement for better facilities; those at Bournemouth West, where the locomotive superintendent was pressing for a new shed during 1886, were even more primitive. The matter was continually postponed until May 1887 when it was recommended that the new shed be constructed at Bournemouth East (Bournemouth Central), a decision that was to burden Bournemouth with cramped facilities for the next 79 years!

The proposals were for a brick-built four-road straight shed, one holding eight engines at an estimated cost of £6,419 and one for 16 engines £8,531, the cheaper option being chosen. The need to save costs was reflected in June 1887 when revised estimates were brought in; the dropping pit was reduced from 510 ft to 300 ft, and at first the lifting shed was cancelled, although quickly reinstated whilst a cover for the coal stage and a dormitory for the enginemen were not proceeded with. In January 1888, again to save expense, it was recommended that the engine hoist for the lifting shed be constructed at Nine Elms works. However, despite these difficulties the new facilities were completed by early summer.

The reconstruction and doubling of the existing 3 mile 40 chain single line between Christchurch and Bournemouth East had been awarded to Messrs Mowlem of Westminster. All the original cast-iron bridges were replaced by double width ones of wrought iron, and the three-span viaduct over the River

The original level crossing near St Clement's church on the Ringwood, Christchurch & Bournemouth Railway between Boscombe and Bournemouth East. The upgrading of this section of line with the construction of the Bournemouth Direct Railway meant that the track was lowered into a cutting and Cleveland Road bridge was constructed at this point.   *Bournemouth Library Collection*

Drummond 'L11' class 4-4-0 No. 170 with an up train of mixed stock heads under the footbridge at the end of Palmerston Road, Boscombe. In the background can be seen Cleveland Road bridge with the line in the cutting following the Direct Railway improvements. No. 170 was constructed in August 1904 and withdrawn in June 1952. In recent years the property on the right has been redeveloped.   *Mike Morant Collection*

Stour was reconstructed under a separate contract by Messrs Firbank, the new wrought-iron lattice spans being carried on brick abutments and piers. Again, as with the Avon viaduct, difficulties were encountered with the foundations.

Between Boscombe and Bournemouth there had been three level crossings, these were replaced by overbridges, resulting in the line being lowered into cuttings, at one point to a depth of 33 ft. The entire work required the removal of 160,000 cubic yards of material. Despite the upheaval caused during these works the train service continued, albeit subject to severe speed restrictions at various times throughout the Christchurch-Bournemouth section.

Construction also commenced on the long-awaited station at Boscombe (Pokesdown) at the end of January 1885. It was a station of unusual design, consisting of a 350 ft-long 30 ft-wide island platform reached by a flight of steps from an overbridge at the east end. The station offices, waiting room and signal box, all of timber construction, were situated on the platform, there were no crossovers and the signal box only contained six working signal levers. The completed station opened on 1st July, 1886 on the same day as double track working was introduced between Christchurch and Bournemouth East. A new station at Christchurch situated to the west of the junction with the new direct line replaced the original buildings on the curve of the branch leading to Ringwood. The new structure of brick construction was of the style of the others on the direct line, it also included a covered footbridge. A new signal box of considerable height to give a view over the top of the nearby Barrack Road Bridge was equipped with a 39-lever frame, seven of which were spare. There was also an East ground frame containing five levers and a West ground frame of six levers.

Mowlem's were also responsible for the construction of the new line between Bournemouth East and Bournemouth West Junction. During the summer of 1884 a steam excavator was working in the cutting at Talbot Woods; although small contractors locomotives had been in use on most contracts for many years, the steam excavator was a recent innovation. A great saver of time and manpower, it was reported that during a 10 hour working day a 'steam Navvy' could move 1,000 cubic yards filling 240 wagons and required 30 men. Previously, to excavate 600 cubic yards a day required 100 men. Steam excavators had also been employed on the site of the new Bournemouth East station. Unfortunately on the Lymington Junction-Christchurch section the waterlogged state of the ground had made working with excavators difficult.

The Direct Line, improvements between Christchurch and Bournemouth East and the new line to Bournemouth West would not have achieved their full potential without the upgrading of the Broadstone-Bournemouth West section, a line that had seen little improvement since opening. The doubling of 3 miles 36 chains of line between Poole Junction (Broadstone) and Poole station was completed at the end of June 1884. Following inspection by Colonel Rich of the Board of Trade, the new line had its connections made on the night of Monday 30th June and the first train to travel over the new double line on the Tuesday morning was the 7.20 am from Wimborne.

The doubling of the section between Poole station and Bournemouth West was a protracted affair. It involved additional earthworks including the widening of several bridges, a new occupation bridge at Whitecliff and a new

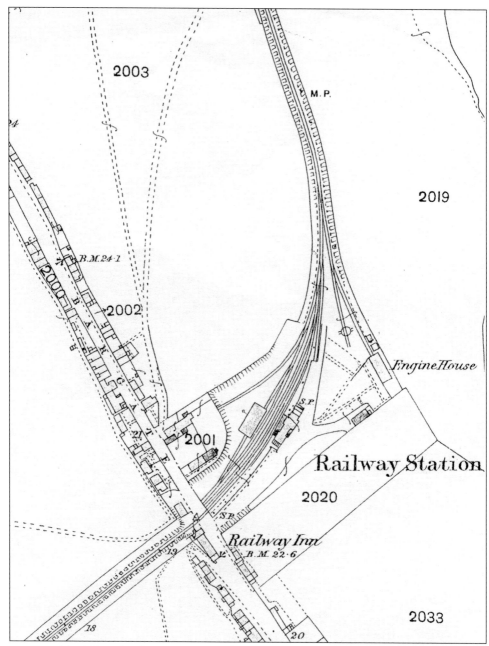

The original Christchurch Railway station, the line to Ringwood running to the top of the map, with the extension towards Bournemouth East to the left. Note the limited development of the period along Barrack Road and Bargate. *Reproduced from the 1874 Ordnance Survey Map*

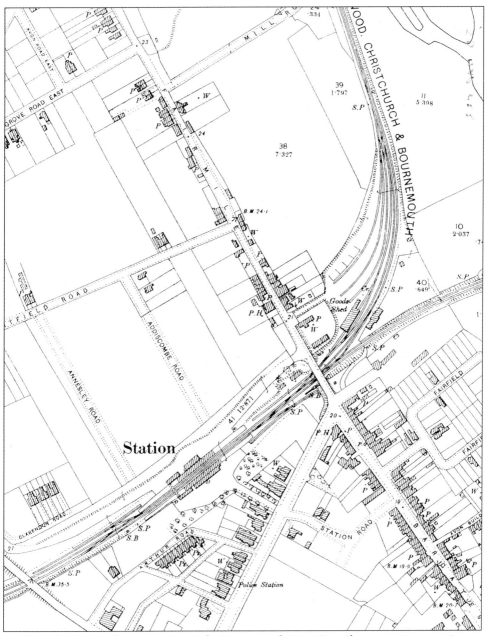

Christchurch after the construction of the Bournemouth Direct line. The new station occupies the lower part of the map with the new line to Brockenhurst curving away to the centre right, with the original Christchurch station and branch to Ringwood leading away to the top of the map.   *Reproduced from the 1889 Ordnance Survey Map*

The exterior of the original Pokesdown station consisted of an entrance door in the wall and a flight of stairs down to platform level. The pre-1914 street scene is full of social history, in the foreground a delivery cart of the Reliance Laundry, whilst in the background is the New Era Laundry, and within half a mile was the Fenton Laundry, just three of a number that served the citizens of Bournemouth.   *K. Hastie Collection*

The original Pokesdown station looking towards Christchurch, a simple island platform structure with buildings and signal box of timber construction. A flight of steps led up to Christchurch Road under which the railway passed in a twin-arched bridge.
                                                                                        Author's Collection

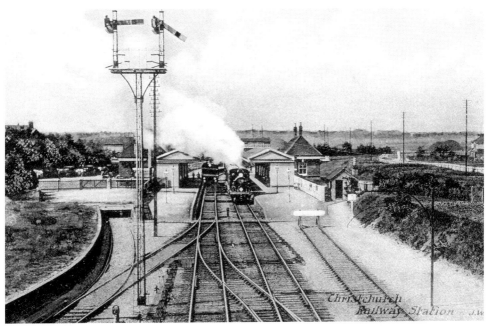

Christchurch new station has a rural air about it looking towards Bournemouth in this pre-1914 view. Standing in the down platform is a steam railmotor, whilst a train on the up line has the signal clear for the Hurn-Ringwood line.
Author's Collection

Staff at Christchurch pose for the camera *circa* 1900. They were of a generation that were proud of their employment on the railway. It was a job for life and there was promotion for those who gained the necessary knowledge, there being many railway families of at least three generations.
G.A. Pryer Collection

A view taken in late 1884 showing construction of the viaduct across the head of the Bourne Valley forming the future Branksome-Gas Works Junction spur making the direct connection between Bournemouth and Poole. The spoil for the embankments is being brought by the contractor's locomotives and tip wagons from the cutting under construction through Meyrick Park. The house surrounded by construction work is situated in Surrey Road.

Bournemouth Library Collection

A view looking north of the embankment works over the head of the Bourne Valley showing the main embankment to join the Bournemouth East extension line to the Poole-Bournemouth West line. The horse and cart tipping spoil to the left, viewed between the houses in Surrey Road, is at what later became Gas Works Junction at the commencement of the second embankment and viaduct curving round to Bournemouth West Junction. The underbridge shown on the extreme right crosses Coy Pond Road.

Bournemouth Library Collection

An unidentified Adams 4-4-2 Radial tank commences the climb towards Parkstone from Poole Harbour embankment with a Salisbury-Bournemouth West working hauling a set of 6 six-wheeled coaches with a passenger brake van at the rear. The type of stock still in use at the turn of the century on secondary and branch line services.   *Author's Collection*

Adams '460' class 4-4-0 No. 474 runs down Parkstone bank towards the Poole Park embankment with a Weymouth-bound train. The buildings in the background on the right are in the vicinity of Sandbanks Road, today one of the more affluent parts of Poole. No. 474 was constructed by Messrs Robert Stephenson & Sons in August 1884 at a cost of £3,296 and was withdrawn from service in October 1928.   *Author's Collection*

An unidentified Adams 'T1' 0-4-4 tank enters Parkstone station with an up train for Bournemouth West. In this pre-1914 view the station has fully developed complete with covered footbridge and a substantial down side shelter.   *Poole Museum Service*

Parkstone station looking towards Bournemouth, in the foreground is the footbridge of 1888. The increase of the incline to 1 in 60 at the end of the station can clearly be seen.
                                                                    Lens of Sutton Association

bridge with floodgates in the embankment across Parkstone Bay thus allowing the development of the present Poole Park.

During these works an incident took place, which in itself demonstrated how easily a locomotive could become derailed, and the subsequent inquiry also gave details of the working of the period. On 22nd July, 1886 a train off the Somerset & Dorset line had arrived at Wimborne where LSWR 4-4-0 'Metropolitan' tank No. 322 was attached to the rear to work the train forward to Bournemouth West. This was the fourth such return working the engine and crew had made that day. Departing at 1.30 pm, the engine was running bunker first and hauling six Somerset & Dorset coaches, this train proceeded to Bournemouth West. At Branksome, where points were being laid for the new line to Bournemouth East, No. 322 became derailed.

Unfortunately a 16 ft length of 2 x 2 inch timber in use as a measuring rod was left along the top of a crossing rail, which formed a ramp to the approaching train allowing the flanges to ride up over the rail causing the engine and the first three coaches to become derailed. Damage was minor, the company fined the ganger 30s. and two platelayers 15s. each, and in the conclusion to his report Major Marindin stated: 'The fact that so very small an obstacle will cause an engine to leave the rails should make permanent-way men very careful where they place their tools and implements when not actually using them'.

Major Marindin inspected both the new line between Bournemouth East and West stations and the doubling works between Poole and Bournemouth West on 28th September, 1886. The latter section opened for traffic on 25th October, 1886, although the Board of Trade requested the lengthening of the platforms at Parkstone within six months. This involved alterations to the gradient of the main line and the sidings, work which the LSWR Board approved in the December at a cost of £1,376. In late 1888 a footbridge was also added at request of the Board of Trade.

At Bournemouth West few improvements had taken place since opening in 1874. However, by the summer of 1885 traffic had developed to such a level that it imposed a severe burden on the two existing platforms. In an effort to relieve the situation minor alterations to signalling, sidings and an excursion platform had been constructed to the south side of the engine shed. Regarded as a temporary measure, it was not properly signalled and could only be used for departures; however, it proved a boom at busy weekends.

With the pending completion of the line from Bournemouth East it was clear the existing layout was entirely unsuitable, as endorsed by Major Marindin who, following a visit to the new works in September 1886, reported:

The accommodation is very inferior, the platforms being too short and only a short length of the up platform covered. The new lines are calculated to bring additional traffic to this station, and I consider the existing platforms and buildings to be quite unfit for a terminal station at a place like Bournemouth. If the Company would give an undertaking to carry out the necessary improvements within twelve months I could recommend the opening of the line. Pending the receipt of such an undertaking I must report that by reason of incompleteness of the works they cannot be opened without danger to the passengers using them.

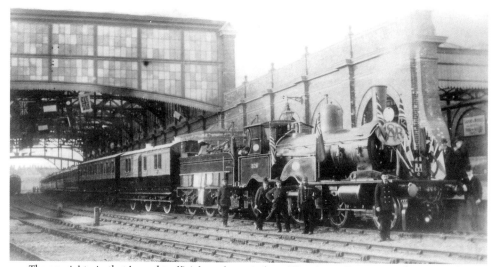

The special train that brought officials and guests from Waterloo to Bournemouth to mark the official opening of the Bournemouth Direct line on 6th March, 1888 waits to return at 4 pm headed by Adams '460' class 4-4-0 No. 526 which is suitably decorated, as is the new Bournemouth East (Bournemouth Central) station.   *Historic Model Railway Society*

An immaculate Sway station looking west with an up train from Bournemouth approaching. The action of the photographer has diverted everybody's gaze from the approaching train, whilst the baby carriage would today be a collector's item.   *Author's Collection*

Despite this situation there appeared to be no great haste in completing the required works at the West station. With the opening of the new Direct Line on 5th March, 1888 a majority of services were extended to and from the West station where the required accommodation was far from ready. A turntable and engine siding, which had been approved in the July at a cost of £550, were still being constructed in the triangle formed by the two new junctions at Branksome. It was not until February 1889 that the LSWR Board approved plans for an additional island platform for excursion traffic and certain siding alterations, the West station improvements not being completed until the summer of 1889. In July the Board of Trade reported that:

> ...the old platforms had been lengthened, the new excursion platform constructed, station buildings enlarged and lines and signals rearranged. All six platforms were signalled for both arrival and departure, controlled from a new seventy four-lever signal box.

Eventually all the difficulties with the 8½ mile Direct Line were overcome and were ready for inspection by the Board of Trade, which in February 1888 allowed its opening with a 20 mph speed restriction over Sway bank until it had been reinspected. Three new stations were provided along the line, Sway, Milton (New Milton after May 1897) and Hinton (Hinton Admiral after May 1888) all of brick construction of the latest design produced by the LSWR. The first three station masters were Messrs Gibson, Gould and Bunny respectively.

On Tuesday 6th March, 1888 a special 11-coach train hauled by '460' class 4-4-0 No. 526, suitably decorated with flags, departed from Waterloo at 9.30 am. Aboard were the Directors and officers of the LSWR, Boards of Directors of several other companies and mayors and burgesses of various boroughs. After a leisurely journey including several stops, Bournemouth East was reached at 12.30 pm. Welcomed by the Mayor of Bournemouth E.W. Rebbeck (an estate agent) the guests were taken by horse-drawn carriages for a tour of the principal parts of the town before adjourning to the Shaftesbury Hall for luncheon provided by the LSWR. Followed by the usual speeches, after which the guests returned to the station for a 4 pm departure, at last the new line was officially open.

The speed restriction over Sway bank was withdrawn on 6th June, 1889. The new line was now fully operational and the journey times of trains to Bournemouth were over the years to reduce. However, in their determination to construct the line there had been a certain amount of opposition from Sir George Meyrick, the owner of the estate at Hinton Admiral. This had been overcome by an agreement that the owner had the right to require any train to stop at Hinton Admiral station, a right that remained until recent years!

Even with the improvements being undertaken and planned to provide a direct line to both Bournemouth and Weymouth, there was still a demand for a further route to both Dorchester and Weymouth. Back in December 1883, frustrated at the poor service they claimed both the LSWR and GWR provided to Weymouth, a public meeting was called with proposals for a Mid Dorset Railway. A line forming a junction with the LSWR West of England main line at Gillingham would run south to Sturminster Newton, there forming a junction with the Somerset & Dorset Railway, then proceed via Hazelbury Bryan,

New Milton station dominated by the town's water tower photographed in April 1984. Apart from the third rail and the loss of goods facilities little had changed since opening, except for the development of shops and housing in the vicinity of the station.   *C.L. Caddy*

Hinton Admiral with a Drummond 'T9' class 4-4-0 approaching from the Bournemouth direction. Situated in the sparsely populated countryside of West Hampshire, the arrival of the railway soon encouraged urban development.   *Lens of Sutton Association*

Bournemouth West looking towards the buffer stops following the alterations connected with the Bournemouth Direct line improvements. In this pre-1914 view the rolling stock of the period and the loaded goods wagons to the left are clearly shown.   *J. Boudreau Collection*

Adams 'X2' class 4-4-0 No. 582 pulls away from Bournemouth West with a Waterloo express on the 11th July, 1902. On the right can be seen the uncovered excursion platforms with a tank engine awaiting its next duty.   *Lens of Sutton Association*

The exterior of Bournemouth West station; additions and improvements over the years brought it up to a standard required by the local population, but never on the grand scale of Bournemouth Central. *Author's Collection*

Just after the turn of the century Drummond 'T9' class 4-4-0 No. 704 approaches Bournemouth West Junction with a Bournemouth West-Waterloo express - note the third vehicle is a Pullman car. In the foreground is an LSWR 'Rat Trap' type ground signal, whilst in the background is the later site of Bournemouth West carriage sidings. *Author's Collection*

Cheselbourne and Puddletown to West Stafford where it would form a junction with the LSWR Dorchester line. It would then proceed through West Knighton, Broadmayne, Sutton Poyntz and Preston before terminating at Weymouth near Westerhall, with a branch to join the Portland branch at Portland Junction just outside the existing Weymouth station. It was intended to utilize the Portland branch and erect a station at Sandsfoot Cove with a dock complex in Portland Harbour to serve cross-Channel steamers.

It was claimed that the advantages of the line would create the shortest and quickest route between Weymouth and Dorchester to Bath, Gloucester, Birmingham, the Midland Counties and the North. It would also enable express trains to run from Weymouth to London via Gillingham and Salisbury, a distance of 138 miles in about 3¼ hours. The entire scheme covered two pages of the *Southern Times*. It was, however, flawed, in particular the West Stafford to Weymouth route was of a similar nature as the 1846 scheme of the Southampton & Dorchester, as was the planned loop to the GWR station at Weymouth, whilst the dock scheme for Portland Harbour had previously been rejected by both the LSWR and GWR. The idea of a fast route to the North via the Somerset & Dorset from Sturminster Newton was wishful thinking.

Towards the end of 1886 further proposals were put forward supported by the Weymouth and Dorchester Railway Improvement Committee, which in general had an affinity to the 1883 scheme. A railway branching off the LSWR West of England line at either Templecombe or Semley with connections to the Somerset & Dorset Railway at Sturminster Newton, to reduce journey times from Bath and the Midlands, was proposed. An independent line between Dorchester and Weymouth was also suggested, including an independent terminus at Dorchester. This would have led to the destruction of a number of properties in the Fordington district, leading to a suggestion of a junction with the Southampton & Dorchester line near Sywards Road bridge, and a terminus at Weymouth near St John's church.

Discussions continued into 1887, however, like many other proposed railways it sounded good, looked good on a map, and gave newspaper proprietors many inches of material, but in reality these lines would never give a return on capital outlay. The ongoing improvements in the Bournemouth area, nearing completion by then and the future plans for the Holes Bay curve would give Weymouth a direct route from Waterloo.

The opening of the Bournemouth Direct line had at once altered the pattern of travel in the area. The importance of the Old Road was immediately reduced, and the future of Holmsley was put into question; whereas before it had been a convenient point from which to complete a journey to Christchurch and other destinations by road this requirement had now been removed. Thus in April 1888 the General Manager suggested the station's closure; however, section five of the 1883 Bournemouth Railway Act stipulated:

The Company shall continue to maintain Holmsley station on the Southampton & Dorchester as a station for cattle, passengers and goods with all the usual accommodation for passengers and for the working of goods and cattle, until the consent in writing of William Drake Esdaile of Burley Manor, Ringwood or his heirs consent to its removal, also her Majesty's Commissioners of Woods & Forests.

Representing the Somerset & Dorset at Bournemouth West is Johnson 0-4-4 tank No. 52 resplendent in its Prussian blue livery and highly polished. The photograph was taken before No. 52 was reboilered in 1902; the locomotive was constructed in December 1884 and withdrawn from service in May 1928.   *Author's Collection*

There is no doubting the Midland Railway parentage of this Somerset & Dorset Johnson small 4-4-0 No. 17 waiting to depart from Bournemouth West with a northbound train. Photographed in original condition, No. 17 was constructed at Derby in May 1891 and withdrawn from service in June 1931.   *Author's Collection*

No further action was taken, the station remaining a rural outpost in the New Forest for the next 76 years.

At the same time the line between Ringwood and Christchurch became almost a little used country branch, whereas its newer section to Bournemouth was transformed into a main line. Bournemouth West could now be reached from Bournemouth East, but there were two missing links, the north side of the Branksome triangle did not exist, and there was no direct line from Poole to Hamworthy Junction. Passengers wishing to travel from any station on the new line to Poole had to change trains at Bournemouth West and if they wanted to travel west of Poole on the Weymouth line, they had to change again at Broadstone.

With these changes Brockenhurst, previously just a junction for the Lymington branch, became an important interchange point, where Bournemouth trains with through coaches for Weymouth divided, the Bournemouth section proceeding via the new Direct Line whilst the Weymouth section proceed via the original route (via Ringwood).

To handle the extra traffic a number of improvements were carried out during the next few years, which amounted to the virtual reconstruction of the station. The plans for a majority of this work were submitted in February 1888 at an estimated cost of £4,509 although the details of the buildings were still to be considered. By April a revised estimate of £7,529 was announced, the work being completed by October 1888. The original upside station buildings were demolished and an up loop laid at the back of the up platform, this resulted in the unusual arrangement of the new booking office and parcel office being

Crossing cottage number 7 situated east of Brockenhurst station, only minor extensions and improvements had been made to this 1847 building by the time this photograph was taken 118 years later.   *South Western, Circle Eyers Collection*

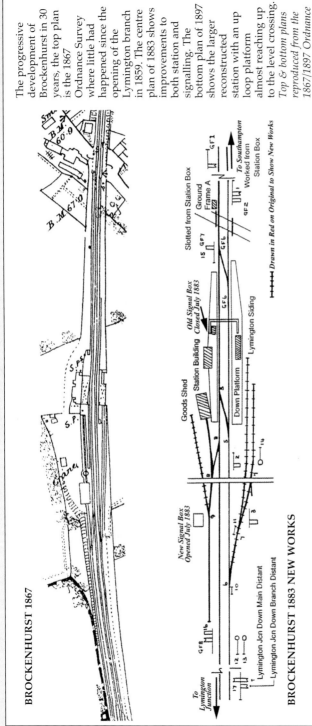

The progressive development of Brockenhurst in 30 years, the top plan is the 1867 Ordnance Survey where little had happened since the opening of the Lymington branch in 1859. The centre plan of 1883 shows improvements to both station and signalling. The bottom plan of 1897 shows the larger reconstructed station with an up loop platform almost reaching up to the level crossing. *Top & bottom plans reproduced from the 1867/1897 Ordnance Survey maps,*

centre drawing by Colin Chivers from a Board of Trade plan

BROCKENHURST 1867

BROCKENHURST 1883 NEW WORKS

BROCKENHURST 1897

Brockenhurst looking towards Southampton following the alterations made during the 1880s. To the extreme left the public footbridge over the goods yard, with the up loop platform left of centre. The up platforms on the left have a later style of canopy than that covering the down platform and Lymington branch bay on the right. *Lens of Sutton Association*

A Drummond 'T9' class 4-4-0 heads a down train through Brockenhurst in the years before World War I. Brockenhurst was at that time an important junction that had been created in the New Forest near a small settlement originally known as 'Brokenhurst'. *John Alsop Collection*

Drummond 'T9' class 4-4-0 No. 728 stands at the down platform of Brockenhurst station around the turn of the century, whilst an 0-6-0 goods engine stands in the Lymington bay with a selection of vintage stock.   *Author's Collection*

isolated from the platform on the upside, access being via a footbridge. It also introduced the rare feature of a movable bridge between the parcel office and the up platform, the bridge when not in use being swung away in line with the parcel office wall. To protect both the up loop and the bridge it was interlocked with the East signal box.

A refreshment room was provided on the up platform during 1889 and one on the down platform the following year. Additional work was carried out in May 1891 when a new turntable was installed and the downside sidings extended, whilst in December plans were approved for alterations to the booking office, new toilets, additional station roofing and alterations to one of the refreshment rooms. In May 1892 it was recommended that the platform waiting shelter be enclosed.

The inconvenience of several crossings in the Brockenhurst area was also eliminated during this period. The closure of one of the two crossings at No. 8 lodge east of Brockenhurst station with the construction of a short diversionary road to give access via the second crossing was allowed by the 1882 LSWR Miscellaneous Powers Act. An Act the following year allowed the closing of a crossing at the west end of the station, the footpath being rerouted via a footbridge. Further west, just east of Lymington Junction, an Act of 1890 allowed the replacement of crossing No. 9 by an overbridge to carry the Brockenhurst-Sway road.

Chapter Twelve

The Final Developments of the Victorian Era

Queen Victoria's Golden Jubilee on 20th June, 1887 was celebrated throughout the country, the railways playing a part in the festivities with the transport of many to special events. Locally the staff at Moreton joined with the Sand & Gravel Company and Brickwork employees in their festivities including luncheon laid on in a large tent near the station. At Hamworthy the station and approach road was decorated with flags and bunting. In the same year the Bath & West show was again held at Dorchester, this event providing a vast amount of traffic for both stations in the town.

The January of 1887 saw the passing of William Mears, the former district superintendent of the Southampton & Dorchester line. Commencing as a booking clerk at Woking he became the station agent at Winchfield about 1840 until appointed station master at Dorchester upon the opening of the line. In 1858 he succeeded Mr Clellan as district superintendent, a post he held until retirement in June 1881 aged 85, when succeeded by Mr Holliday. Mr Mears' business capacity and loyalty were rewarded with a handsome pension and he was permitted to retain the occupation of the superintendent's residence at Dorchester for the remainder of his life.

Improvements to Poole station were approved, in February 1888 the General Manager recommending at a cost of £159 'that the gates at Poole station level crossing be fitted with appliances for opening and closing on either side of the line simultaneously'. A year later in February 1889 it was agreed that an additional siding be laid and in April a crossover and lengthening of the down platform were approved, this was amended in the November when extensions to both platforms were approved as were new waiting rooms and a footbridge.

Across the harbour at Hamworthy in February it was recommended that the wharf be dredged to accommodate vessels. In April the company was given notice by the town council to remove the siding and shed constructed by them at Hamworthy Quay under an agreement of November 1865. In June the Bournemouth & Swanage Steam Packet Company offered £60 for the purchase of the shed, whilst the council, having second thoughts, then proposed that the siding should remain under the terms of the 1865 agreement.

Further east, the inhabitants of Lyndhurst were pressing for railway accommodation direct to the town, a scheme that the company would not entertain. However, in July they approved the alteration of the crossover and the laying of an additional siding at the east end of the station. An estimate of £260 to provide a ladies waiting room and additional roofing on the up platform at Moreton was approved, as was £430 to provide a footbridge at Totton and £170 to allow the gates at Wool to be worked mechanically from the signal box. The Moreton scheme was amended in the August of the following year to a new booking hall and ladies waiting room, platform roofing and an additional bedroom to the station house.

Whilst all these fairly minor improvements were taking place, a letter in the *Hampshire Independent* in late 1887 from a Shirley resident complained of the

The original Millbrook station looking towards Southampton, and showing the one siding on the up side. In this turn of the century view the shoreline came up to the down platform.

Lens of Sutton Association

Totton station viewed towards Lyndhurst Road in the early years of the 20th century. To the right is the mill served by a private siding.   *G.A. Pryer Collection*

poor arrangements at Millbrook, a station he claimed had an expanding area serving almost 14,000 people. Recently he had had 50,000 bricks delivered from Chandlers Ford, but as there was only one short siding, the bricks and luggage all came together and when they wished to get the luggage vans away the bricks were shunted down the line. In consequence, as the trucks were partly unloaded, the bricks were damaged during the shunting. Also a number of local tradesmen having their goods delivered there had had them damaged as there was no covered accommodation to keep them dry, and there was a need for the company to erect a suitable goods station.

Despite the failings at Millbrook, there were at that period a number of private sidings and additional ordinary sidings added along the line. In October 1889 Messrs Osman & Barnes applied for a private siding to their brick works at Lytchett Crossing. During 1890 an application was received from Mr George Jennings of Parkstone for a siding to be laid into his pottery works from Parkstone station. Approval was given in the April, the LSWR bearing the cost of £400 of the same up to its boundary and supplying Mr Jennings with old materials at reasonable charge for the portion on his land. The fact that the LSWR was prepared to accept the entire cost of the connection demonstrated the confidence they had in the value of the traffic on offer!

In February 1891 Mr Carter applied to alter the siding into his brickworks at Hamworthy Junction. At Totton additional goods sidings and accommodation were agreed to, and in November 1892 there was an application by Messrs Rose & Andrew for a siding into their timber yard. Other minor improvements approved the following year included the provision of a 50 ft turntable and associated sidings at Dorchester at an estimated cost of £850, extension of a siding at Christchurch and the construction of a crossing keeper's cottage at Woodfidley.

Further improvements had been carried out in the Bournemouth area during this period; during 1889 a portion of land that had become available at Branksome was purchased for future development and in the same year an additional island platform for excursion traffic at Bournemouth West and the alteration of several sidings was approved. In May 1890 it was agreed to improve the facilities at Bournemouth East goods depot by removing the platform of the old passenger station to provide space for a cart road between sidings, construct a cart road at the east end of the depot to provide an access into Southcote Road, and build a new goods and inquiry office at a total outlay of £925.

Apart from a few minor incidents in the early days, the Southampton & Dorchester and its associated lines had a good accident record until Tuesday 23rd December, 1890 when a collision took place at Broadstone Junction that, although serious, could well have had far worse consequences. LSWR 0-6-0 double-framed Beyer, Peacock goods engine No. 290 was returning light engine from Wimborne to Bournemouth. At Broadstone the 2.10 pm from Bath to Bournemouth was signalled from the cut-off line resulting in the light engine having to wait at signals on the Wimborne side of the junction. The driver moved forward against the signal, upon hearing a shout from the signal box he stopped by which time he was in the path of the approaching train. Although the signalman at once put the signals to danger the train, hauled by Somerset & Dorset Johnson 0-4-4 tank No. 54, ran into the rear of the goods engine obstructing its path. The goods engine was pushed forward 280 yds, its tender crushed and rear wheels ripped off. No. 54 with the tender wheels trapped underneath slewed sideways across the up and down Poole lines, the smokebox front was smashed in and the boiler forced back 11 inches in the frames. The train was severely damaged with the telescoping of the stock, the front van torn apart by the coaches in rear. The guard was flung out onto the track to escape with minor injuries, three passengers received serious injuries and one, a Miss Elizabeth Worthington, was killed.

An inquest was held in the Parish Room, Broadstone. The Broadstone signalman said that he made sure that the light engine had stopped at the signal before he released the signals to allow the Somerset & Dorset train to enter the station. After making an entry in the book he looked up and saw the light engine creep past the box, he ran out of the box shouting at the driver and ran alongside the track to try and draw his attention, he then ran back to the box and placed the Somerset & Dorset line signals at danger. By this time the approaching train was between the distant signal and the stop signal but was unable to pull up in the distance available.

The driver of the light engine told the Coroner that whilst at a standstill he saw the stop signal and the junction signal drop to clear, which would authorize him to proceed, he did so and as the engine was passing the signal box he heard the signalman say, 'Where are you going to?' He could not say if the signalman was in the box or alongside the line as he did not see him. The engine had proceeded a few yards past the signal box when his fireman shouted, 'Look out mate the Somerset is close on us'. He opened the regulator in order to move ahead but almost at the same time the collision occurred. The fireman of the light engine said that upon climbing back aboard the engine after checking that the locomotive oil lights were burning, he saw that the stop and junction signals were 'off'. As they passed the signal box he saw the signalman holding up his hands and shouting, 'Where are you going?' He then saw the signalman reverse two or three levers, before leaving the box and running down the track and shouting 'stop'; he applied the brake telling the driver that the signalman was stopping them, he then saw the Somerset train approaching. However, the fireman's evidence is a little contradictory as to the signalman's described actions. Seen from a moving engine at 5.20 pm on a December evening it would have been dark, he certainly would have had difficulty to see if the signalman pulled levers in a dimly lit box!

The signal linesman told the inquest that after the accident he examined the signals and points, the signals were all correct but the points had been 'run through' damaging the point rods. The jury returned a verdict of culpable negligence by William Charles Squires, driver, and Albert John Stone, fireman, of the light engine who were both arrested and taken into police custody.

The same day Major Marindin of the Board of Trade arrived at Broadstone and conducted his inquiry from a saloon coach placed near the signal box. As both the driver and fireman were in custody he could not interview them until the following day when they were released on bail. Added to their evidence was that of Frank Cribb the driver of the Somerset & Dorset train and Edward White his fireman. Driver Cribb said he watched the signal as he approached and it did not return to danger, his speed was 15 mph reducing to 10 mph in readiness to hand the single line tablet over at the signal box. They both saw the signalman out on the signal box landing, as they passed the box he saw the light engine ahead of him but despite a full application of the brake he could not stop before the collision took place.

On Saturday 3rd January, 1891 before Wimborne police court the crew of the light engine appeared charged with manslaughter. The signalman Walter Gosney said he did not alter the stop signal for the light engine after signalling the Bath train, he could not do so owing to the interlocking. George Clarke a carpenter employed by the LSWR had gone to the signal box to enquire about a train to Wareham, and said, 'As soon as the signalman took off the signal for the Somerset train to pass into the station, the light engine passed the stop signal'. But he had to admit 'He did not know which lever the signalman pulled first, he didn't understand signals a bit'. After due deliberation it was decided that there was a case to answer, the driver of the light engine being committed for trial at the County Assize Court.

The trial took place at Dorchester on Wednesday 18th February, and took a most unusual course, the prosecution offering no evidence against Stone the fireman who was discharged. James Annetts, the signalling superintendent of the LSWR, explained the principles of signalling and interlocking, describing that how once the road had been set for the Somerset & Dorset train it would have been impossible to release a signal allowing the light engine to proceed. The evidence of the other persons involved was heard. Clarke could not give details of the levers pulled and he said that the Somerset & Dorset train came into the station at a tremendous pace! The driver of the train had stated that he had reduced his speed from 15 mph to 10 mph ready for the fireman to give up the single line tablet. Both Clarke and Stone, the fireman of the light engine, saw Gosney the signalman reverse some levers, the driver of the Somerset & Dorset train said the signals were not returned to danger. John Willcox, foreman porter, said he saw all signals at danger, five minutes later he saw the light engine standing about 40 yards on the Poole side of the signal box, and the Somerset & Dorset train approaching the stop signal which was in the all clear position. Following the collision he looked again and saw that all signals were at danger.

There was a conflict of evidence, it was in the interest of the crews of both engines to 'have clear signals' but the signalman could only have one clear road (backed up by the interlocking). If the drivers' evidence was correct, the only course the signalman could have taken was to have cleared the signal for the light engine and then returned the signal quickly and changed the points for the Somerset & Dorset before the light engine passed over them (in those days there was no track circuit lock). The signalman was distracted by Clarke who was in the box but did not know which levers were pulled.

The case then took a strange twist when the judge said he could see no proof that Miss Worthington was the lady taken from the wreckage of the train, owing to the failure of the Crown to provide necessary proof and he instructed the jury to return a not guilty verdict. The inquiry had highlighted the long

Beyer, Peacock double-framed goods 0-6-0 No. 290, the LSWR engine involved in the Broadstone collision of 23rd December, 1890. Photographed in later life when fitted with an Adams boiler and Drummond chimney and renumbered as 0351. As almost by poetic justice 0351 was standing in the bay platform at Salisbury when struck by the engine and derailed stock involved in the Salisbury disaster of 1st July, 1906, her fireman being fatally injured. No. 0351 was withdrawn in December 1913 having travelled a recorded 864,913 miles.

South Western Circle, Norman Collection

'Q' class 0-6-0 No. 30539 passing Broadstone signal box with the 4.15 pm Brockenhurst-Bournemouth West service (a strengthened school train) on 15th July, 1960 demonstrates the point of collision in December 1890 when Beyer, Peacock Goods No. 290 overran signals shown to the rear of the approaching train and was struck by Johnson 0-4-4 tank No. 54 which was approaching under clear signals off the Somerset & Dorset line seen joining the main line from the left under the front coach of the train.   *H.C. Casserley*

hours worked by Victorian railwaymen: the crew of the light engine had the previously worked 14¾ hours and after only five hours off duty had commenced shunting at Bournemouth at 6.25 am that morning and were still on duty at 5.20 pm when the accident occurred.

If long hours was not the cause, sheer neglect was certainly responsible for an accident on 22nd February, 1894 when the 2 pm Christchurch-Hamworthy passenger train started away from Hamworthy Junction against the signal and ran to Hamworthy on the up line as a result of neglect of the crew. Indeed it is difficult to understand in daylight how they failed to realise they were not travelling on the left-hand track but were running 'wrong road'.

The long hours, in this case those of the signalman, were also raised by the Board of Trade Inspector and a misunderstanding as to the meaning of the authorized suspension of absolute block working within station limits at the inquiry into the collision at Wimborne station on 29th November, 1894. The 12.20 am goods from Nine Elms hauled by 'A12' class 0-4-2 No. 532 had run into the rear of the 5.50 am Wimborne-Bournemouth workmen's train. The accident was caused by a combination of circumstances; when approaching the Wimborne down distant signal a gauge glass broke and the crew had difficulty in shutting off the cocks. Becoming disorientated by a cab full of steam, they were upon the down home signal before the driver realised his position; unfortunately an application of the steam brake failed as the steam pipe had broken. Although travelling at reduced speed the goods, consisting of 29 loaded wagons and two brake vans, ran into the rear of the 8-coach passenger train and its rear brake van No. 62 being smashed beyond repair. By good fortune only one of the two passengers aboard the train was injured. Good fortune was also on the side of the LSWR during the evening of 1st November, 1899 when a portion of a goods train ran back 'wrong road' from Boscombe through Christchurch station before being brought to a stand about 300 ft beyond the platform. Fortunately, there was no down train in the section at the time!

On 1st November, 1892 the LSWR purchased Southampton Docks from the Southampton Dock Company for £1,360,000. Although at the time only consisting of part of the Eastern Docks, it was a far-sighted vision on the part of the company. The docks' subsequent enlargement and development were to ensure Southampton's status as a major port and railway centre up to the present day. At that stage not directly connected with the Southampton & Dorchester, the construction of a large dry dock and success in drawing American liner traffic away from Liverpool was eventually to make Southampton the premier liner port.

This prestigious traffic required a service of superior trains, whilst Bournemouth continued with its rapid expansion as a select seaside resort, Pullman cars having been introduced on certain trains from 1st April, 1890. Indeed so popular was the town that the town council feared detriment of its established trade. In November 1891 the council sent a letter to the LSWR with a resolution they had passed by the town council asking the company to consider whether the cheap day excursions to Bournemouth might be discontinued after 31st July each year. It was felt that the large numbers of such trains which had been running might deters visitors who would otherwise go

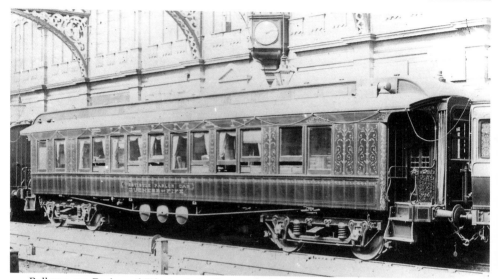

Pullman car *Duchess of Fife* stands in the up platform of Bournemouth Central station, the opulence of the vehicle making the best LSWR carriage look second class. Pullmans commenced to run on selected trains between Bournemouth and Waterloo in 1890 and continued until October 1911.   *Author's Collection*

The Weymouth portion of a down Waterloo express, joins the Holes Bay curve at Holes Bay Junction. The signal box and the original Poole & Bournemouth Railway line from New Poole Junction (Broadstone) are visible behind the train.   *Author's Collection*

there for longer periods. The company in its reply stated it could not agree with the suggestion, however, the following May an application by the National Sunday League for an excursion to Bournemouth was declined! At the same time the residents of Boscombe had complained to the company over the change of name of Boscombe station to Pokesdown in 1891.

Returning to the situation at Poole, the inhabitants still lacked a good direct connection with Southampton and London. The lack of a direct connection with Bournemouth East resulted in prospective passengers either having to change at Bournemouth West, Broadstone Junction, or Wimborne and a journey in the Dorchester direction also resulted in a change at either of the latter two stations. The matter that was not resolved until the construction of the Holes Bay curve for which authorization was obtained on 4th July, 1890 to construct a new length of railway from a point 63 chains west of Poole station to Hamworthy Junction. The contract was awarded to Messrs Lucas & Aird who commenced work in October 1891.

The residents of Branksome had petitioned the LSWR Board in October 1888 for the provision of a station. This the Board declined until in November 1891 a letter was received from Bournemouth Town Council expressing the hope that in the new arrangements connected with the Poole and Hamworthy Junction line, the company would consider the question of a station at Bourne Valley. During March 1892 the Engineer was instructed to prepare plans and estimates for a station at Branksome Junction and a short length of railway eastwards to a point to become known as Gas Works Junction. These were presented to the Board at the June meeting, scheme A £8,300 and scheme B £7,500, the latter being accepted. The short line to Gas Works Jn completed the triangle at Branksome and enabled trains to bypass Bournemouth West.

The new line to Hamworthy was laid across Holes Bay in the upper reaches of Poole Harbour, built entirely on embankment for its 1 mile 47.21 chain length. In its construction there was two three-span iron viaducts crossing the Upton and Creekmoor Lakes, a public road bridge, an occupation bridge and a culvert. Over 279,000 cubic yards of material were tipped to form the embankment much of it coming from the side of a cutting at Hamworthy Junction. When first tipped the embankment sank considerably with the alluvial soil at the bottom of the bay but later stabilised. The southern face of the embankment was faced with Swanage stone.

At the east end a junction was formed with the Poole-Broadstone line, the signal box, Holes Bay Junction, was situated in the fork and contained 23 working and two spare levers. Hamworthy Junction station was rebuilt, except the station master's house, which was renovated. Two 452 ft platforms were constructed a subway being provided to reach the down platform which was an island, the outside edge used by Hamworthy branch trains; 160 ft-long canopies covered both platforms. On the upside there were two additional sidings each capable of holding 50 wagons, and three on the downside, each holding 15 wagons, were added. A new signal box situated on the down platform contained 53 working and three spare levers and a subsidiary cabin was also provided at the west end containing 12 working and two spare levers . The signalling was inspected in late March 1893 and brought into use, although the station buildings

An Adams '46' class 4-4-2 tank No. 133 heads away from Hamworthy Junction with a Wareham-bound train. The down bay platform is to the right with the Hamworthy branch curving away in the right foreground.   *Author's Collection*

Hamworthy Junction looking east on 16th August, 1957 with a rake of coaches standing in the bay platform. Apart from the upper quadrant signals the station stood in a time warp, both over-sized for its later requirements and having not seen a paintbrush for many years.
                                                   A.E. West Collection South Western Circle

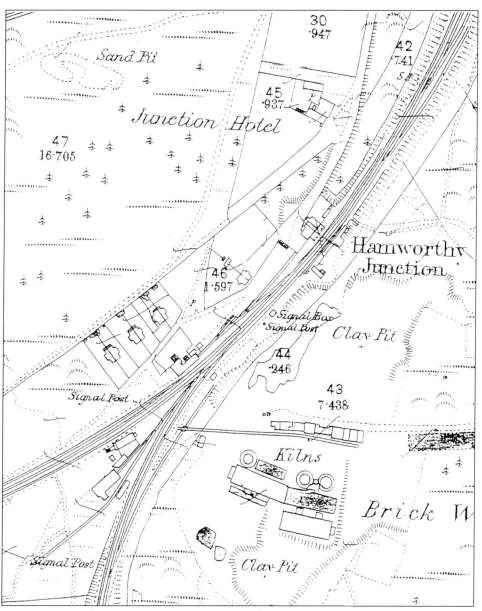

A section of the 1883 Ordnance Survey map showing Hamworthy Junction before the construction of the Holes Bay curve. The Hamworthy branch runs towards the bottom of the drawing. *Reproduced from the 1883 Ordnance Survey Map*

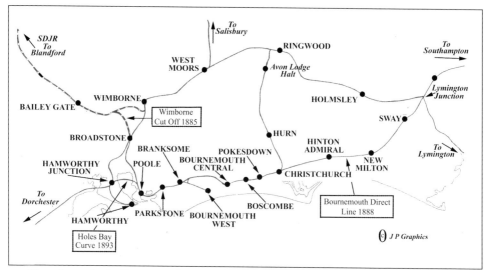

The railways in the Bournemouth-Poole area at the turn of the century, the Wimborne cut-off, the Lymington Junction-Bournemouth Direct line of 1888 and the Holes Bay curve of 1893 having all been completed, the latter two forming a direct route to Weymouth. This greatly reduced the status of the original main line between Lymington Junction and Hamworthy Junction via Ringwood and Wimborne, it thereafter being referred to as The Old Road.

Branksome, opened in June 1893, was part of the final direct link between Bournemouth and Weymouth. The station was situated in a cutting at the top of the steep Parkstone bank thus the booking office was on the up side at road level. The station name board proclaimed 'Branksome for Sandbanks' a rather salubrious district, which is more than could be said for Branksome station which for many years looked very shabby.   *Author's Collection*

were not quite complete at that time, and it was reported, 'There is at present no gas lighting in the station, oil being the general illuminant'.

The opening of the Holes Bay curve forged the final link in a direct line to Weymouth. To celebrate the event the Directors ran a special train to the town on Friday 19th May, having arrived in Bournemouth on the Thursday afternoon. They inspected the new station at Branksome before proceeding to the Bath Hotel where the Mayor and other leading figures from Bournemouth were entertained to dinner. On the Friday morning a special train for the Mayor and other important townspeople and consisting of two corridor coaches, an inspection saloon and van left Weymouth at 9.55 am. After picking up the Dorchester civic party the train proceeded via Broadstone Junction to Bournemouth West where the Bournemouth civic party and officials of the LSWR were waiting. The train then proceeded to Poole where a brief stop was made to pick up the mayor and other dignitaries of the town before proceeding over the new line to Weymouth. Here the Mayor Mr T.J. Templeman entertained the 230 guests to luncheon at the Jubilee Hall. Mr Scotter, the LSWR General Manager, in his after-dinner speech told those present that the new section of line would shorten the London to Weymouth journey time by 1 hour 15 minutes, and made it clear that the LSWR were interested in other places than Southampton and Bournemouth: 'They wished to run to every watering place on their line'.

The *Poole & Dorset Herald* said of the new line, 'The event is almost a complete revolution in the railway traffic of the district, and gives Poole the advantage of a large number of new trains to Bournemouth, Christchurch &c, and better facilities for travel generally than have ever before been offered'.

The new works at Branksome had also been proceeding well and were inspected by the Board of Trade in May 1893, and opened for traffic on 1st June, 1893, forming the final piece in the jigsaw. The new direct route also resulted in most Weymouth trains being routed via Bournemouth. The section of the original main line between Lymington Junction and Hamworthy Junction via Ringwood and Wimborne became a secondary route, becoming known as the 'Old Road' to future generations of railwaymen. The completion of the latest works saw the Southampton-Dorchester section of the LSWR reach its peak, apart from the Fawley branch and a few private sidings added later.

Hamworthy during the latter part of the 19th century was still a small community and since the arrival of the railway in Poole at the end of 1872 passenger traffic on the branch had declined. After the branch was inspected by the Directors during August 1881 closure was suggested. However, the Traffic Committee realised the branch was still used by passengers travelling to and from the Dorchester direction as there was then no direct service from Poole. The opening of the Holes Bay curve and the rearrangement of services was to change the situation, resulting in a weekday service of 11 trains each way running over the 1¾ mile-long branch. Following the opening of the Holes Bay curve services over the branch were rearranged with certain Ringwood-Christchurch-Bournemouth trains extended to Hamworthy.

Although the Old Road had declined Holmsley was still a topic raised at Traffic Committee meetings. In September 1893 the inhabitants of Burley suggested the removal of Holmsley station and the erection of a new one about

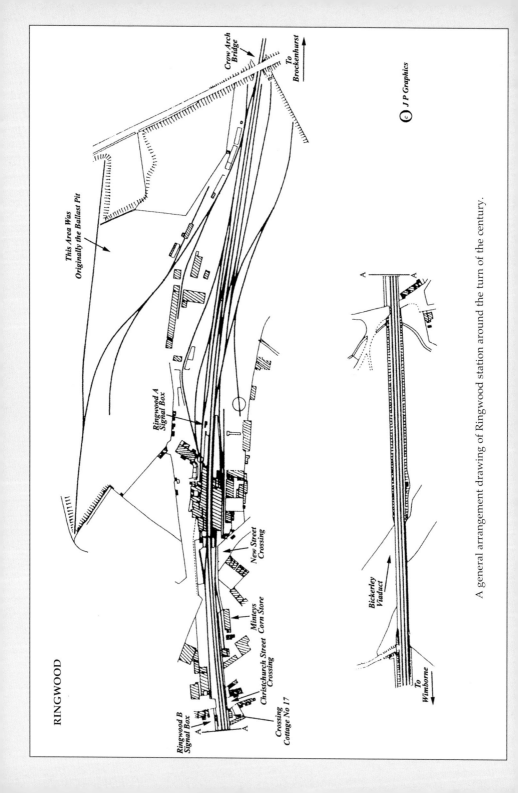

RINGWOOD

This Area Was Originally the Ballast Pit

Crow Arch Bridge

To Brockenhurst

© J P Graphics

Ringwood A Signal Box

Ringwood B Signal Box

Crossing Cottage No 17

Christchurch Street Crossing

Minteys Corn Store

New Street Crossing

Bickerley Viaduct

To Wimborne

A general arrangement drawing of Ringwood station around the turn of the century.

1½ miles nearer to Ringwood. Persistent in the matter, another memorial from the inhabitants of Burley in December 1895 suggested the removal of Holmsley station to a point about half a mile from Burley village, or that a platform should be provided there for the stoppage of trains. This request was declined, as was a request a year later from Hampreston Parish Council asking for a small station to be provided at Uddens crossing.

In the New Forest the situation at Beaulieu Road where the station had been closed for a number of years was changing. In January 1892 the Horse Guards had enquired whether, in the event of rifle ranges and a camping ground being established at Blackdown, the company would be willing to re-open Beaulieu Road station to afford accommodation for troops and stores during the season. The company officers were instructed to prepare plans and estimates if sufficient traffic could be provided.

By February 1894 the company had received the licence from the Office of Woods for the land required for the station, and at the end of May the necessary plans were prepared for a station containing passenger and goods accommodation and four cottages for staff at an estimated cost of £4,380. A new station was opened at Beaulieu Road in November 1895. In February 1898 Lord Montagu of Beaulieu had written to the company suggesting that the company should erect the stable and coach house at the station which he had proposed to provide at his own expense under arrangements with the Engineering Committee two years previously. However, for reasons not explained in the minutes his offer was refused.

In 1894 it was also decided to provide a bicycle shed at New Milton station which was going to cost the company £50. At Moreton where goods facilities were inadequate it was decided to convert the former crossing keeper's cottage into a goods store for the modest outlay of £30. This gave good value as it survived until the station's reduction to an unstaffed halt. Wool, the next station up the line, although in the late 19th century only serving a small village, its importance was growing with the regular army summer camps at Lulworth and the popular attraction of Lulworth Cove to which a horse-drawn conveyance was running daily. It was decided to add the words 'For Lulworth Cove' to the station name boards.

With the extensive improvements carried out along the line during the past 10 years the situation at Southampton West was far from suitable for the increasing amount of traffic handled, or indeed the requirements of the western part of the town which was rapidly expanding. In answer to previous complaints, a footbridge had been provided at the level crossing during 1885 and two years later the LSWR purchased a house in Kingsbridge Lane, 'Alessandro' as a residence for the station master. However, it was clear that the station had become unsuitable for the requirements of the public and plans were made for its replacement. It was decided to construct a new station west of the level crossing. But this was not without controversy and resulted in a public inquiry during July 1884 following an objection that the price asked by Southampton Corporation for the land for the new station was too low. In the event it was considered the £3,500 was perfectly fair and reasonable for the area consisting of field and shoreline.

Beaulieu Road station situated deep in the New Forest, this second station opened in November 1895 with the hope of increased trade including a seasonal Army training camp, but, situated in a poorly populated area, income was low.   *G.A. Pryer Collection*

Southampton West (Blechynden) looking towards Southampton tunnel. Taken prior to the opening of the new station in 1895, the original photograph and many others of the Southampton area in the Lankester Collection were destroyed during the bombing of 1939-1945.
Southampton Echo

A pre-1894 view showing an unidentified Adams 4-4-0 approaching Blechynden station with a Bournemouth West-Eastleigh train. The train is standing on land that became the site of the new Southampton West station in 1895. *B. Moody Collection*

Southampton West station viewed from Four Post Hill, in this pre-World War I scene the water still comes up to the down platform of the station. Although the Corporation power station had been built the massive infilling of later years had not commenced. *Author's Collection*

Southampton West shortly after the turn of the century, the 82 ft-high clock tower situated behind the up platform dominating the scene. With over 60 trains a day stopping here, the station was a much-needed improvement on the previous arrangements.   *B. Moody Collection*

Southampton West showing the up side approach in 1953 where, apart from repairs to war damage and modern motor vehicles, including the ubiquitous Morris Commercial Post Office van, little had changed since 1895.   *R.B. Gosling Collection*

Owing to the closeness of the site to the water's edge in a field subject to tidal flooding, foundations about 30 feet deep were required, concrete supporting brick arches on which the platforms were constructed. The up platform was 600 ft long and the down platform 800 ft in length with a down bay platform of 500 ft at the west end; a covered footbridge was provided at the London end. The buildings of brick were of the style of the period; on the upside an 82 ft-high clock tower with a cupola top was a distinguishing feature. The previous signal box remained, situated on the upside between the new station and level crossing it then contained a 24-lever frame assisted by a 16-lever ground frame 'A' near the tunnel mouth and a 19-lever ground frame 'B' at the west end of the layout. It opened without ceremony on 1st November, 1895, except for the discharge of a number of detonators as the first down train steamed into the station at 6.25 am. Not all the work was completed, the *Southampton Times* stating:

When the refreshment rooms are opened and Messrs Smith's bookstall has been refurbished the place will present quite a finished appearance. The approach to the down platform has not been completed owing to the subsidence which took place at that point. A large number of workmen are, however, engaged under the personal supervision of Mr Adkins, District Superintendent in putting the finishing touches to the work, and in a few days the whole of the station and its approaches will be opened for traffic.

However, despite these small setbacks the new station provided the Dorchester line with modern facilities as befitted a town of Southampton's importance. At the time it was recorded that over 60 trains daily stopped at the station.

The opening of the Wimborne cut-off in 1885 had somewhat reduced Wimborne's importance as a motive power depot for the Somerset & Dorset, indeed with the increased traffic over the line a shed in the vicinity of Bournemouth West was a requirement. The Joint Committee submitted a plan in January 1895, which had been approved by the Midland company's officials, for an engine shed in the triangle at Bournemouth West Junction, the original estimated cost having been reduced from £4,200 to £2,800.

Work on the wooden-framed corrugated structure was undertaken by the LSWR and completed by the end of the year. However, being a joint property and situated on the land of one of the participants there were many clauses included in the agreements. At a meeting of the Joint Committee held at Waterloo on 6th February, 1896 it was agreed that as the LSWR turntable adjoining the new shed was used almost exclusively by Joint engines the value of the turntable, £668, be included in the agreed price which eventually came to £2,822 19s. 4d. for the shed, £865 the turntable, and £141 3s. superintendence, totaling £3,829 2s. 4d. It was also agreed that when the LSWR obtained water they be charged 2s. 6d. for tender engines, 1s. for tank engines, 2s. 6d. for washing out engines and £1 for any LSWR engines stabled in the new shed.

In late 1895 Mr Pope of the Dorchester brewing family who owned a considerable amount of land to the east of the railway just south of Dorchester Junction suggested that the LSWR and the GWR companies build a new joint station on land he was prepared to offer on easy terms. Had the scheme proceeded a station erected on land between Herringston Road and the railway would have seen the South Court Avenue-Manor Park area developed 50 years earlier than it was. However, there is little doubt that its distance from the town of the late 19th century did not encourage a facility that would have, in the light of later economies, benefited both companies and relieved the LSWR of the operational difficulties at their station.

To the east of the county the service on the Hamworthy branch was in decline, by the summer of 1896 having been reduced to four down and five up trains. The first down train from Hamworthy Junction departed at 9.15 am, returning from Hamworthy at 10.22 am and the last down train left the junction at 4.56 pm returning from Hamworthy at 6.10 pm. Indeed, the idea of operating a service unsuitable to users is nothing new!

The LSWR announced that the service would be withdrawn from 1st July. Poole Town Council discussed the situation at their June meeting and considered it was a matter for the inhabitants of Hamworthy to consider, but any action that the Hamworthy Overseers take would no doubt receive the support of the council.

The Poole Town Clerk received a letter from the LSWR in reply to a petition sent by the residents of Hamworthy,

> I beg to state that your Council and the petitioners do not seem to be aware that that there was virtually no passenger traffic to and from Hamworthy station, and it is therefore useless to keep the station open. The passengers are so few that they do not average one per train. Passengers who formerly travelled to and from Hamworthy now find it more convenient to use Poole station, and especially is this the case since the new curve line across Poole Harbour has been opened. Hamworthy station ought to have in fact been closed when the new curve line was opened. The traffic has practically dwindled to nothing so that some of the trains carry no passengers at all and others only one or two. Under these circumstances the Directors have decided that the station shall be closed for passenger traffic on and after 1st July next.

In response to this Alderman Dugdale told fellow Councillors,

> There was no question about the trains running empty, and that state of things had been brought about by the Railway Company, who had taken the trouble to make the trains so inconvenient that nobody could possibly use them. The Company themselves had driven away the traffic from the station by making the connections so bad at the Junction.

Indeed these words from the Alderman have had a familiar ring to them over the years. Thus on 1st July, 1896 the Hamworthy branch was the first in Dorset to lose its passenger service, ironically the first passenger-carrying branch in the county!

Whereas terminal decline had set in on the Hamworthy branch further development was taking place on the main line with the opening of a station at Boscombe on 1st June, 1897. A ceremonial opening took place on 29th May by the Chairman of the LSWR Sir Charles Scotter accompanied by other company officials and the Mayor of Bournemouth. The Chairman stated at the opening that 'he knew of no other town of 50,000 inhabitants that had five stations'. Indeed, if one looks at today's conurbation area, Hamworthy to Christchurch

13¾ miles apart, had eight stations in place by 1897, such was the development potential of the Poole-Bournemouth area.

With the opening the new station complete with goods facilities, the previous Boscombe station situated in a cutting only 726 yards to the east was renamed Pokesdown. Further improvements were carried out at Poole after approval to extend several sidings and enlarge the goods shed was given in 1896; although plans for station buildings were not proceeded with until after March 1897 when, following a deputation from Poole, improvements estimated to cost £2,398 were carried out. Three years later in February 1899 sanction was granted for the erection of a wooden footbridge across the line at Sterte, west of Poole station, and two new signal boxes, Poole A and Poole B. On the GWR section between Dorchester Junction and Weymouth during the summer of 1899 the longitudinal sleepers and bridge-rails were replaced on the up line by transverse sleepers and bullhead rails, the railways were moving into a new age.

Since their inception railways had made remarkable progress, in particular with express passenger services that regularly eclipsed their own high standards. However, this was only part of the picture, the ability to move goods long distances had transformed the manufacturing industry which was now able to supply the nation and beyond with little difficulty. The forward thinking towards railways for the mass movement of troops had also been proved. A fine example of the latter was during August 1898 when the greatest army manoeuvres to date took place over the countryside from Wareham in the south to the Wiltshire border in the north with an estimated 29,000 troops involved. The logistics for this exercise were enormous in the days before motorised transport. Many troops arrived at Wareham where a base camp had been established north of the town at Trigon. The press carried many pages full of detailed reports of the event giving mention to almost every regiment in the British army.

On one day, Tuesday 9th August, nine special trains brought 432 men, 306 horses and 64 wagons to the station, five of these trains arriving between 3.47 am and 6.52 am. Supplies from two ships were also unloaded at Poole quay and brought to Wareham by rail. Amongst the various detachments were troops from Ireland arriving from Holyhead in London & North Western Railway stock, which had travelled via the GWR, together with at least six other trains that were handed over to the LSWR at Dorchester Junction. A further report expected over 70 special trains to be run by both the LSWR and Somerset & Dorset companies, the latter for a further encampment at Blandford. Indeed, the exercise put the LSWR in good stead the following year with the outbreak of the Boer War.

Thus we come to the end of the 19th century by which time the principal expresses between Waterloo and Bournemouth had had their timing reduced to 2 hours 5 minutes for the 107¾ mile journey. In July the LSWR introduced two new express trains each way between Waterloo and Weymouth with the 10.30 am and 4.10 pm down services and the 7.50 am and 3.35 pm up services. The down trains with stops at Winchester, Eastleigh, Southampton West, Bournemouth Central, Poole, Wareham and Dorchester covered the 142½ miles in 3 hours 4 minutes, and the up trains with the same stops took 3 minutes

From a railway viewpoint little had changed since 1900 when this pre-1939 view of Poole was taken. The curve of the railway swings across the picture with the station in the centre, beyond is the long narrow goods shed and behind the sidings are allotments, these making way for additional sidings in September 1941. Today Poole's third station still sits awkwardly on the curve whilst the redevelopment of the town has seen most of the buildings in the picture replaced.

R.B. Gosling Collection

Poole West signal box at the time of its opening in 1899, and at the time of writing still in operation. Referred to by the Signalling Record Society as an LSWR type '4' box, the design had been introduced in 1894.   *Historical Model Railway Society*

A pre-1914 view of the level crossing at Poole High Street looking towards the junction with Towngate Street. An up train is just passing Poole 'A' signal box. Today apart from the rails the scene has changed, the entire area having been redeveloped, that beyond the gates forming Falklands Square and the Dolphin Centre.   *Author's Collection*

The London Express crossing the High Street.

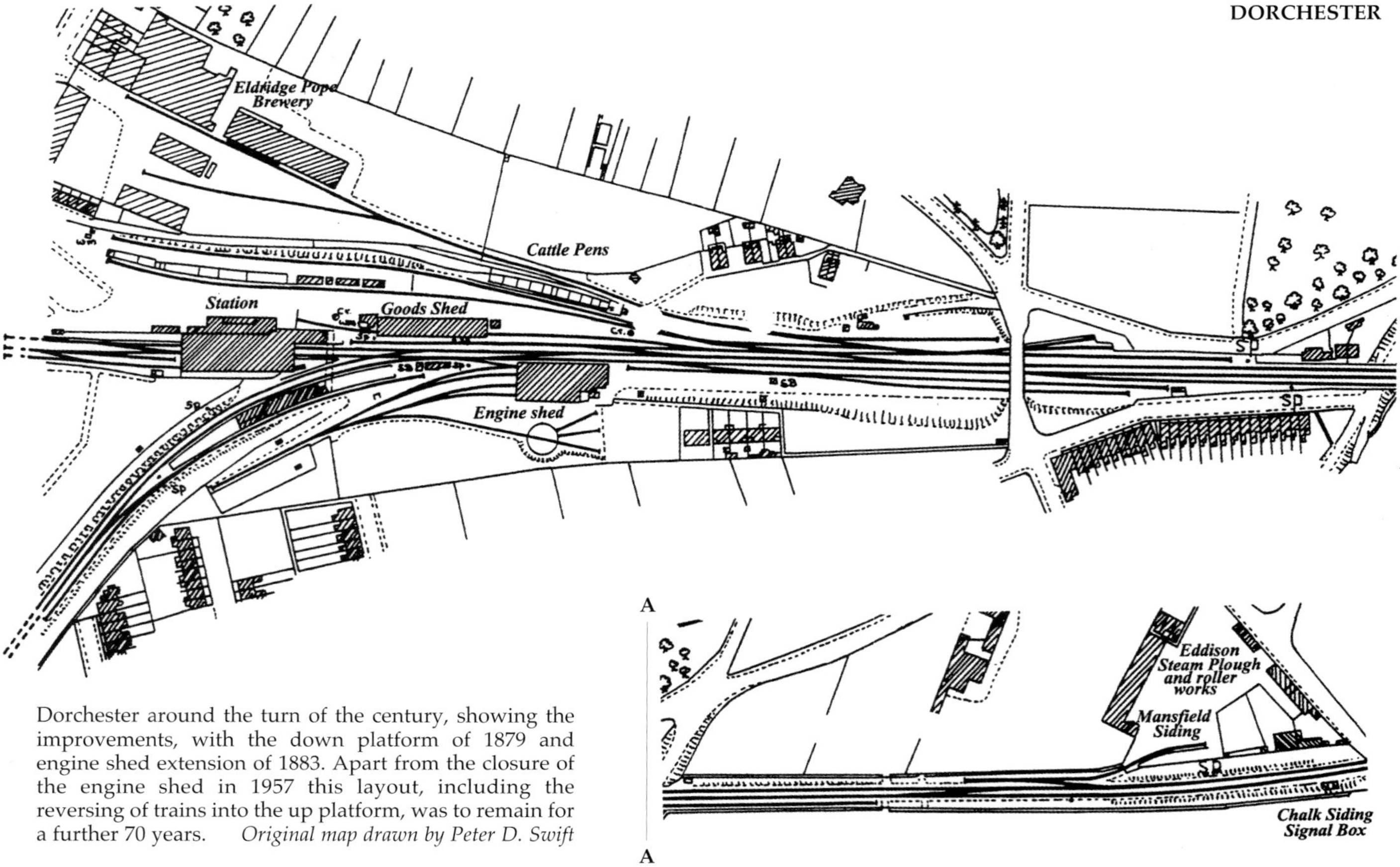

DORCHESTER

Dorchester around the turn of the century, showing the improvements, with the down platform of 1879 and engine shed extension of 1883. Apart from the closure of the engine shed in 1957 this layout, including the reversing of trains into the up platform, was to remain for a further 70 years.   *Original map drawn by Peter D. Swift*

Eldridge Pope Brewery

Cattle Pens

Station

Goods Shed

Engine shed

Eddison Steam Plough and roller works

Mansfield Siding

Chalk Siding Signal Box

GENERAL VIEW
DORCHESTER 20

After 1900 little changed at Dorchester station, the practice of reversing up trains into the platform continuing for a further 70 years. This pre-1914 view is from Maumbury Rings with the train shed of the up platform in the centre of the picture. By this time the outer side screens had been removed along with the covered section to the left originally used by down trains. The 1879 down platform stands on the curve (*right*) leading to Dorchester Junction, above the roof of the down platform the goods shed can be seen, with the signal box and engine shed to the right.

Author's Collection

A glimpse of the Somerset & Dorset engine shed at Branksome in original condition in April 1928. Standing in the doorway are Somerset & Dorset 4-4-0 No. 71 on the left and Urie 'King Arthur' class 4-6-0 No. 748 *Vidien*.   *H.C. Casserley*

Adams 'T6' class 4-4-0 No. 680 storms through Boscombe with a down express in the early years of the 20th century, note the second coach is a Pullman car. No. 680 was built in December 1895 and withdrawn from service in June 1937. Boscombe station changed very little in its 68 year life, closing in October 1965.   *Lens of Sutton Association*

longer. The 15 miles 9 chains between Dorchester and Wareham was covered in 15 minutes stop to stop, thus requiring speeds well in excess of 60 mph.

However, proving that nothing changes, there were complaints: a leading Weymouth councillor was upset that the trains were not faster, and commenting on a non-stop run from Waterloo to Bournemouth complained that the train then stopped three times before reaching Weymouth. On up journeys there had been a number of occasions when the late arrival of the Bournemouth West portion caused delays. A further complainant was aggrieved that passengers between Bournemouth and Waterloo could obtain cheap weekend tickets, a privilege denied to Weymouth, the writer pointing out that by booking to Bournemouth and then re-booking with a weekend ticket a considerable amount could be saved.

The seaside resorts served by the LSWR in the area also provided a wide selection of steam boat excursions by paddle steamer which were very popular with both the Victorian and Edwardian holidaymaker, a market both the railway and steamer owners were quick to exploit. Over the years there had been various through bookings between the various paddle steamer operators, a majority of these allowing either outward or return journey to be made by rail; such as arrangements between the Southampton, Isle of Wight & South of England Steam Packet Company (Red Funnel) and Messrs Cosens of Weymouth, the two principal steamer operators along the coast between Southampton and Weymouth. Arrangements with the latter company were in place by 1886, their sailing bills stating: 'Messrs Cosens & Co have made arrangements that throughout the season their steamers will be timed as far as practicable to meet the requirements of excursionists visiting Swanage, Bournemouth and Weymouth by the London & South Western Railway and the Midland Company's trains'. In addition there had over the years been a number of rail excursions to Southampton, Bournemouth and other resorts allowing the passengers to partake of a steamer trip included in the excursion fare.

The LSWR itself also entered into the excursion trade properly following the construction of the *Duchess of Fife* in 1899, after which excursions were run from Portsmouth as far west as Bournemouth and Swanage. On these sailings various combinations of ticket were obtainable, and in later years steamer cruises to Southampton docks and a visit to a liner were also available. Unfortunately, these activities ceased with the outbreak of World War II, never to return,

Thus we come to the end of the 19th century, during the second half of which Dorset and West Hampshire had been put firmly on the railway map. Every town and village along the line had benefited from its development, and although the aspirations of the original Directors of the Southampton & Dorchester had not fully come to fruition, the later development in the Bournemouth area had more than made up for any other failings. Having risen from an obscure settlement to County Borough in 1900 with an estimated population of 58,820, Bournemouth had also become established as a high class resort and the railway centre of the area.

An interesting view at Dorchester around 1860. In front of the goods shed stands Sharp Jones 2-2-2 No. 8 *Vesta*, behind the tender stands a goods brake van complete with a roof-mounted guard's look-out and to the left a goods van with a corrugated iron body. *Vesta* constructed as early as September 1838 cost £1,750 and was originally fitted with inside cylinders Shown here in its rebuilt form of 1854 with outside cylinders and other additions, there appears to very little of the original engine remaining such were the extensive reconstructions of many early locomotives.

Dorset County Museum

Chapter Thirteen

Locomotives of the Victorian Era

Unlike a branch line that was often worked by a small selection of locomotives, over the years the Southampton & Dorchester and associated lines were served by a majority of the classes of locomotive operated by both the LSWR and the Southern Railway. In the circumstances it is impossible to give a complete locomotive history covering the events of over 150 years, this can be found in the excellent publications of the RCTS and other publishers. However, a general outline with details of a few of the more interesting and historic examples that are known to have worked in the area will fulfil the requirements of the reader in following the history of the line.

Before the development of Bournemouth, the opening of the Direct Line, and the Holes Bay curve, all of which changed the entire pattern of train working, the 'Doset' as the Southampton & Dorchester was referred to by old enginemen was something of a rural backwater serving an agricultural community with trains travelling at a rather pedestrian speed, often reflected in both rolling stock and locomotives that were well past their prime.

An engine with local connections was No. 16 *Southampton*, a 2-2-2 built by Messrs Summers, Groves & Day of the Millbrook Foundry, Southampton, in June 1839 at a cost of £1,338. Rebuilt in 1844 it served at various locations on the LSWR appearing on the Southampton & Dorchester in late 1856 when it was relegated to unspecified stationary duty at Ringwood, a situation that usually saw out the final years of a useful boiler. However, in the summer of 1859 *Southampton* was rebuilt and as No. 176 survived until 1869, latterly operating the Gosport branch.

One of the first engines recorded as working over the Southampton & Dorchester was *Reindeer*, which was employed hauling several trial trains before the line's opening. One of a class of six 2-2-2s built in 1838 by G. & W. Rennie they were soon found to be underpowered and developed other problems resulting in their rebuilding in 1842 by Fairburn, of Manchester, in which form they ran until again reconstructed in 1855/56. Nos. 23 *Antelope* and 25 *Reindeer* were then employed on the Southampton & Dorchester line. It was recorded that a broken rail at Moreton derailed *Reindeer* in October 1869; receiving only minor damage she survived as the last member of the class until withdrawn in January 1872. Unfortunately, *Antelope* suffered boiler failure after the fire was lit whilst the boiler was empty at Wimborne resulting in her withdrawal in November 1871.

During the early years only two engines appear to have been stabled at Dorchester, in August 1849 these were recorded as two Sharp, Roberts 2-2-2s No. 7 *Venus* and No. 10 *Aurora*. Built in 1838, like many engines of the early period, they were quickly out-classed resulting in *Aurora* being withdrawn in October 1856. However, two members of the class, No. 7 *Venus* and No. 10 *Vesta*, were reconstructed in 1855 and survived until July 1870 and May 1872 respectively, both ending their days at Dorchester.

Beattie 'Hercules' class 2-4-0 No. 40 *Windsor* standing at Dorchester about 1860. With the exception of a modified safety valve the locomotive is in original condition including round coupling rods and a 1,200 gallon four-wheel tender. Built at Nine Elms in July 1852 at a cost of £1,749 she only received minor modifications before being withdrawn in May 1884.

Dorset County Museum

Beattie 'Hercules' class 2-4-0 No. 37 *Arab* constructed in 1853 at a cost of £1,732. Photographed after the fitting of a 1,950 gallon six-wheel tender and other modifications including flat coupling rods, enclosed splashers and a Stirling type cab, *Arab* was finally withdrawn from service in June 1880.   *Author's Collection*

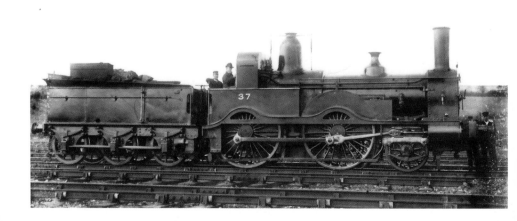

Several of the Rothwell singles also appeared on the Southampton and Dorchester line, two ending their days as stationary boilers, No. 79 *Harpy* at Ringwood and No. 81 *Herod,* a former Bournemouth engine, at Bournemouth East until 1873. Other singles that saw service on the line were members of the 'Vesuvius' class. No. 123 *The Duke* was in her earlier years a favourite for Royal Trains and other important specials. At the end of her life she resided at Dorchester and after travelling a recorded 567,038 miles was withdrawn in June 1878. Sister engine No. 116 *Stromboli,* latterly stationed at Hamworthy Junction, worked the Hamworthy branch until withdrawn in April 1880.

The opening of new lines during the latter part of the 1840s required additional motive power, resulting in 10 Fairbairn singles Nos. 63-72 and a further six singles Nos. 109-114 supplied by Messrs Christie, Adams & Hill. Of the latter class both No. 111 *Test* and No. 114 *Frome* are recorded as having been allocated to Dorchester at various periods.

We now arrive at the final batch of singles built for the LSWR, Joseph Beattie's 'Canute' class, a group of 12 engines constructed between 1856 and 1859. Again when deposed from express working they descended to secondary workings, by May 1864 Nos. 130 *Harold,* 131 *Rufus,* 133 *Crescent* and 135 *Canute* were allocated to Northam. Amongst other duties they worked Southampton-Weymouth services, with No. 132 *Conqueror* allocated to Dorchester.

At first the management of the LSWR had omitted to provide suitable motive power for goods traffic, apart from the seven 0-4-2 Luggage (goods) engines of 1841/42 of which little is recorded. The matter was not rectified until the construction of 10 0-6-0 goods engines of the 'Bison' class between 1845 and 1848. When built they were capable of handling the heaviest duties required of them. A frequent heavy train was the up Dorchester goods; in August 1849 No. 50 *Buffalo* was recorded as being employed on this working. In March 1856 Beattie ordered the class be restricted to local goods duties, however, six of the class were rebuilt during the 1860s and survived into the 1880s. To replace them on goods services and other duties it was clear that additional motive power was required. Joseph Beattie produced three classes of 2-4-0 small-wheeled locomotives between 1851 and 1863, the 'Hercules', and 'Saxon' and 'Gem' classes providing a total of 27 engines, the first class with 5 ft 6 in. driving wheels, the other two classes with 5 ft driving wheels. In theory any of the above engines allocated to either Nine Elms or Northam could have put in appearances on the Dorchester line. However, only a few members of the 'Hercules' class are documented, No. 40 *Windsor* was working around Dorchester by 1860 and by the mid-1860s the class was reduced to light goods, shunting and light passenger duties. No. 21 *Prince* and *Windsor* by March 1878 were allocated to Wimborne from where they worked both goods and passenger trains to Ringwood, over the Christchurch branch to Bournemouth East, and from Wimborne to Poole and Bournemouth West. No. 26 *Gazelle* and No. 37 *Arab* from Northam often worked the 6.15 am Bishopstoke-Dorchester goods, returning at 12.50 pm.

For passenger work Beattie produced a series of 2-4-0s between 1855 and 1875 consisting of 109 engines divided into nine classes with driving wheels ranging from 6 ft to 7 ft diameter. These classes were allocated across the LSWR and the following are recorded as having a local connection. By the late 1870's 'Eagle'

Beattie 'Falcon' class 2-4-0 No. 84 *Styx* waits to depart from Bournemouth West with a Salisbury train, photographed in later years when fitted with an Adams type chimney. Built in October 1866 at a cost of £3,012, she ended her days working local services from Bournemouth until withdrawn in April 1897.

G.A. Pryer Collection

Beattie 'Volcano' class 2-4-0 No. 25 *Reindeer* built at Nine Elms in July 1872 at a cost of £2,993, she was the second engine working on the Southampton & Dorchester line to hold the name. Photographed in her original condition before April 1886 when she was rebuilt with an Adams boiler, she was finally withdrawn in December 1892 having covered a recorded 804,922 miles.
Author's Collection

A family photograph reputedly taken at Dorchester shows Beattie 'Undine' class 2-4-0 No. 174 *Naiad*. The locomotive cost £2,993 when built in June 1860, serving the LSWR for 26 years until withdrawn in September 1886. *Author's Collection*

Beattie 'Vesuvius' class 2-4-0 No. 294 stands inside the new engine shed at Bournemouth Central in July 1896. Built in April 1873 at a cost of £3,285, she was one of the engines involved in the derailment between Downton and Breamore on 3rd June, 1884 resulting in the death of four passengers. No. 294 was withdrawn in January 1899 having covered a recorded 879,548 miles.

Author's Collection

'Vesuvius' class 2-4-0 No. 1 *Sussex* stands outside Bournemouth engine shed towards the end of her days. She was the first LSWR locomotive to be fitted with vacuum brakes in late 1878 when she undertook trials equipped with Smith's simple vacuum brake; unfortunately as it was not automatic it failed to meet the approval of the Board of Trade. *Sussex* had been built in July 1870 at a cost of £2,992 and was withdrawn from service in May 1898.   *Author's Collection*

class No. 27 *Eagle* was allocated to Dorchester to work the Weymouth-Wimborne-Southampton service until withdrawn at the end of 1886 having travelled 691,059 recorded miles.

The policy of sending older engines to work the Southampton & Dorchester continued with members of the '231' class, when No. 231, which had been on hire to the M&SWJR, was sent to Dorchester in the summer of 1893 until withdrawn two years later. No. 64 *Acheron* of the 'Volcano' class had also been allocated to Dorchester by March 1878 where it was recorded that her regular working was the 1.10 pm Weymouth-Salisbury returning at 7 pm. By 1885 Nos. 5 *Ganymede*, 26 *Reindeer*, 61 *Snake*, 63 *Alecto*, 91 *Spitfire*, 116 *Stromboli* and 118 *Etna* were allocated to Northam, Bournemouth and Dorchester for local services. By March 1894 Nos. 114 *Frome* and 115 *Vulcan* were working local services from Bournemouth and one of the class would often act as pilot at Southampton West.

Whereas the previous passenger 2-4-0s had 6 ft diameter driving wheels the 'Undine' class built between 1855 and 1860 had 6 ft 6 in. wheels. Again by 1878 Nos. 163 *Undine*, 170 *Cupid*, and 171 *Sylph* were at Northam and 164 *Psyche* at Dorchester.

Members of the 'Falcon' class also migrated to the Southampton & Dorchester line in later years with Nos. 86 *Shark* and 88 *Sirius* at Northam often working the Southampton-Wimborne-Weymouth service. Nos. 83 *Siren* and 84 *Styx* were allocated to Bournemouth and, following the opening of the Direct Line in 1888, worked Bournemouth-Wimborne-Brockenhurst services and Bournemouth West to Salisbury services. By 1894 both engines, together with Nos. 86 *Shark* and 88 *Sirius*, had moved to Dorchester.

We now move forward to the 'Vesuvius' class the largest group of 2-4-0s consisting of 32 engines built between 1869 and 1875 and used on the principal express trains. In their declining years a number of the class were allocated to Northam, Bournemouth and Dorchester sheds. The year 1883 saw Nos. 41 *Ajax*, 119 *Vesuvius*, 121 *St George*, 294, 295, 296, 316, and 317 at Bournemouth with Nos. 14 *Mercury*, and 15 *Mars* at Dorchester. No. 294 had been involved in the fatal accident between Downton and Breamore on the Salisbury & Dorset line on 3rd June, 1884.

Fourteen members of the class were rebuilt, being fitted with Adams type boilers and cabs, and a number were again allocated for local services. However, two unrebuilt engines ended their days at Dorchester: No. 316, withdrawn in February 1899 having run 880,749 miles, and No. 19 *Briton* in the July at 854,567 miles, the last Beattie 2-4-0 in service.

Finally there were two classes of 2-4-0s fitted with 7 ft diameter driving wheels, the 'Clyde' class. Consisting of four engines constructed in 1859 and named after Directors of the company, Nos. 157 *Clyde*, 158 *Lacy*, 159 *Castleman* and 169 *R.H. Dutton*, they were the first British standard gauge locomotives with coupled wheels of 7 ft diameter. In 1864 three further engines were added to the class, Nos. 73, 74 and 75, *Fireball*, *Firebrand* and *Fireking* respectively.

Again by 1878 the class had been reduced to secondary duties with *Fireball*, *Firebrand*, *Fireking* and *R.H. Dutton* at Notham and appropriately *Castleman* at Dorchester. Interestingly, from August 1884 *Castleman* ran with the boiler from

The last Beattie 2-4-0 in service No. 19 *Briton*; built in July 1871 at a cost of £2,960 she was one of the members of the class not rebuilt and allocated to Bournemouth in her original condition until withdrawn in July 1899 having run a 854,567 recorded miles. *Author's Collection*

Standard Well Tank No. 36 *Comet*, photographed in later life at Northam shed by which time she had received an Adams stovepipe chimney and other modifications. When new *Comet* was working a goods train at Wool when the driver was struck by an arrow from a boy's bow. *Comet* was hired to the Isle of Wight Junction Railway during 1874-5 and following the introduction of larger locomotives was withdrawn in December 1884, only 22 years old. *Author's Collection*

the previously withdrawn *Clyde*. On withdrawal from Dorchester in 1887, *Castleman* had run a recorded 869,309 miles, the highest of the class, the boiler being sold to the Vauxhall Steam Laundry for £68 14s. 10d. where it served until 1902-03. *Fireball* and *Fireking* also ended their days at Dorchester, withdrawn in March and May 1888.

The final batch of 2-4-0s were six engines of the 'Centaur' class constructed in 1868. Again constructed with 7 ft diameter coupled wheels, they were employed on the principal expresses until the early 1880s and by 1884 three had been allocated to Northam for employment on locals services. By March 1890 No. 95 *Centaur* and 99 *Phlegon* were working from Dorchester on local services to Bournemouth and Southampton and also performing piloting duties at both Dorchester and Weymouth. No. 100 *Python* was for a period allocated to Bournemouth and when withdrawn in February 1899 had the distinction of being the first LSWR locomotive to exceed a million miles (1,061,915).

The last surviving 2-4-0 No. 19 *Briton* spent her final years on light duties at Bournemouth. She was taken to Dorchester and cleaned with a view to her purchase by a deep ploughing contractor who had plans for her boiler; however, the arrangements fell through and *Briton* was towed to Nine Elms and broken up in 1900.

Thus we conclude a brief outline of the early singles and the 2-4-0s that formed the backbone of LSWR motive power in the early years and continued to give good service on secondary routes for many years after. To the casual observer in the 1880s Dorchester shed must have resembled a working museum! However, many of these engines had been extensively modified and rebuilt over the years and served well.

Their livery had also changed; prior to 1850 the main engine colour had been described as both bottle green and holly green, this was then changed to Indian red until 1865 when chocolate brown was introduced. After 1872 a paler chocolate defined as purple-brown was applied, this remaining until Adams introduced umber to be quickly followed by pea green.

Running alongside the express engines on the Southampton & Dorchester line were a number of diminutive tank locomotives used for branch line work, local passenger, goods traffic and shunting duties. Colloquially known as the 'well tanks' their first recorded appearance on the line occurred between 1852 and 1856 when No. 34 *Crescent* was reported as working the Hamworthy branch, however, this engine had a short life being broken up in 1856 after only four years' service.

The 'Tartar' class was more successful, No. 52 *Albert* was recorded as being introduced in 1852, and present at the opening of the Christchurch branch in November 1862. No. 17 *Queen* was working the line during 1865-66 being involved in two accidents during that period. No. 53 *Phoenix* was working the Lymington branch in 1868 and allocated to Bournemouth East following the opening of the extension in 1870, whilst 'Sussex' class No. 15 *Mars* worked between Wimborne and Poole following the opening of the line from New Poole Junction (Broadstone) in 1872.

Whereas the previous well tanks had been of the 2-2-2 wheel configuration, by 1858 a modified version of the 2-4-0 wheel arrangement had arrived. A

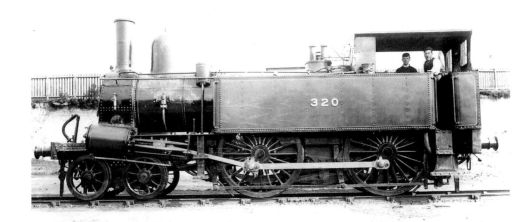

With its distinctive front end appearance 4-4-0 Metropolitan tank No. 320 poses with her crew outside Bournemouth Central shed. The last survivor of the class, she was withdrawn in December 1913 with a recorded mileage of 807,120. *Author's Collection*

Single-framed Beyer Goods 0-6-0 No. 370 stands outside the LSWR shed at Weymouth during 1893. Built in May 1878, the photograph shows the locomotive after rebuilding in May 1890 when an Adams boiler and cab were fitted, the engine remaining in service until withdrawn in July 1924. *Author's Collection*

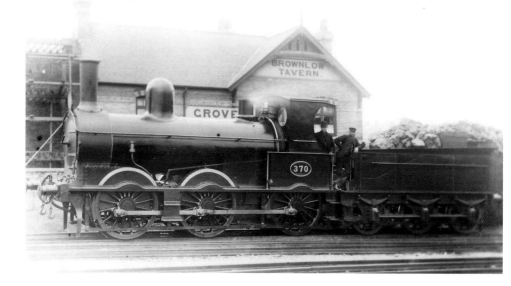

group of three known as the 'Nelson' class was constructed for the opening of the Lymington branch. In the event only No. 143 *Nelson* was sent to Lymington; allocated to Dorchester during the early 1870s the locomotive was often employed on the Weymouth-Portland branch.

The success of these engines led to the standard well tanks of which 85 were placed in service. Only the first five carried names, one of these No. 36 *Comet* was allocated to Northam shortly after entering service. When working a goods train at Wool on 3rd April, 1872 the driver was injured by an arrow shot at the train by a boy!

These useful machines were spread across the LSWR system. No. 198 was allocated to Bournemouth East during March 1873, around the same period Nos. 184, 185 and 189 were also in the Bournemouth area with Nos. 303, 208 and 214 at Dorchester. Five years later the allocation for March 1878 consisted of Nos. 198 working the Lymington branch, 267 at Bournemouth East, 190 and 256 at Bournemouth West, and 246 and 248 at Dorchester. By 1887 Nos. 201, 202, 243, 256, 258 and 270 were at Bournemouth, frequently working the Swanage branch, and Nos. 197, 198 and 199 were allocated to Northam often appearing on the Brockenhurst-Lymington service. March 1890 saw Nos. 250, 259 and 267 at Bournemouth, No. 260 at Wimborne with Nos. 246 and 327 at Dorchester.

Between 1884 and 1887 no fewer than 31 of the class were rebuilt as tender engines, many reboilered and all fitted with Adams-type cabs, stove pipe chimneys, injectors, vacuum ejectors and steam brakes. Again a number were allocated to the area in March 1887: Northam had Nos. 187, 192, 210, 214, Wimborne Nos. 181 and 207, whilst Dorchester had Nos. 177 and 186. This had changed by June 1888 to Nos. 183, 185, 192, 206, 209 and 217 at Bournemouth, with Nos. 177, 178, 180 and 181 at Dorchester.

Withdrawal of members of the class increased following the introduction of the Adams 'O2' 0-4-4 tanks and other new engines, and with the exception of the celebrated 'Wenford Three' in Cornwall, the entire class had been withdrawn by 1898.

Another class that served the Southampton & Dorchester line were the Beyer, Peacock single-framed 0-6-0 goods engines, a class of 35 constructed between 1874 and 1878 having 17 inch diameter cylinders with a stroke of 22 inches and 5 ft diameter driving wheels. In 1878 six members of the class were allocated to Northam. Between 1886 and 1894 thirty-two members of the class were rebuilt with Adams boilers and cabs. In 1895 No. 347 was reported as allocated to Bournemouth and No. 345 to Dorchester, by 1911 No. 162 was at Bournemouth and No. 342 was noted as working the Lymington goods. Although a few members of the class were withdrawn just prior to World War I many remained in service until the 1920s, No. 345 being the last withdrawn in September 1925.

We now move forward to a selection of locomotives constructed under the superintendency of W.G. Beattie, the son of Joseph Beattie. Firstly the 'Metropolitan', known as such because of their likeness to a class in service with the Metropolitan Railway, these six 4-4-0s had 17-inch diameter cylinders with a stroke of 24 inches and were fitted with 5 ft 9 in. diameter driving wheels. Constructed by Beyer, Peacock during 1875, and numbered 318-323 they were intended for service in the Plymouth area, unfortunately they proved unsuitable.

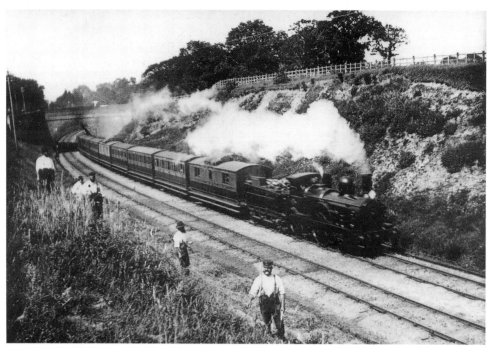

A Beattie 2-4-0 as modified by Adams is seen climbing away from Wimborne at Merley having just passed under the Poole to Wimborne road bridge. The Broadstone Permanent Way gang are in view; their train looks to be in fine condition.   *Terry Saunders Collection*

Adams '135' class 4-4-0 No. 138 stands in Dorchester shed yard, in the background can be seen the rear of the signal box and the water tank. No. 138 built by Messrs Beyer, Peacock in December 1880 at a cost of £2,685 was withdrawn in December 1913 having covered a recorded 1,123, 047 miles.   *Author's Collection*

The Engineer's Department employed No. 323 during 1877 whilst remedial work was carried out between Poole and Branksome, the following year Nos. 321 and 322 were allocated to Dorchester, No. 322 later being loaned for a period to the contractors building the Bournemouth Direct Line, after which she worked from Bournemouth West mainly on Wimborne services.

With the opening of the Direct Line in 1888 Nos. 319, 321, 322 and 323 were transferred to Bournemouth East (Bournemouth Central) where they were employed on a variety of local services including the Swanage branch. It is recorded that No. 321 was derailed at Poole in May 1894 whilst working a goods train and No. 319 ran out of control on Parkstone bank the following year. By the turn of the century the class had moved away from Bournemouth, being withdrawn between 1906 and 1908, with the exception of No. 320 which survived until 1913 having a recorded mileage of 807,120.

The '348' class 4-4-0 express engines were constructed by Sharp, Stewart in 1877. Unfortunately there were a number of design and construction faults causing many problems when the engines entered service which resulted in Beattie's resignation.

It was not until after eight of the class had been reconstructed with Adams boilers and other improvements that reliability and performance was obtained. Amongst those not rebuilt Nos. 361, 363 and 364 were allocated to Dorchester to work out their mileage on local services until withdrawn in 1894. Of those rebuilt No. 356 was allocated to Dorchester and Nos. 348, 349, 353 and 357 to Bournemouth where, during the summer months, they often worked Swanage branch trains. This unhappy saga in LSWR locomotive history ended in March 1905 when the final five were withdrawn.

At this point we revert back 20 years to January 1878 when William Adams became mechanical engineer of the LSWR at a time when more powerful locomotives would be required for heavier trains and more intensive services. In his 17 years in charge Adams produced 524 elegant and robustly-designed locomotives that served the company well.

Adams' first tender locomotives were the 12 members of the '380' class 4-4-0s appearing in 1879, equipped with 5 ft 7 in. diameter driving wheels and intended for fast goods, secondary passenger, and excursion work with Nos. 387/8 allocated to Northam shed. Following the opening of the Bournemouth Direct Line in 1888 members of the class frequently appeared on Sunday excursions, and by the same time Nos. 385/6 were also at Northam working the Bournemouth line. No. 389 was allocated to Dorchester regularly working the up night goods. Eight members of the class survived into Southern Railway ownership, the last withdrawn in December 1925.

The next design to follow, the '135' class 4-4-0 express engines, had 6 ft 7 in. driving wheels, the batch of 12 delivered between November 1880 and January 1881. In March 1888 Nos. 135/6/7 were allocated to Bournemouth for working expresses over the Direct Line; in 1895 the Bournemouth allocation was Nos. 135-140 with Nos. 142, 145 and 146 at Dorchester. Following the introduction of the later Drummond engines, after 1902 the entire class was at Eastleigh working local services until laid up during 1913. The international events of the following year saw them return to service on the duplicate list with Nos. 0312 and 0370 at Dorchester in 1916 for Weymouth-Bournemouth slow services, and Nos. 0307, 0310 and 0347 at Bournemouth as pilots at both stations and banking duties on Parkstone bank. The extended career of No. 0347 came to an abrupt end in December 1916 when, working a naval special from Weymouth to Portsmouth, she failed with a fractured cylinder approaching Brockenhurst. Having travelled a recorded 1,116,947 miles she was officially withdrawn in November 1921.

With further engines required for both the Waterloo-Southampton and Waterloo-Salisbury expresses, Adams again ordered a dozen new locomotives from Robert Stephenson & Co., this time with 7 ft 1 in. diameter driving wheels. Referred to as the '455' class, Nos. 455-456 were delivered in the summer of 1883 with the entire class allocated to Nine Elms. The opening of the Direct Line in March 1888 saw Nos. 452-454 moving to Bournemouth to work the principal Bournemouth expresses, with other members of the class over the years becoming Bournemouth based. The class was considered the freest running of all Adams 4-4-0s. Between 1888 and 1891 Adams experimented with compounding, No. 446 being the chosen engine working on the Wordsell-Von-Borries compound system. In trials conducted in conjunction with conventional engine No. 448, the latter was recorded as having achieved 80 mph near Wool whilst compound No. 446 was credited with 78 mph. In general the compound showed few advantages over the conventional locomotive.

Later usurped by more modern locomotives and some members of the class suffering from a reduced performance after the fitting of Drummond boilers, the years leading up to World War I saw 11 of their number working slow passenger trains and other secondary duties between Southampton and Weymouth. The entire class eventually was withdrawn in 1924-1925.

Adams' next design was for a mixed traffic 4-4-0 with 6 ft 7 in. driving wheels, the '460' class, of which originally 30 were ordered, 10 each from Robert Stephenson, Messrs Neilson, and Kitson. In the event the Kitson order was cancelled following a disagreement concerning additional payments, the remaining 20 locomotives being delivered during 1884. An additional member of the class constructed by Stephenson for an exhibition at Newcastle to celebrate Queen Victoria's Jubilee in 1887 was later purchased for £2,500. No. 526 was a bargain finished to exhibition standard, often employed on Royal Trains and other specials including the inaugural special for the opening of the Bournemouth Direct Line on 5th March, 1888. From this date Nos. 569, 575 and 576 were transferred to Bournemouth East (Central) for working Waterloo expresses. For a number of years No. 470 was loaned to Dorchester during the summer months to handle the additional traffic there.

Again the introduction of newer locomotives saw the class relegated to lesser duties. In March 1896 Nos. 147, 463/73/7 were at Northam, Nos. 460/2/76/8 at Bournemouth and No. 475 at Dorchester. By 1911 Bournemouth was allocated Nos. 460/2/76/7, often working the Salisbury-Bournemouth service and local passenger and goods services to Dorchester, Weymouth and the Swanage branch. Placed on the duplicate list in 1912, the entire class passed into Southern Railway ownership in 1923. The following year saw Nos. 0465, 0468, 0472 and 0475 allocated to Bournemouth working Salisbury and Weymouth services, the Swanage branch, local goods and piloting at both Central and West stations. No. 0465 was the first to be withdrawn in December 1924, with the last two going in April 1929.

The opening of the Direct Line, together with other improvements on the LSWR system including heavier trains and improved schedules, were to tax the earlier Adams 4-4-0s of the '135', '445' and '460' classes, although in their time they ranked amongst the largest and most powerful express engines of the day. The need for further improvement led to Adams designing the 'X2' class 4-4-0s with 7 ft 1 in. driving wheels, completed at Nine Elms works between June 1890 and May 1892 and intended for the heaviest and fastest Salisbury and Bournemouth expresses. The 20 members of the class were initially allocated to Nine Elms, Salisbury and Bournemouth, the latter's allocation being Nos. 585, 586, 589 and 594.

Relegated to secondary duties following the introduction of Drummond's 'T9' class between 1899 and 1901, they were to be seen on Waterloo-Bournemouth semi-fasts, Eastleigh-Bournemouth-Weymouth slows and often worked summer reliefs and excursions. By 1925 none were allocated to Bournemouth, although Nos. 586 and 592 of Salisbury often worked the Salisbury-Bournemouth West service. Withdrawal commenced in December 1930 and by August 1937 only No. 586 remained, to be condemned in March 1939, but owing to the war situation she was repaired and returned to service in November working a variety of duties including Southampton-Weymouth goods via the Old Road. On 20th March, 1941 she was reported as working a train of refrigerated meat vans from Southampton to Bournemouth West, and later piloting at the Central station. Returning to Eastleigh she was eventually withdrawn in November 1942 having covered 1,323,177 miles.

Striving to improve performance still further Adams introduced the 20 'T3' class of 4-4-0 express engine during 1893. Equipped with 7 ft 1 in. driving wheels they were numbered 557-596 with Nos. 566 and 567 allocated to Northam and 573 and 575 at Bournemouth. It is recorded that No. 559 was loaned to Dorchester during the summer of 1895 working a Weymouth-Waterloo service on alternate days. Later replaced on top duties by newer engines they became scattered around the system. With the formation of the Southern Railway No. 567 was at Bournemouth and No. 557 at Dorchester, by which time a number appeared on summer Saturdays working Waterloo-Bournemouth semi-fast reliefs, and taking over cross-country services from the GWR at Basingstoke for Bournemouth. In 1929 Bournemouth had No. 576 and Dorchester Nos. 557 and 560, both employed as pilots on heavy Southern Railway trains between Weymouth and Dorchester.

The first member of the class was condemned in October 1930 with only 563 and 571 surviving into the war years. The former was condemned in August 1945 after travelling a recorded 1,571,150 miles but was restored for the Waterloo Centenary celebrations of 1948 and subsequently became an exhibit at the former Clapham Transport Museum and today resides in the National Railway Museum at York.

The 'T6' class of ten 4-4-0 express engines (Nos. 677-786) delivered from Nine Elms works in late 1885/early 1886 again had 7 ft 1 in. driving wheels and were an enlarged and improved version of the previous 'X2' class. Again they were employed on the best Bournemouth and Salisbury expresses with Nos. 680, 683

Adams 'X2' class 4-4-0 No. 592 in her later years on pilot duty at Bournemouth Central. Built in March 1892 No. 592 was withdrawn in December 1936. *Author's Collection*

Adams 'T3' class 4-4-0 No. 569 stands outside Dorchester shed in Southern Railway days, and was withdrawn from service in May 1932. Built at Nine Elms in June 1893 one of a class of 20 locomotives the last of which No. 563 was withdrawn in August 1945 and today is preserved at the National Railway Museum, York. *Author's Collection*

and 684 allocated to Bournemouth and Nos. 677-682 and 686 at Nine Elms on duties they retained until being relegated to secondary work in 1911. By the mid-1920s two were allocated to Dorchester often working Weymouth-Southampton slow trains, piloting London expresses on summer Saturdays and working a daily pick-up goods to Bournemouth.

Eight members of the class were withdrawn between 1933 and 1937 with No. 684 going in May 1940. The survivor No. 681 was loaned to Bournemouth in September 1940 working Weymouth 'slows' for a few weeks and returned as station pilot at Central over the Christmas of 1942. Her final duty was the Hamworthy Junction-Ringwood-Eastleigh goods on 24th February, 1943, being withdrawn in the April with a recorded mileage of 1,506,148.

Adams' final express design was the 'X6' class 4-4-0s - a modified version of the previous 'T6' class but fitted with 6 ft 7 in. driving wheels. Primarily built for the West of England and Portsmouth services, they rarely put in appearances on the Bournemouth line until around 1905 when they moved to secondary duties During August 1911 Nos. 662 and 665 were reported working Weymouth-Dorchester-Eastleigh services, and the following summer Nos. 660, 662, 663 and 664 were at Bournemouth with No. 661 at Dorchester.

During World War I the class were spread around the system. After 1923 Nos. 661 and 665 were at Dorchester working Weymouth-Bournemouth stopping services and Dorchester-Ringwood-Eastleigh goods. By 1932 they were replaced by Nos. 659 and 660 with only the former remaining the following year. Withdrawal commenced in 1933 with several of the survivors putting in appearances at Southampton and Bournemouth during the war years, the final member of the class being withdrawn in December 1946.

Concurrent with the development of Adams' handsome express engines there were a large number of goods engines and various tank engines to fulfil the requirements of the expanding services. Adams' first goods engine, the 0-6-0 '395' class of which Messrs Neilson constructed 70 between 1881 and 1885, were to take over from the ageing Beattie classes.

Spread across the system the October 1883 allocation saw No. 444 at Bournemouth with Nos. 398 and 443 at Northam, the expanding Southampton Docks traffic seeing 12 of the class at Northam by March 1888, with Nos. 159, 163 and 509 at Bournemouth and Nos. 164 and 510 at Dorchester two years later. The class handled the heaviest freight traffic and could also be seen on excursion and other passenger workings until after the turn of the 20th century when, replaced by the new Drummond classes, they took over local and branch freight workings. World War I saw 50 members of the class commandeered by the Government for foreign service, the resulting shortage being made up by the loan of engines from other companies, including Great Northern Railway 'J4' class 0-6-0 No. 846 allocated to Bournemouth between November 1917 and November 1920.

The return of peace saw the remaining members of the class still active, with No. 0154 allocated to Dorchester during 1925, two were withdrawn during 1933 and apart from No. 3101, noted shunting at Poole and Dorchester during November 1943, their visits to the Southampton & Dorchester line ceased. Withdrawal of the remaining stock commenced in 1950, the final two surviving until late 1959.

Adams '395' class 0-6-0 goods engine No. 442 forms a backdrop as railway staff pose for their photograph to be taken at Dorchester shed. No. 442 was constructed in May 1883 and survived until August 1957 proving the benefits of a solid yet simple design.

G.A. Pryer Collection

Although the '395' class goods engines were suitable for the purpose for which they were built, Adams required a further class of engine capable of working fast freights, van trains and available for use on semi-fast passenger services. The result was the 'A12' class 0-4-2 locomotives known as the 'Jubilees' owing to the first series entering service in 1887, Queen Victoria's Golden Jubilee year. They were also the first locomotives to be constructed by the LSWR at Nine Elms for a number of years, a total of 90 being constructed by 1895, although a batch of 40 were built by Messrs Neilsons.

When new in 1889 Nos. 552 and 554 were allocated to Bournemouth and by 1892 members of the class were working the fast Dorchester-Nine Elms freights with No. 532 being involved in a collision at Wimborne two years later. Throughout the years there were usually one or two working around the Bournemouth area. In 1932 Nos. 624 and 656 were based there, the former often employed on carriage heating duties at Bournemouth West.

After a lifetime of varied and heavy work withdrawal commenced in 1928 with only 32 remaining 10 years later. By then an Eastleigh working was the Hamworthy Junction-Bournemouth-Eastleigh goods, and Eastleigh-Dorchester goods via the Old Road, returning with the 7.34 pm milk vans, whilst Dorchester-allocated No. 612 often worked goods to Eastleigh over the Old Road. The outbreak of war in 1939 gave the remaining engines a further lease of life: No. 555 was reported working at Bournemouth, Poole, Dorchester and Weymouth during April 1940 and No. 644 made appearances at Bournemouth in the June. Four remained in traffic to enter British Railways stock in January 1948 with the last being withdrawn in the November, all having given a lifetime of exceptional service.

Adams 'Jubilee' class 0-4-2 No. 536 passes Wimborne Junction signal box with a down goods shortly before the closure of the box and the original Dorset Central section to Corfe Mullen Junction in 1933.   *Mrs E. Edwards*

Adams also designed 245 tank engines during his time at Nine Elms. His first design in 1879 was 12 class '46' 4-4-0 tank locomotives for Waterloo suburban services. Rebuilt as 4-4-2 tanks with larger bunkers and increased water capacity they remained in the London area until 1907; by then renumbered on the duplicate list Nos. 0374, 0375, 0376 and 0133 were transferred to Bournemouth. Two of the class were sub-shedded at Hamworthy Junction to work local services where their ponderous actions quickly earned them the sobriquet 'Hamworthy Buses'. Later joined by Nos. 0124, 0132 and 0378, despite their reputation they gave good service. The last of the class No. 0375 was withdrawn in 1925 having accrued 1,318,510 miles.

Further increases in traffic and the need to replace older locomotives saw the introduction of the '415' class 4-4-2 tanks with 5 ft 7 in. driving wheels, intended for suburban, slow and branch passenger services. A improvement on the previous '46' class, they were fitted with well tanks under the cab and bunker holding 680 gallons of water with only 320 gallons being carried in the unusually small side tanks. The first 12 engines were delivered from Messrs Beyer, Peacock between August and November 1882 and proved very successful; by October 1885 the class consisted of 71 locomotives with batches supplied by Messrs Stephenson, Dübs, Neilson and Kitson. The following year saw No. 52 allocated to Bournemouth East, and Nos. 54, 57 and 519 to Bournemouth West.

By 1905 a number had been displaced from the London area. In August 1911 Nos. 0416, 0420, 0424, 0425, 0487, 0519 were recorded as working in the Bournemouth area on local services including Bournemouth-Salisbury, Bournemouth-Brockenhurst via the Old Road, Bournemouth-Ringwood via

Adams '46' class 4-4-2 tank No. 378 stands outside at the back of Bournemouth Central shed. Built by Messrs Beyer, Peacock in August 1879 as a 4-4-0 tank, the entire class were later rebuilt as 4-4-2 tanks, No. 378 receiving attention in August 1885. In August she was allocated to Bournemouth where with other members of the class she worked local services. Owing to their ponderous movements they were locally referred to as the 'Hamworthy Buses'. No. 378 was withdrawn in May 1923. *R.K. Blencowe Collection*

Adams Radial Tank No. 52 runs down the 1 in 50 gradient towards Bournemouth West with a local train in the years before World War. I On 20th January, 1890 No. 52 with a driver unfamiliar to the class was approaching Bournemouth West with a train from Brockenhurst, when he miscalculated his distance and struck stock standing at the head of the platform. *J. Boudreau Collection*

Hurn, and the Swanage branch. Following the Grouping in 1923, Nos. 0416, 0431, 0480, 0483 and 0485 were at Bournemouth covering the same services. However, their time was running out, by 1927 the entire class except Nos. 0125 and 0520 had been withdrawn, the two survivors later being joined by a repurchased No. 0488. This engine remained to work the Lyme Regis branch until withdrawn in 1961; fortunately No. 582 is today preserved by the Bluebell Railway.

June 1888 saw the introduction of the first of 50 'T1' class 0-4-4 tanks, Adams having abandoned his previous idea of outside cylinders and leading bogies for tank locomotives. With 5 ft 7 in. driving wheels the new engines were large machines and following the success of the initial batch the class was increased to 50, all constructed at Nine Elms. A majority of the class when new was allocated to London area sheds. There is some doubt as to the early allocation at Bournemouth, although Nos. 18 and 75 were recorded as being there in March 1897, and Nos. 1, 6, 20, 67 and 75 there by mid-1905 and No. 15 in August 1911. During July 1917 Nos. 4 and 20 were equipped for push-pull working over the Old Road; in March 1918 No. 11 was working the Lymington branch being exchanged for No. 18 the following month.

Withdrawal of the class commenced in 1931, Bournemouth continuing to have a varied allocation which in June 1937 consisted of Nos. 2, 7, 362, 364, with Nos. 7 and 364 withdrawn during 1939. But hey were quickly reinstated and the following year were often working the Swanage branch with No. 2 as Bournemouth West pilot until late 1941 when with a number of other members of the class loaned to the Somerset & Dorset line to alleviate a locomotive shortage. By mid-1945 No. 363, the sole 'T1' at Bournemouth, was often rostered to work the Swanage Goods.

In December 1889 the first of the 'O2' class 0-4-4 tanks appeared in service; introduced as replacements for the ageing Beattie well tanks these small but powerful engines with 4 ft 10 in. driving wheels were to prove to be excellent performers. Some 60 members of the class were soon distributed around the system. No. 180 was named *Alexandra* for the opening of the Bisley Camp branch in July 1890, the name being removed during the Drummond regime.

Dorchester received a number of these tanks in the early days to replace the well tanks employed on the Portland branch; the allocation in March 1896 was Nos. 215/6/21 with Nos. 200 and 208 at Bournemouth often employed on Bournemouth West-Salisbury services. The class also appeared on the Lymington branch, in 1911 No. 203 was recorded as working the branch, whilst Dorchester had five members of the class. Following the formation of the Southern Railway in 1923 a number of these useful engines were transferred to the Isle of Wight, over the years 23 making the voyage, all receiving the name of an island town or village.

In 1939 Dorchester, always a stronghold for the class, had an allocation of six and still retained five at the end of December 1945. The closure of the Portland branch to passenger traffic in 1952 reduced their number; of these, No. 177 had been at Dorchester for long periods since at least 1928. Two of the class remained, one of their duties being the daily Dorchester-Easton goods, until reorganisation in 1954 saw all Portland goods duties transferred to Weymouth, thus ending Dorchester's 65 year association with the class.

Adams 'T1' class 0-4-4 tank No. 1 shunts wagons in Poole goods yard on 19th June, 1934. A close examination of the cab roof reveals the pulleys still in position from when the engine was push-pull fitted with the LSWR wire operated system. No. 1 was built in April 1894 and gave useful service for 55 years until withdrawn in June 1949.   *Author's Collection*

In immaculate condition Adams 'O2' class 0-4-4 tank No. 108 waits to depart from Bournemouth West with a Salisbury train on 7th August, 1902. Built in December 1891 No. 108 survived 75 years until December 1966. Shipped to the Isle of Wight in May 1930 and renumbered as W17 *Seaview* she remained until the end of steam operation on the Island's rail system.

Author's Collection

At nationalisation, of the original 60 engines 48 were still in service, 25 on the mainland and 23 on the Isle of Wight. In 1949 Nos. 30204 and 30412 were allocated to Bournemouth replacing 'M7s' on station pilot duties. However, the closure of a number of branch lines and the availability of new BR Standard tanks saw the gradual demise of the class, the final mainland withdrawal taking place in late 1962. On the Isle of Wight a reduced number survived until the end of steam in December 1966, fortunately No. 209 as W24 *Calbourne* was saved and today can be seen in action complete with vintage stock on the Isle of Wight Steam Railway.

Horses undertook shunting in a number of smaller goods yards until the 1890s, whilst a number of unsuitable engines and elderly saddle tanks were employed in other places. With expanding traffic and the desire to speed up proceedings in general Adams designed a small but powerful 0-4-0 side tank, the 'B4' class, constructed in two batches of 10 between October 1891 and December 1893. With 3 ft 9¾ in. driving wheels, a wheelbase of 7 ft and a total weight of 33 tons 9 cwt they were ideal for their purpose in particular in yards with sharp curves and weight restrictions.

Initially spread across the system from Plymouth in the west to Nine Elms in the east they performed proficiently at their task of shunting and as station pilots. However, their use in larger yards proved less successful, the small amount of coal stored in small bunkers on the footplate limiting their range.

The acquisition of the Southampton Docks Company and its assorted collection of small saddle tanks saw two members of the class, Nos. 81 and 176, transferred to the Docks Department in November 1893 and named *Jersey* and *Guernsey* respectively. With the exception of the temporary naming of No. 185 *Alexandra* they became the first Adams engines to receive names.

Success in their new found employment and the expansion of the docks complex resulted in the transfer of a further 10 members of the class in the following eight years. On the main line the 0-6-0 'G6' class (*see below*) superseded their employment. However, their short wheelbase ensured their survival at a number of locations where restrictions precluded the use of other engines. Drummond had four additional engines with minor modifications made in 1908 and classed as 'K14'; of these two went to the Docks Department and as with previous transfers received names, also until November 1933 their maintenance was the responsibility of the Docks Department.

Bournemouth received its first allocation of the class in April 1904 when Nos. 88, 94 and 103 arrived, one employed as Bournemouth Central station pilot with two sub-shedded at Hamworthy Junction working the Hamworthy branch and the Poole Harbour Tramway. From that time, apart from assorted saddle tanks appearing to cover repairs, and the loan of No. 94 to Messrs Kynock Ltd between April and December 1915, the 'B4' tanks became the regular Poole Quay engines, the allocation changing over the years as the class moved around to cover visits to Eastleigh works.

World War II effectively ended the separation of the main line and Dock Department members of the class; following the fall of France reduced shipping movements at Southampton resulted in less shunting duties. By August 1940 Nos. 81 *Jersey*, 89 *Trouville* and 101 *Dinan* were recorded as being in store at

Adams 'B4' class No. 30096 stands alongside Hamworthy Goods station during 1953. Built in November 1893 and originally named *Normandy* she was the last of the class to remain in service. When withdrawn she was sold to a coal merchant and returned to Southampton shunting at Dibbles Wharf. Sold to the Bulleid Preservation Society for £1,000 in 1972, today she is preserved on the Bluebell Railway. *R.B. Gosling*

Adams 'G6' class 0-60 tank No. 262 stands outside Dorchester engine shed. From the time of their introduction until the later years Dorchester usually had one member of the class to handle shunting duties and in earlier days the Portland goods traffic. No. 262 was built in September 1894 and withdrawn from service in November 1949. *Author's Collection*

Hamworthy Junction, and in October 1941 No. 102 *Granville* was allocated to Bournemouth, working the Poole Quay tramway. With the build up to D-Day all had returned to Southampton by April 1944. The slow return to normality saw Nos. 92, 99 and 100 working at Bournemouth with No. 88 in store.

However, the purchase of 14 'USA' 0-6-0 tanks in 1946 for shunting within Southampton Docks saw the 'B4s' replaced by November 1947 from which time only occasional visits were made to the docks. Fourteen members of the class were withdrawn of which 11 were sold to various contractors for £700 apiece. The remaining 11, a mixture of former dock tanks and others, were allocated where needed. In April 1947 No. 93 *St Malo* was sent to Bournemouth where the allocation in June 1949 consisted of Nos. 86 *Havre*, 87 and 93 *St Malo*. Again there were changes as engines went to Eastleigh works, No. 87 as 30087 remaining at Bournemouth until condemned in December 1958, her replacement being No. 102 (30102) *Granville*. No. 93 *St Malo* as 30093 was transferred to Winchester in February 1960 leaving No. 30102 *Granville* to work the last train over the Poole Harbour Tramway on 26th April, 1960. No. 30102 was the last 'B4' to depart Bournemouth shed a month later, thus ending a 56-year relationship where they were synominous with the Poole Harbour Tramway.

A further requirement for a shunting engine with greater power and range than the previous 'B4s' saw Adams introduce 10 'G6' 0-6-0 tanks between June and December 1894; with 4 ft 10 in. driving wheels they had many features common with the previous 'O2' class. Their success saw Drummond order the construction of a further 24 between 1896 and 1900, the class being spread across the system.

Dorchester had received 'G6' class No. 358 new in August 1894 for yard shunting and working the Portland goods traffic. In 1901 the allocation was two, Nos. 258 and 273 to shunt the yard and handle the LSWR goods traffic over the Portland branch which in 1900 had been extended to Easton. However, within a few years the usual allocation was one member of the class at both Dorchester and Bournemouth.

In May 1922 No. 263 was equipped with vacuum brake and carried out trials over the Portland branch with passenger traffic, but in the event was less successful than the 'O2' class and had the equipment removed and returned to shunting duties. Withdrawal of the class commenced in August 1948 at which time the pattern of one allocated to Dorchester and one to Bournemouth still applied with No. 30162 at the latter until departure in mid-1954, thus leaving the depot without a 'G6' since their introduction. No. 30260 remained shunting Bournemouth Central goods yard until withdrawn in April 1959 to be replaced by No. 30274. Within months Bournemouth received its first diesel shunter resulting in No. 30274 being withdrawn in October 1960.

A deposited plan showing the proposed arrangements at Weymouth for the Southampton & Dorchester Company station on land now occupied by the Park District. Had these plans been proceeded with, the station would have been situated on the lower line on the plan terminating in the present Victoria Street behind the Hotel Prince Regent. The line curving across the centre would have joined the future GWR Wilts, Somerset & Weymouth Railway on the site of the present station. Had these plans come to fruition very little if any of the present housing in the Park District would have been constructed.

Courtesy Dorset History Centre

Chapter Fourteen

The Weymouth Branch and
Dorchester Extension Plans

At this point in the narrative it is desirable to outline two schemes that had they proceeded would have had a significant impact on the Southampton & Dorchester Railway and the railway map of the West of England in general. Even before the Southampton & Dorchester had been constructed the company considered two possible extensions, an independent line to Weymouth, and secondly an extension from Dorchester to Exeter, the latter a strongly felt desire of both Moorsom and Castleman.

A Proposed independent line to Weymouth

During 1845 the Southampton & Dorchester company considered the construction of an independent line to Weymouth with its own station and an extension to the harbour, the LSWR not wishing to see the port of Weymouth with its potential Channel Islands traffic in the sole hands of the GWR.

The planned route was to have left the main line east of Moreton station on the Wool side of 'Red Bridge'. It would have run across heathland before crossing the present Bere Regis-Warmwell Cross Road (B3390) on the level before following it on the west side, passing through Warmwell and then crossing the Warmwell Cross-Broadmayne Road. Skirting the west of the Weymouth Road (A353) just before Poxwell the line would have reached its summit 300 ft above sea level, and been in a 75 ft deep cutting less than a hundred yards from Poxwell Manor House before entering a 1,210 yds-long tunnel to emerge just north of Osmington village.

Taking advantage of the fold in the hills the line was to descend on a gradient of 1 in 1,000 through the valley below the White Horse and then pass between Sutton Poyntz and Preston to follow the north side of Preston road. Curving with the road at Chalbury Lodge it would, after passing through Southdown Farm, strike out at a tangent across the salt marsh at Lodmoor on a low embankment before entering Weymouth via Greenhill. The Dorchester Road would have had to be raised 14 ft to allow the line clearance to reach its terminus in an area now known as the Park District. Had the scheme proceeded the prospects for that area now densely packed with terrace houses would have been entirely different.

The exact location and details of the proposed terminus are not known as only the basic route of the line is shown in the surviving plans. The Weymouth Council minutes for 1st February, 1847 state:

> The Council assented to the passing of the Moreton branch of the Southampton & Dorchester Railway on condition that the terminus be placed to the west side of the carriage road [now known as Crescent Street and Victoria Street] set out on the east side of the park and not less than 80 feet behind the old quay wall behind 'Belvedere Cottage' [today the site of the Crescent Street Surgery].

A class '47' stands with a ballast train on the down line at Redbridge, east of Moreton during electrification works in 1988. It was at this point the planned direct line to Weymouth would have curved away to the right. *Author*

Plan for the proposed Southampton & Dorchester Company direct railway to Weymouth, leaving the Dorchester line at Red Bridge, east of Moreton it would have passed Warmwell Cross, Poxwell and Osmington before running in the valley under the White Horse to Preston and Chalbury before turning south across Lodmoor salt marsh and entering Weymouth from the east.

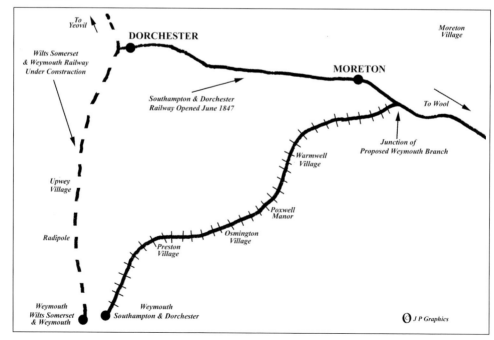

This suggests that the station would have taken in an area of the present Grange Road, Victoria Street, and land to the west thereof.

Just after passing under the Dorchester Road a spur was to have curved away across the north end of the present Park area, turning left to run into what became the Weymouth station of the Wilts, Somerset & Weymouth Railway, which was later constructed within a ¼ mile of the proposed Southampton & Dorchester station.

Objections to the scheme were minimal, the east end of the proposed line crossed empty heathland, and the Park area of Weymouth was undeveloped and becoming a deep embarrassment to the Corporation which had originally planned to landscape the 50 acres of marshy land that had been reclaimed from the Backwater into a public park. However, after many years of argument, and the construction of the GWR station on the west side of the reclaimed area, the park scheme was finally abandoned and after 1861 the remaining land was developed with densely-packed terraced housing. Today known as the Park District it covers the ground between the railway and the Esplanade.

The principal objector to the scheme was John Trenchard, Lord of the Manor of Poxwell, who informed the company that he intended to speak against the Bill in Parliament unless certain conditions were met. His main objection was that the line running close to the Manor House would cut through the gardens of his farm cottages. Eventually it was agreed to insert clauses in the Act to protect Trenchard's estate and an agreement between Trenchard and Castleman stipulated that either the tunnel would be extended to 1,370 yards in length, partly on a curve to conceal it from the manor house, or the railway would pay Trenchard £5,000 to build a new residence well away from the line and convert the existing manor into a farmhouse. Castleman and the Board no doubt thought they had solved the problem but became involved in further disputes which culminated in an agreement on 18th August, 1847 by which the company were to pay Trenchard £5,000 straightaway, plus a further £175 for every acre of land taken and a deposit of £6,000 against any future claims. The company also agreed to 'make a passenger and goods station within 250 yards of the boundaries of the parishes of Warmwell and Poxwell'.

Poxwell Manor viewed from the east. Had plans for the branch to Weymouth proceeded the line would have passed behind the manor house in a cutting before entering a tunnel under the hill on the left.   *Author*

After much delay the Southampton & Dorchester Railway's Weymouth Branch Bill received the Royal Assent on 2nd July, 1847. However, the takeover of the company by the LSWR the following year and the signing of a working agreement with the GWR for running rights between Dorchester and Weymouth made the project, estimated at £90,000, unrealistic and the powers were allowed to lapse. An appeal by one of Weymouth's two members of Parliament, Col W. Lockyer Freeston, frustrated at the lack of progress with the Wilts, Somerset & Weymouth line, to the LSWR Directors during 1849 to reconsider the matter was unsuccessful. Thus Weymouth never obtained a second railway route and station, and Trenchard received nothing, his attempts to improve his estate at the railway's expense having failed!

The Proposed Dorchester-Exeter Extension

The Exeter extension was surveyed by Moorsom and went before Parliament in 1845 with a Bill under the title of the 'Exeter, Dorchester, Weymouth Junction Railway', and included a line from a junction east of Bridport cutting across to Weymouth. It was a bold scheme in view of the recommendations concerning company boundaries recently drawn up by the 'Five Kings', and the geology of the route west of Dorchester was difficult. However, the Government for defence purposes was desirous to see a continuous line of railway along the coast to Plymouth. Other contenders at that time included schemes under the titles of the Exeter, Great Western Railway, and the Exeter, Yeovil & Dorchester Railway. These two schemes envisaged utilizing the proposed Bridport Railway to Maiden Newton then joining the proposed Wilts, Somerset & Weymouth line. Although with both schemes the Exeter end was well suited for westward connections, the east end terminating at Maiden Newton on a north-south route was not conducive of direct travel eastwards, and these were two of the many schemes that failed to materialize.

Little else was heard of the Southampton & Dorchester extension until late 1851 when Castleman and Moorsom revived the scheme as the Dorchester & Exeter Coast Extension Railway, with the Weymouth branch omitted and several other minor alterations made. Although the existing LSWR station at Dorchester was a terminal facing west, owing to the proposed Wilts, Somerset & Weymouth line crossing the path of any extension in less than 100 yards to the west, the LSWR had to choose a circuitous route to proceed westwards. Plans of the proposed extension show the line leaving the existing line to the east of the existing Dorchester station and curving north to take the course of the present Cornwall Road before crossing the Bridport Road (A35) and skirting the edge of the later Barracks site curving west to cross the Wilts, Somerset & Weymouth Railway north of the Bridport Road. The line would then curve south re-crossing the Dorchester-Bridport Road heading south-west to pass the north side of the villages of Martinstown and Winterbourne Abbas before descending through the Bride Valley to Burton Bradstock. After this the proposed route would skirt around the north of Bridport before crossing the Marshwood Vale towards Axminster, from where it would virtually take the route to Exeter of the later Yeovil & Exeter Railway.

A further proposed railway, which lacked the impact of the proposed LSWR coastal route, was the Great Western & Exeter Coast Railway. Announced at the July 1852 Board meeting of the Bristol & Exeter Railway, it was a joint scheme by the Great Western and the Bristol & Exeter Railway companies to construct a railway from the Bristol & Exeter main line at Stoke Canon, north of Exeter, to Maiden Newton to join the Wilts, Somerset & Weymouth line of the Great Western Railway. *En route* it was to pass through or near the towns of Honiton, Axminster and Bridport (with such branches as were mutually agreed). The line would have been about 50 miles long and - with an allowance for branches - cost an estimated £800,000. However, as with earlier schemes involving the Bridport branch no further progress was made.

Early in 1853, it being anticipated that the GWR would apply to Parliament for powers to construct the above mentioned line, a special general meeting of LSWR shareholders was held. Following a ballot, a resolution was passed giving full power to the Directors to raise capital and to take necessary steps for the construction of the line from Dorchester to Exeter, via Bridport and Axminster. The number of votes in favour of the resolution was 20,645 whilst against it there were only 3,441, giving a majority of 17,205 votes. The resolution having been passed, the Chairman wrote to the Chairman of the Parliamentary Committee of Railways during May, pledging the Directors to proceed with the construction of the line, upon which the Bill of the Great Western company was rejected.

During that period events both northwards and eastwards were moving fast.* The Directors of the LSWR received a report from their Engineer, Mr Errington, who was of the opinion that a single line of railway from Dorchester to Exeter with land to allow for conversion to double track could be constructed for £700,000 and that a connection with the Exeter & Crediton Railway and the Bristol & Exeter lines might be completed for £100,000.

The application to Parliament was to be for powers to construct, within five years of the passing of the Act, a single line of railway from Dorchester to Exeter, there to be connected with the Bristol & Exeter and Exeter & Crediton lines, with land for a double line.

The Bill contained an obligation to make the extension line double between Exeter and Axminster within five years after the opening of the line, and also between Dorchester and Axminster within the same period, unless in the meantime an Act was passed for making a narrow gauge railway from Salisbury to Axminster. The latter statement was to have significant bearing on future events! A branch had served Salisbury from Bishopstoke (Eastleigh) since March 1847. Although not the most direct route from London, its existence was later to form part of an important route to Southampton and Portsmouth, and the presence of the LSWR at Salisbury was an important stepping-stone in the South Western's expansion to the West.

Firstly, an Act was passed in 1848 allowing the construction of the Salisbury and Yeovil Railway, with further schemes for the continuation of that line westwards from Yeovil and Exeter, and a direct line linking Basingstoke to Salisbury. This cast a shadow over the Dorchester-Exeter scheme, added to which there was pressure from the Military for a continuous line of railway

* See *Yeovil; 150 Years of Railways*, B.L. Jackson, Oakwood Press, 2003 for full details.

from Dover to Plymouth, preferably without a break of gauge. Faced with a choice of two routes, the 'Coastal Route' (Dorchester-Exeter), and the 'Central Route' (Yeovil-Exeter) opinions were divided within the LSWR Board and amongst the shareholders. At a special meeting held on the 15th November, 1853, the report of the Directors recommended the construction of the Dorchester-Exeter extension. However, an amendment was moved:

> That this meeting declines to take any liability for raising the capital to construct the extension of a railway between Dorchester and Exeter, being of opinion that such extension is impolitic and unremunerative, especially in the present unlooked for state of public affairs, and would involve considerable injustice to a large body of shareholders individually protesting against the measure, and further, that this meeting is not bound to adopt the deviations made by the Board from the terms of the pledge given to the committee of the House of Commons.

The amendment was carried with a considerable majority and a poll was demanded, in which the amendment against any further extension of the line was carried by only a majority of three votes. If this itself was not a narrow enough decision, the outcome was further complicated by claims of tampering with some votes and creating others of a fictitious character for the purpose of carrying out the scheme. These claims resulted in a libel case being brought against *The Times* newspaper by the Hon. F. Scott, Chairman of the LSWR, and seven Directors.

However, the matter was far from dead. Further discussions had taken place resulting in the company preparing a consolidation Bill, the principal purpose of which was to embrace many of the company's powers into a single Act, which received the Royal Assent the following year. In August 1855 the LSWR Board appointed a committee for the purpose of investigating the extension to Exeter, and the Board also discussed the matter, arriving at the same conclusion,

> ...that if the extension were to be made from Dorchester it should form a new line throughout, and any savings of cost achieved by adopting and running over a part of the sanctioned broad gauge lines under the control of other companies and the necessary mixture of gauge was inconsistent with the interests of the LSWR. A further consideration respecting the traffic of the two rival lines was which of them would be least liable to invasion by other proposed railways or future developments.
>
> It was felt that the Yeovil-Exeter line could not be considered apart from the Salisbury and Yeovil Railway, and could not be adopted without adequate security that the latter railway would in fact be constructed and worked under proper agreements with the LSWR. The proposed line from Dorchester to Exeter would be 58 miles in length and the distance from London 191½ miles, whereas the proposed line from Yeovil to Exeter would be 50 miles in length, and 171½ miles from London, showing a difference in favour of the Yeovil to Exeter [or 'Central Line' as it was usually known]. The cost of construction of the Yeovil-Exeter line would be somewhat under £600,000 whilst the Dorchester and Exeter line came to nearer £700,000! The two lines were identical for 30 miles between Axminister to Exeter, the difference in cost being due to the greater length and heavier works between Dorchester and Axminster, where there would be no less than 8 miles of gradients of 1 in 80, while on the Yeovil to Axminster line there would be no more than 3 miles of that gradient. There was also consideration in the expense of the working, it being calculated that the haulage cost per trip on London-Exeter traffic via Yeovil would be 12% less than via Dorchester.

The Dorchester line would receive the benefits of traffic coming from the West that would materially increase receipts on the existing Southampton & Dorchester Railway, whereas the Yeovil route would make a very large addition to the traffic of the Salisbury-Basingstoke line and the Salisbury-Bishopstoke (Eastleigh) line.

The Yeovil line would carry all the traffic of the district which it transversed, whereas the Dorchester line would, for more than half its length have a competing line, which, from the character of the Bridport trade, would draw the greater portion of the traffic from the only place of importance between Dorchester and Axminster and also compete for a share of local traffic. It was also considered that although the Salisbury and Yeovil line would prevent any of the traffic from the Company's line at Axminster being carried over the Dorchester line, the abstraction of traffic in the Bridport area by the broad gauge branches would not make the additional outlay on the Dorchester-Axminster section a viable proposition. Taking into account increase of traffic which would be secured permanently to the Company's Salisbury and Bishopstoke (Eastleigh) lines, the committee recommend the Board to obtain an Act for making the line from Yeovil to Exeter.

However, the question of extending westwards from Dorchester refused to fade away, and schemes for both Dorchester and Yeovil was again mooted, plans for both being deposited during 1856, and tenders duly received. The engineering difficulties and greater cost of the coastal route plus Great Western activity in west Dorset went against that scheme, whilst the easier country and anticipated extension from Salisbury to Yeovil brought the Central Route into favour. Powers for the construction of the Yeovil-Exeter line were obtained on 21st May, 1856 and the 'coast line' was allowed to fade away. The battle was over, ending many years of acrimonious arguments within the Board and amongst the shareholders, and thus the die was cast for the future of railways in the South-West.

The Basingstoke line opened on 2nd May, 1859, Salisbury to Yeovil opened to traffic on 1st June, 1860, the extension to Exeter following on 19th July. There was now a through standard gauge route between London and Exeter. The broad gauge Wilts, Somerset & Weymouth line was completed to Weymouth in January 1857, ending the end of the battle of the gauges, and apart from the fanciful schemes of the Abbotsbury Railway Company no further plans unfolded to connect Dorchester directly with the West of England.

The sharp curvature of the Eling Tramway is shown at the point where it turns away from Totton station.   *South Western Circle, Eyers Collection*

Photographed in September 1966, Eling Tramway and sidings at the point where they passed under the Totton bypass.   *South Western Circle, Eyers Collection*

Chapter Fifteen

The Eling Tramway and the
Poole Harbour Tramway

The Eling Tramway

The Eling Tramway was one of the first private sidings on the Southampton & Dorchester line, and over the years served a number of industrial and waterside premises. Provision for the tramway was made on 2nd July, 1847 when the Southampton & Dorchester Railway was authorized to construct a branch railway to commence and proceed from the Southampton & Dorchester Railway in the parish of Eling and terminate at or near a quay in the same parish belonging to Sir John Barker Mill abutting onto the Southampton Water, which branch railway would be called the Eling Branch Railway. However, apart from official documents the line was always referred to as the Eling Tramway.

Work on the line's construction was not begun immediately, in fact the Southampton & Dorchester company had been absorbed into the LSWR when the latter signed an agreement with Sir John Barker Mill on 17th April, 1851 to acquire the necessary land and construct the line. In the event the LSWR only constructed the junction and the section of line within its boundary, resulting in Sir John Barker Mill at his expense employing a contractor to complete the remainder of the line, which it appears opened later the same year. As originally constructed the line was less than a mile in length. However, it is known that in the early years the LSWR made various additions to the tramway in particular after 1868, but the dates and details, like those of the line's construction, are not fully recorded. Neither was any lease or agreements signed between Sir John Barker Mill and the LSWR. The matter was not raised until after 1884, by which time the estates had passed to Sir John's third cousin Mrs Marianne Vaudrey who later assumed the name Barker Mill by Royal Warrant.

Realising that no agreement existed covering the tramway, this was rectified with an agreement signed on 22nd October, 1886, which gave her the lease of the railway for 999 years at the yearly rent of one peppercorn, if demanded. In addition she undertook to pay the LSWR a rental of £25 per annum in respect of the additions made to the tramway by the LSWR, with the option to purchasing the additions at any time for the sum of £400. She also undertook to maintain the railway and the additions in default of which the LSWR would carry out the work at her expense. The LSWR agreed to maintain the junction and the portion of the railway on its land. In the event of the railway beyond the company's boundary falling into complete disuse and remaining so for three years, the LSWR could give notice to determine the lease.

Mrs Vaudrey Barker Mill devoted a great deal of time to the management of the estates and was involved in the sale of a certain amount of land for the construction of the Southampton Western Docks, before she died aged 86 in 1932. She had, however, relinquished her interest in the Eling Wharfs in July 1923 when the lease was transferred to Messrs Burt, Bolton & Haywood Ltd.

An aerial view of the Eling Wharf estate, its junction with the main Southampton-Dorchester line is just visible to the top left.
Totton & Eling Historical Society

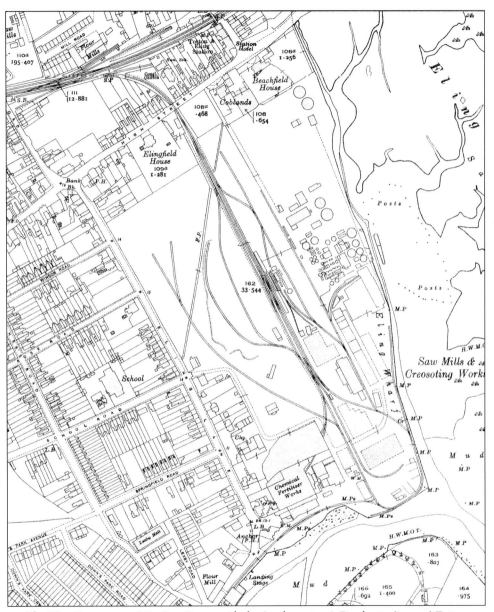

The Eling Tramway and Trading Estate, with the Southampton & Dorchester line and Totton station crossing the map on the top left. *Reproduced from the 1933 Ordnance Survey Map*

From the beginning traffic consisted of timber, agricultural products building materials and other associated trades, and in the early days of Redbridge sleeper works timber and rails were landed at Eling.

In November 1918 plans were prepared to take over part of the tramway and wharf for Admiralty use to store and tranship materials being sent to Marchwood magazine by water. However, in the event no traffic of this nature was handled.

The construction of the Agwi oil refinery at Fawley resulted in 5,208 tons of construction materials being transshipped from rail wagons to barges and taken by water to Fawley between August 1920 and April 1921. Between June and August 1922 seventy-seven wagons were dispatched containing oil products, some in drums the remainder pumped from coastal tanker into rail tank wagons. However, by September the following year this traffic had ceased, the oil being taken by sea. It was not until the opening of the Fawley branch in July 1925 that rail tank traffic was established direct with the refinery.

During the 1930s the staple traffic was timber, telephone poles, stone, tar and chemicals. Figures available for 1931 show the South Western Tar Distilleries both inwards and outwards was double that of the second highest user, timber merchants Burt, Boulton & Hayward. Traffic remaining constant during World War II when benzene was produced for the Air Ministry and dispatched by rail.

No instructions for working the tramway appear to have been issued until October 1917 when a printed notice was issued by the LSWR, these instructions subsequently being published in the 1921 appendix to the working timetable. A level crossing over Totton High Street was approached by a sharp curve off the trailing connection from the down main line at Totton station. The crossing was actually 70 yards past the railway company boundary. As the trains were propelled onto the tramway it was only a matter of time, given the curve and other circumstances, before an accident would occur. In June 1931 a motor car was damaged during a shunting move, resulting in two pairs of crossing gates being erected the following year, the cost of £63 3s. 6d. being shared between the railway and Messrs Burt, Boulton & Hayward Ltd.

Railway locomotives only propelled the wagons to a point approximately 140 yards beyond the crossing from which point the wharf operators moved them into position. Until 1923 it would appear that horses were used for the purpose, in that year Messrs Burt, Boulton & Hayward introduced two industrial locomotives, *Cameronian* an 0-4-0ST Manning, Wardle No. 653 of 1877 vintage, and *Benton* an 0-4-0ST Black, Hawthorn No. 1098 of 1896. In April 1948 *Benton II* arrived, an 0-4-0ST Andrew Barclay No. 1290 built in 1912. By 1950 the two original engines had been scrapped but *Benton II* survived until 1966 when replaced by an 0-4-0 Ruston & Hornsby diesel shunter No. 218944 of 1942. The diesel remained until sold in 1975, from which date no shunter was employed. However, the rail-mounted steam cranes remained and over the years these had been used on many occasions to assist with shunting.

Despite the steady decline in general freight traffic the tramway carried a reasonable amount during the early 1960s. Figures for the November of 1963 record 142 loaded wagons arriving, including 55 wagons of fertiliser, 64 tanks of tar and 16 wagons of roadstone. A total of 79 loaded wagons departed, 19 with poles from the timber merchant and 60 wagons from the South Western Tar Distilleries, this including 24 wagons of creosote for British Railways.

The 1970s saw a change in direction for both the freight traffic and the trading facilities at Eling. The Amalgamated Roadstone Corporation Ltd (ARC) brought a roadstone processing plant into operation during 1973 connected to a new siding off the tramway. Block trains of stone up to a maximum of 24 wagons were brought from Whatley Quarry, Frome, the trains being divided in Totton goods yard before each half was taken separately onto the tramway for discharge.

During 1987 a further siding was added to serve the new depot and warehouses for Redland Tiles, the facility being served by a Speedlink service with a short working from Eastleigh. This new traffic brought main line locomotives onto the tramway, with both class '47' and class '56' locomotives on the ARC workings, and class '33' and class '47' on the Speedlink services.

However, the sight of heavy locomotives on the tramway was to be short lived; the ARC workings gradually decreased and had ceased by 1988, with the Redland's traffic following two years later. British Rail took advantage of the wording of the 1886 lease: 'That in the event of the railway beyond the Company's boundary falling into complete disuse and remaining so for three years' the lease could be determined', resulting in the closure of the Eling Tramway with the removal of the points connecting it to the main line in December 1993, ending a further part of Southampton & Dorchester Railway history.

The Poole Harbour Tramway

The original Act of the Poole & Bournemouth Railway included a clause for the construction of a tramway to Poole Quay; although the line from New Poole Junction (Broadstone) to Poole opened in December 1872 there had been little effort to provide the tramway, the LSWR seeking an extension of time to its Bill in early 1873. Largely due to the efforts of Poole Council applying pressure, work on construction had commenced by the September when the Council expressed dissatisfaction at the way in which the tramway was being laid. Eventually the work was completed and officially opened for traffic from 6th June, 1874.

One mile 13 chains in length it ran from the down side of Poole station along Nile Row after which a right-hand turn took it along West Quay Road, the track running along the west side before turning left onto the quay at Poole Bridge, then terminating opposite the Jolly Sailor public house. The line was provided with a loop siding in West Quay Road and a further loop on the quay between the Custom House and the Jolly Sailor. Between 1893 and 1895 the quay wall was extended at the east end past the pottery, the tramway being extended at the same time by one chain in the form of two lines and a crossover to extend the previous run-round facilities.

Originally horses were employed to haul wagons to and from the station. As early as February 1878 Mr Scott the LSWR General Manager recommended that

The Quay, Poole

Poole Harbour tramway looking west viewed from the run-round loop. In this turn of the century scene the masts of sailing vessels are prominent, whilst to the left on the Hamworthy side a steam paddle tug can be seen.   *Author's Collection*

Several wagons stand on the Poole Harbour Tramway in this pre-1914 view taken from Poole bridge and the masts of sailing vessels still dominate the scene.   *Author's Collection*

Standing behind Poole station at the entrance to the Poole Harbour Tramway is 0-4-0ST No. 407 *Pioneer*, the first steam locomotive to work the line in 1899. A standard Manning, Wardle 'E' class saddle tank it was supplied new to contractors R.T. Relf in 1876 and purchased by the LSWR in August 1881. In 1904 *Pioneer* was transferred to engineering duties and other assorted tasks until withdrawn in 1919. *R.K. Blencowe Collection*

Vulcan a Vulcan Foundry 0-4-0 saddle tank No. 836 built in 1878 and supplied to the Southampton Docks Company. Taken into LSWR stock in 1892 as No. 118. Sent to Bournemouth in 1900 as shed pilot and a spare for Poole Quay, also transferred to engineers duties in 1904 being involved in works between Brockenhurst and Pokesdown from 1906 until the end of 1908 when returned to the Southampton area. Saved by World War I, *Vulcan* was sold in 1924 to contractors Taylor, Tunnicliffe of Stoke, Staffs, and scrapped during 1931. *R.K. Blencowe Collection*

a small locomotive should be purchased to work the tramway similar to the engines working the traffic between Southampton station and Town Quay. However, there the matter rested but as trade increased the limitations of horse power became a problem resulting in trials being conducted with a small 0-4-0 saddle tank No. 407 *Pioneer* in June 1899, prior to an Act being passed in the August allowing the use of steam engines over the tramway. Following adjustments for clearance in Nile Row and alteration to pointwork at West Quay the regular use of steam locomotives commenced. *Pioneer* was joined by two former Southampton Dock Co. 0-4-0 tanks, No. 111 *Vulcan*, and No. 408 *Bretwalda*, the three working both the tramway and the Hamworthy goods branch. Trials were carried out with 'B4' class 0-4-0 tank No. 94 in October 1903, and, following minor alterations to the track to give additional clearance, two 'B4s' arrived in April 1904 with a third joining the following month. From then, with the exception of visits to works and shortages when a selection of former Southampton tanks deputized, the 'B4' tanks remained for the next 56 years.

The outbreak of World War I saw a sharp decline in coastal shipping as traffic was switched to rail, one example being coal for the gasworks which then was situated on the quay. The use of Poole as a Naval base required additional sidings for handling supplies, so in late 1914 and early 1915 various timber sheds and other buildings along West Shore were demolished and sidings laid on the site. They were known as West Bay Military Sidings and a large stores complex was set up here. The sidings ran parallel with the Poole Quay Tramway from a behind the platform at Poole station to Poole Bridge where they connected again to the Tramway. At the end of the war there was disagreement with the previous owners and the local authorities until the stores were removed in late 1919, with the sidings taken out of use in January 1920 and quickly removed.

During and after the 1920s traffic was never to return to pre-1914 levels as the motor lorry claimed some of the short haul traffic with firms such as Southern Roadways setting up a depot specifically to handle goods traffic. Again World War II saw disruption to coastal shipping, whilst the build up to D-Day saw vast amounts of American stores brought to Poole Quay including large quantities of petrol in rail tankers. To minimise the fire risk the wagons were propelled by the engine from the station to the quay with troops keeping the public clear whilst this operation took place.

In the years following the war there was an upsurge in traffic until the end of fuel rationing when motor transport again began to gather favour. This, with the continual development of Hamworthy Quay, saw a gradual decline in the fortunes of Poole Quay as shipping concentrated on the Hamworthy side and various traders along the tramway either closed or changed their transport requirements. By the late 1950s trade had declined requiring only two trips a day, one in the morning and a return working in the evening. A further decrease in traffic saw the last train hauled through the streets on 30th April, 1960 by 'B4' No. 30102, the line officially closing on 5th May. Most of the track was removed shortly after and today road improvements and the reconstruction of parts of Poole have obliterated much of the route of the line, whilst on Poole Quay the tourist trade has taken over where commerce once thrived.